Dedicated to Savy and Peanut, who make every day an adventure. Thank you for traveling the world with us.

# GREECE

## Educational Resources, Crafts & Activities for Kids

*Sarah M. Prowant, MSN-Ed, RN*

**Savy** Activities
Colorado, USA

Savy Activities© All Rights Reserved

# TERMS & CONDITIONS

This product is licensed for single use only (single home or classroom). Redistributing, selling, editing or sharing any part of this product in any part thereof is strictly forbidden without the written permission of Savy Activities. You may make copies for your personal use but will need to purchase separate licenses for use in additional classrooms and/or schools. Failure to comply is a legal copyright infringement and will be prosecuted to the full extent of the law.

When posting photos of any part of this product on social media, please give credit to "Savy Activities" by hyperlinking to our website and tagging us as @SavyActivities on social media.

We reserve the right to change this policy at any time. If you have any questions regarding this or other of our materials, please contact us directly.

# FOR BEST RESULTS:

 When assembling a 3D model, glue a second piece of thick paper with a craft glue stick to back of each sheet of model pieces (prior to cutting pieces) to provide additional stability when assembled.

 Laminate all cards & posters with at least 3 ml lamination for additional protection.

 If printing from an ebook, cardstock paper (>60 lbs) provides best results for cards, models and manipulative activities, while standard printer paper is adequate for recipes, lessons, etc. Please set printer to "FIT TO PAGE" when printing for best results.

# FOLLOW US ON SOCIAL MEDIA!

 @savyactivities

 /SavyActivities

www.SavyActivities.com

# WHATS INCLUDED:

- Educational Placemat/Poster & Flag
- Greece Landmark Three-Part Cards
- Greece Landmark & Cities Map Pinning
- Greece Regions Poster & Continent Flag Pinning
- Greece Fun Facts
- Greek History Poster & Timeline Period Cards
- Parthenon 3D Model & Parts of Poster
- Greek Column Matching
- Ancient Greek Persons
- Theater Masks
- Ancient Greek Pottery Art
- Olympians - Greek Mythical Gods (Ring Cards)
- String the Lyre
- Iynx Wheel
- Clepsydra (Water) Clock
- Plato (Playdough) Mats & Cards
- Ancient Greek Catapult
- Toilet Roll Trojan Horse
- Hoplite Armor Poster
- Daedalus & Icarus Minibook
- Kotinos Olympic Wreath
- Abacus Craft
- Evil Eye "Mati" Pendent
- Mykonos Windmill
- Greek Alphabet Cards
- Magnetic or Not? Sensory Bin
- γύρος (Gyros) Recipe
- Greece Fauna Three-Part Cards
- Life Cycle Dolphin, Tracing, Felt Puzzle
- Greek Currency: Euro
- Greek Language Cards

# Greece

**National Flora:** Bear's Breech
**National Fauna:** Dolphin
**Capital City:** Athens
**Currency:** Euro €
**Language:** Greek
**National Holiday(s):** March 25
**Famous Landmarks:**
Acropolis (Parthenon, Odeon of Herodes Atticus, Erechtheion, Propylaia)
Metéora Monasteries
Church of St. George
Delphi
Paraportiani
Samaria Gorge
Navagio
Myrtos Beach
Mykonos Windmills
Corfu Fortress

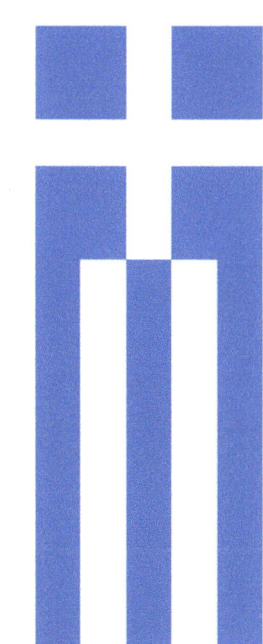

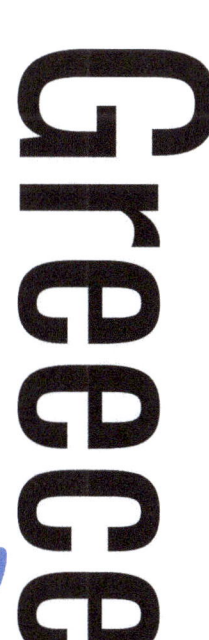

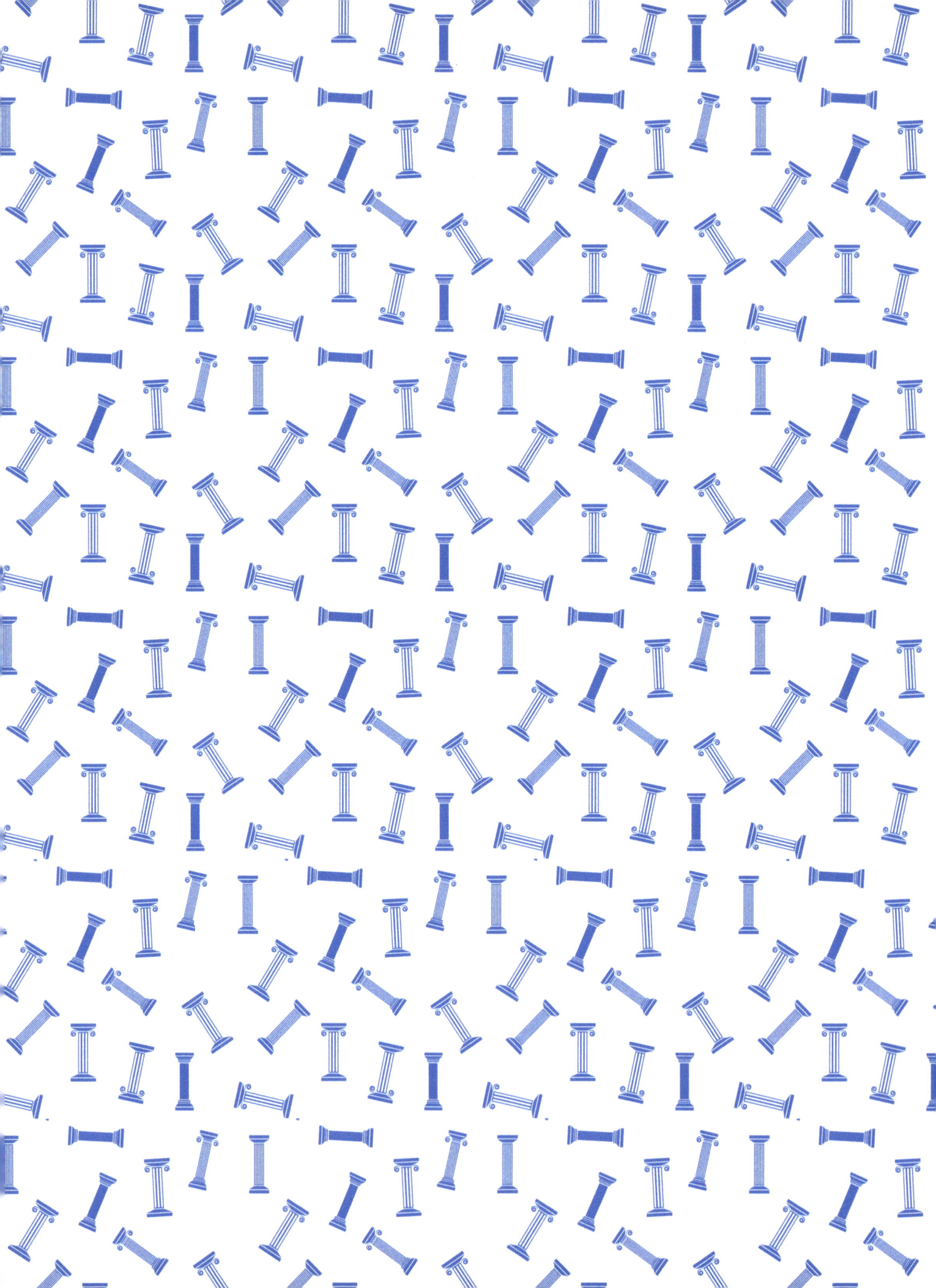

# Greece

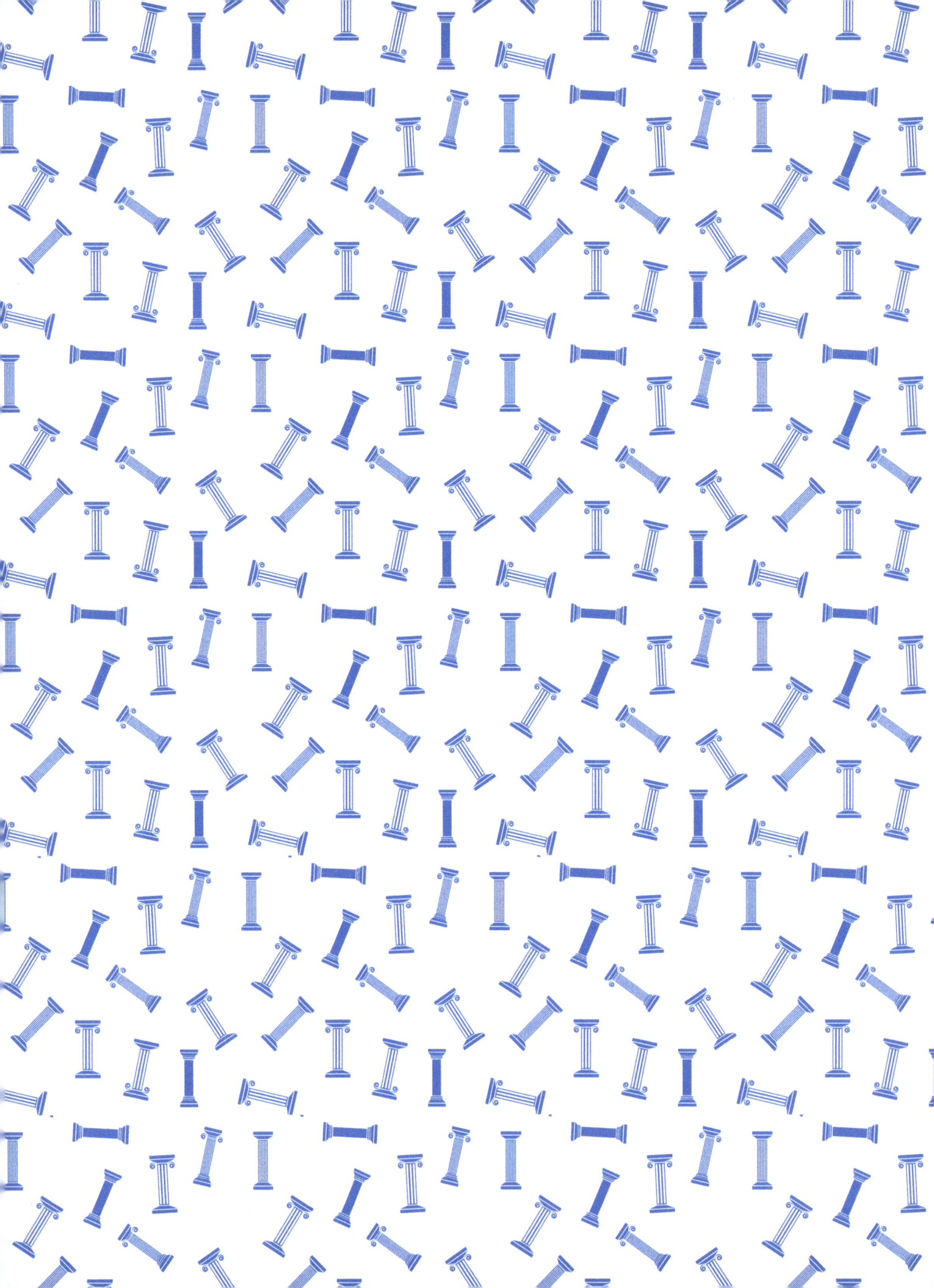

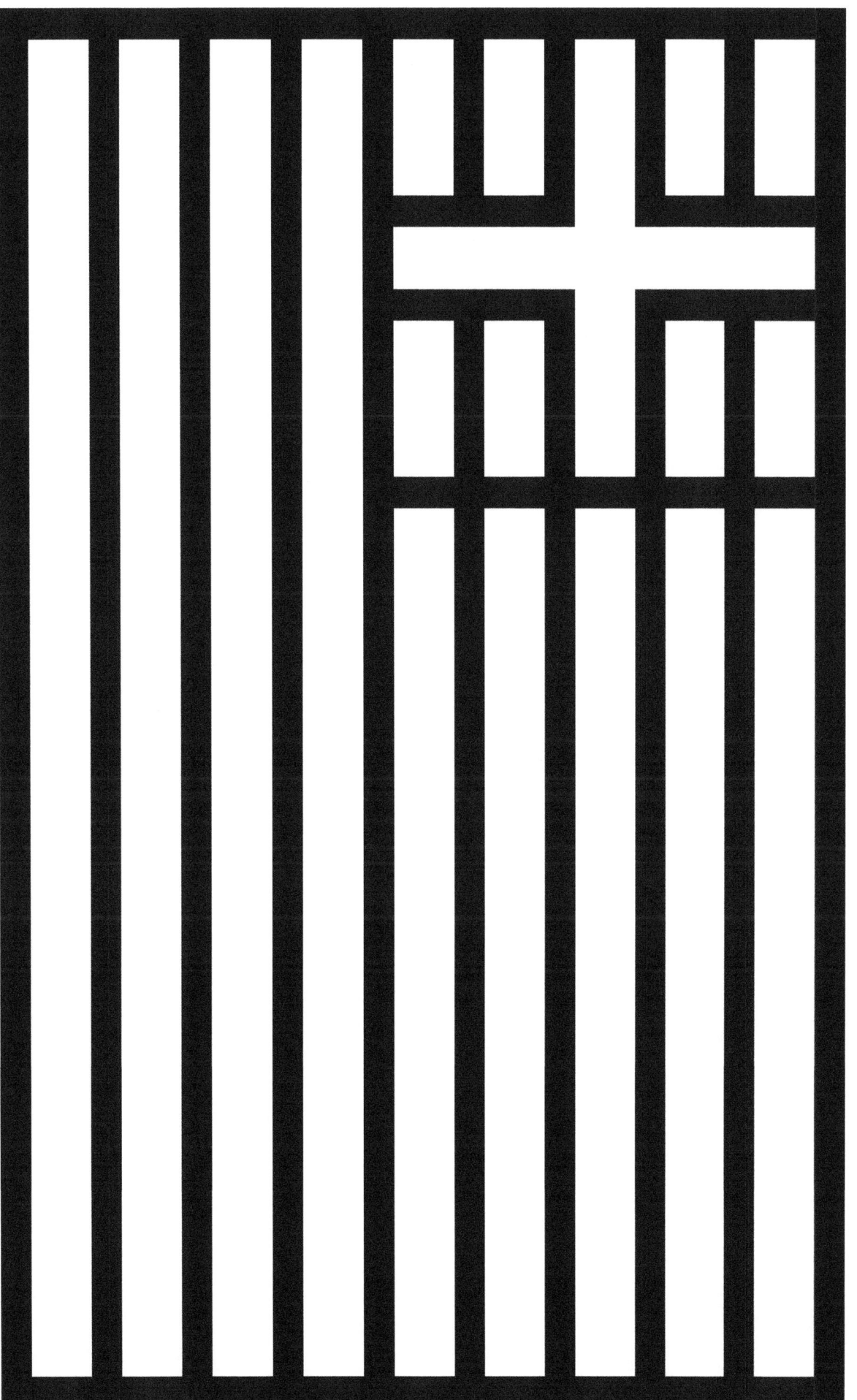

Greek Flag Coloring Page

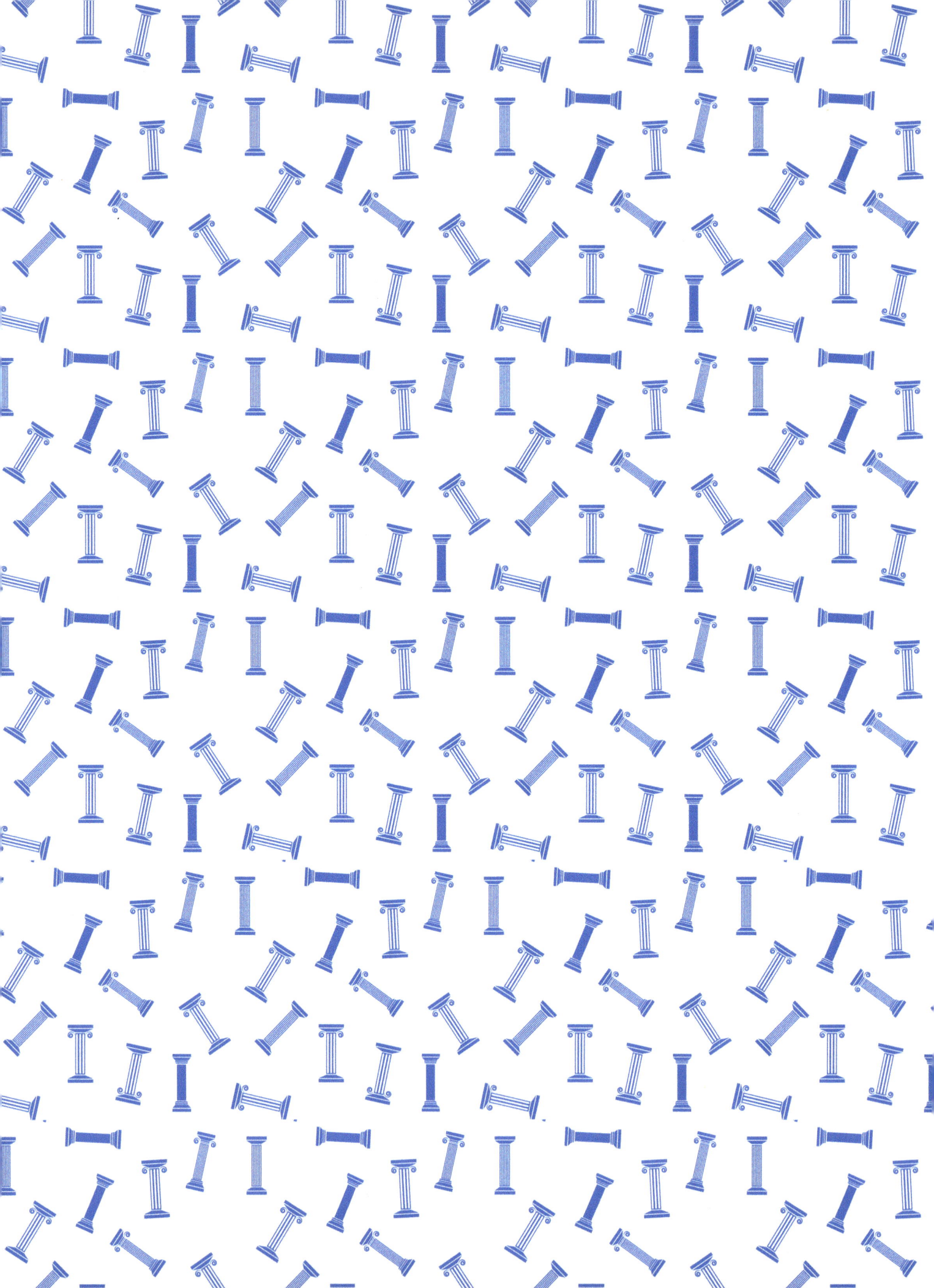

# Greece Landmarks (3-Part Cards)

**Acropolis**

**Church of St. George**

**Metéora Monasteries**

**Delphi**

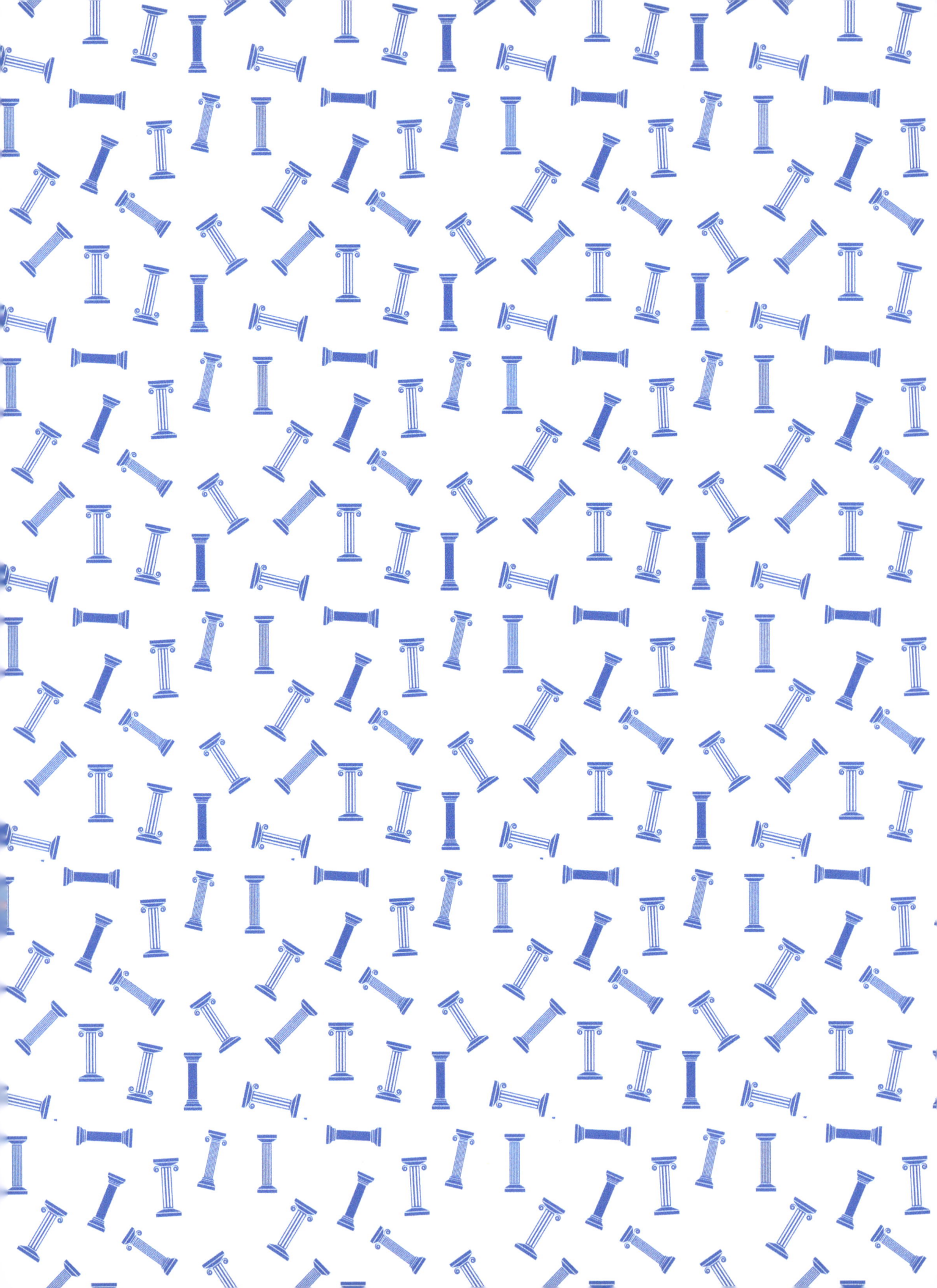

# Greece Landmarks (3-Part Cards)

**Acropolis**

**Church of St. George**

**Metéora Monasteries**

**Delphi**

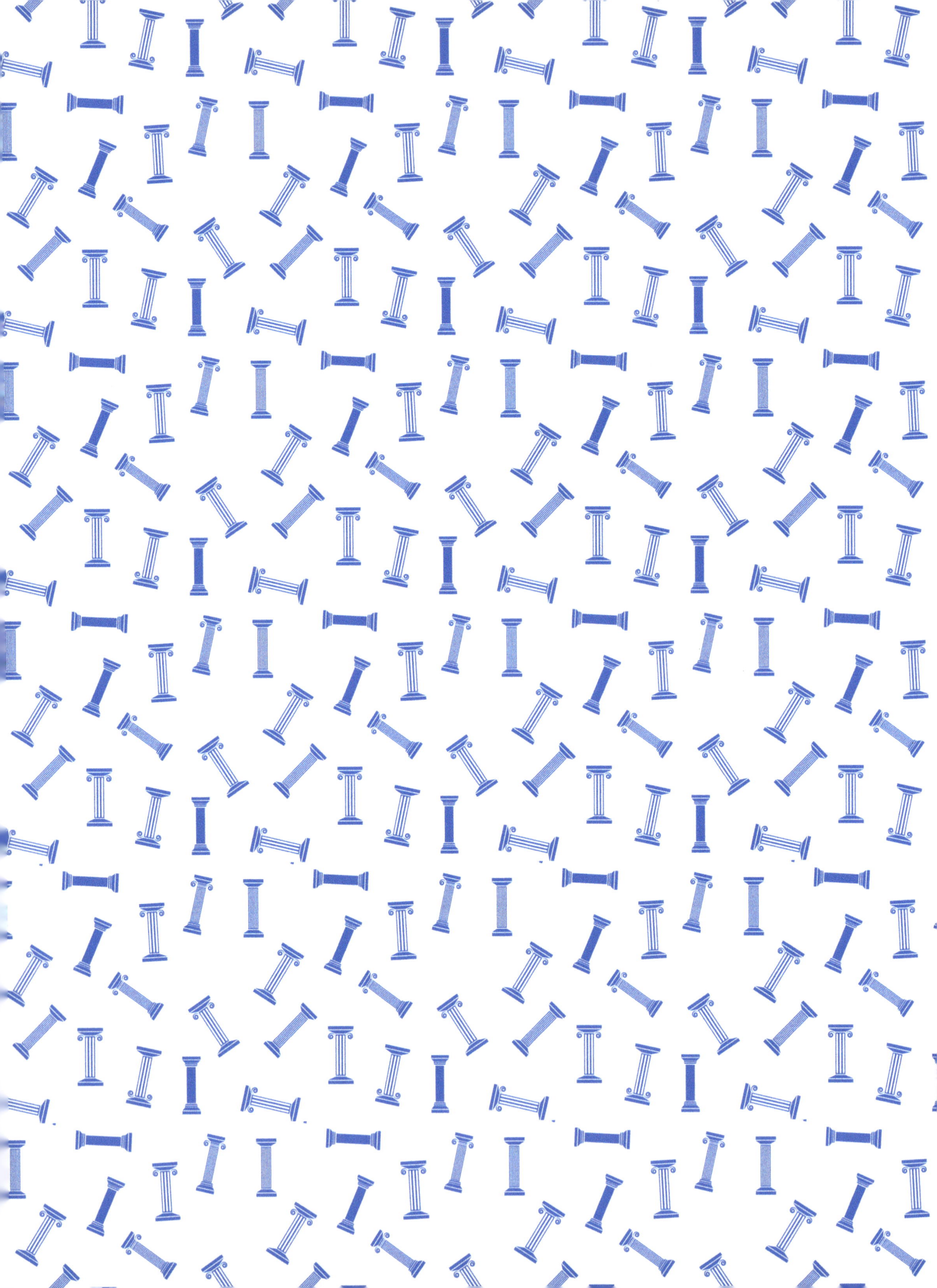

# Greece Landmarks (3-Part Cards)

**Paraportiani**  **Samaria Gorge**

**Navagio**  **Myrtos Beach**

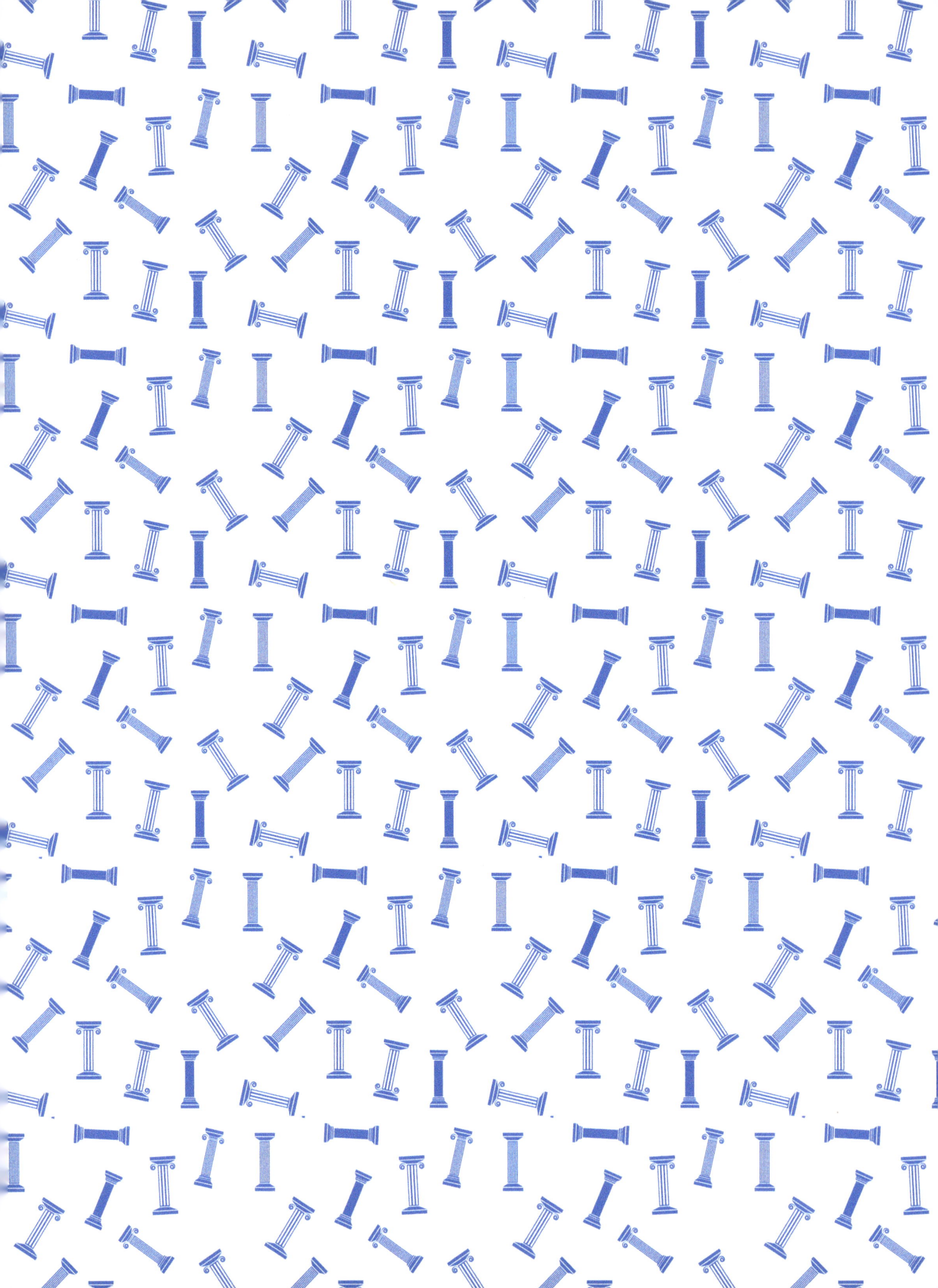

# Greece Landmarks (3-Part Cards)

**Paraportiani**  **Samaria Gorge**

**Navagio**  **Myrtos Beach**

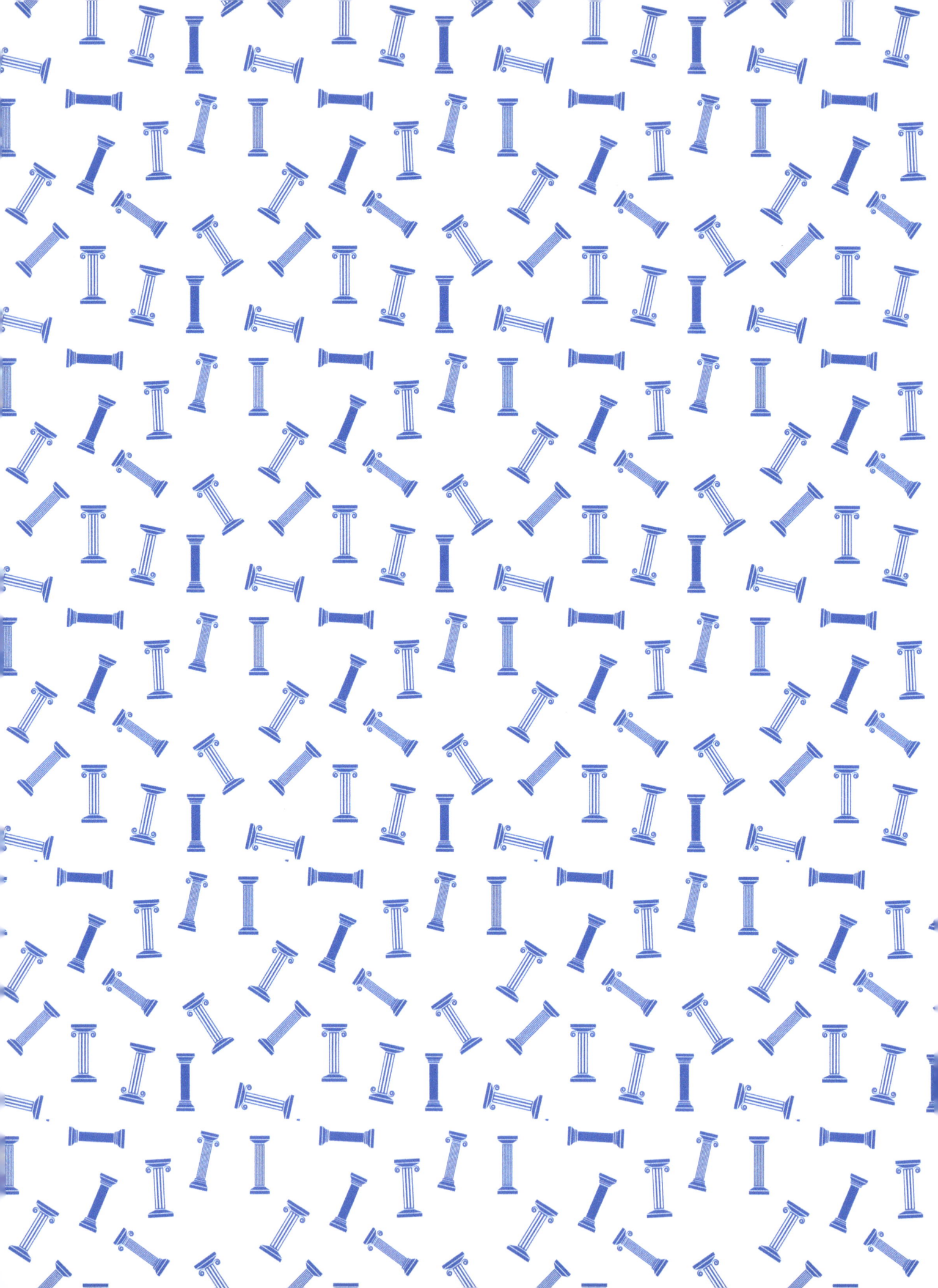

# Greece Landmarks (3-Part Cards)

**Mykonos Windmill**

**Mykonos Windmill**

**Corfu Fortress**

**Corfu Fortress**

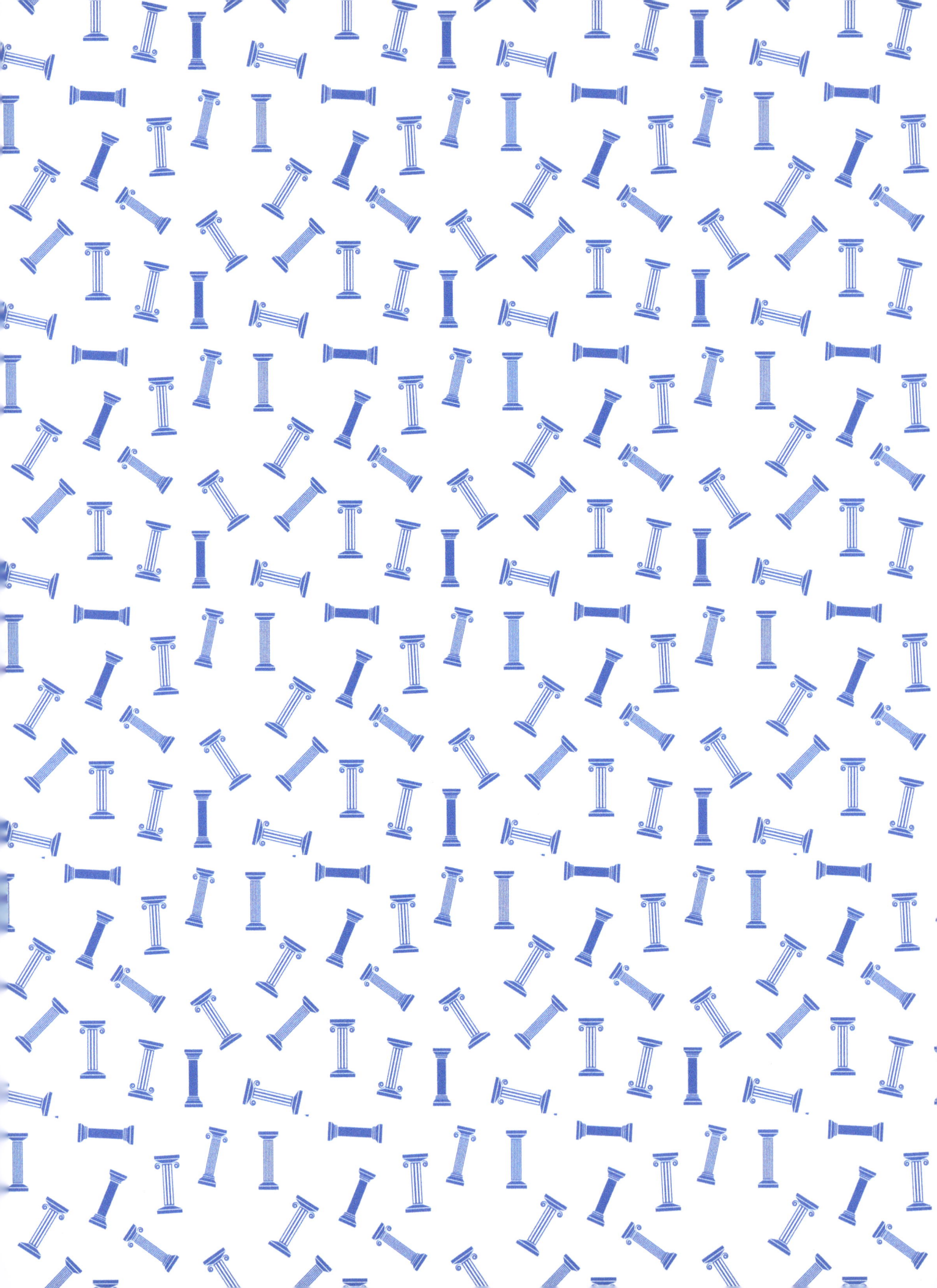

# Greece Landmarks

*Cut out circles using a 1" circle punch or scissors. Place circles on map where the landmarks are located. Refer to the control version for help if needed.*

# Greece Cities

*Cut out the labels and attach them to the diagram*

| Athens | Thessaloniki | Patras | Piraeus |
| Larissa | Heraklion | Chania | Thera |
| Ioannina | Mykonos | | |
| Kalamata | | | |
| Corfu | | | |
| Rhodes | | | |

## Instructions

Paste included map illustration onto foamboard, cardboard or corkboard. Glue straight or T-pin to back of labels or photo circles and pin into map at appropriate location of landmark or city.

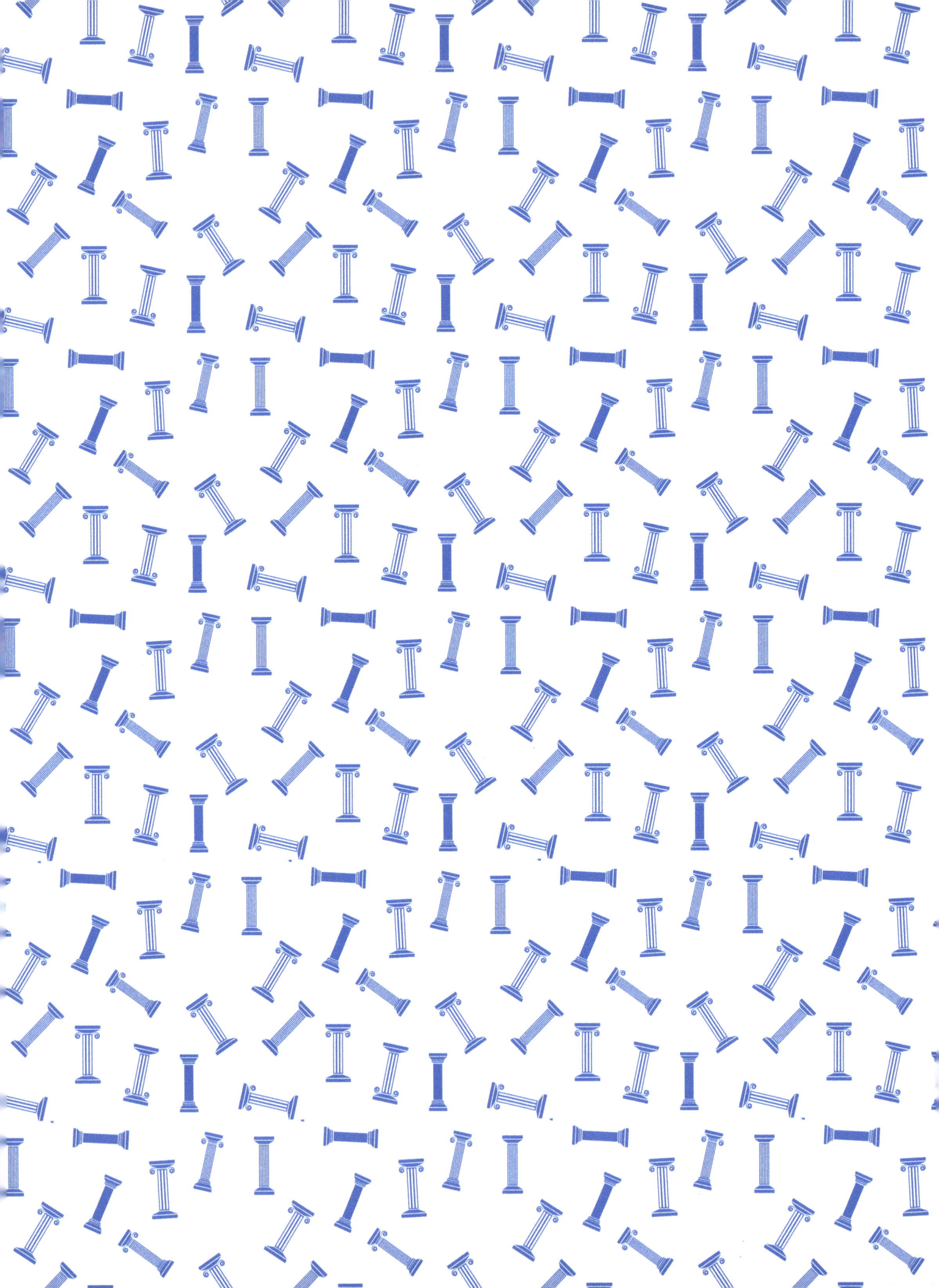

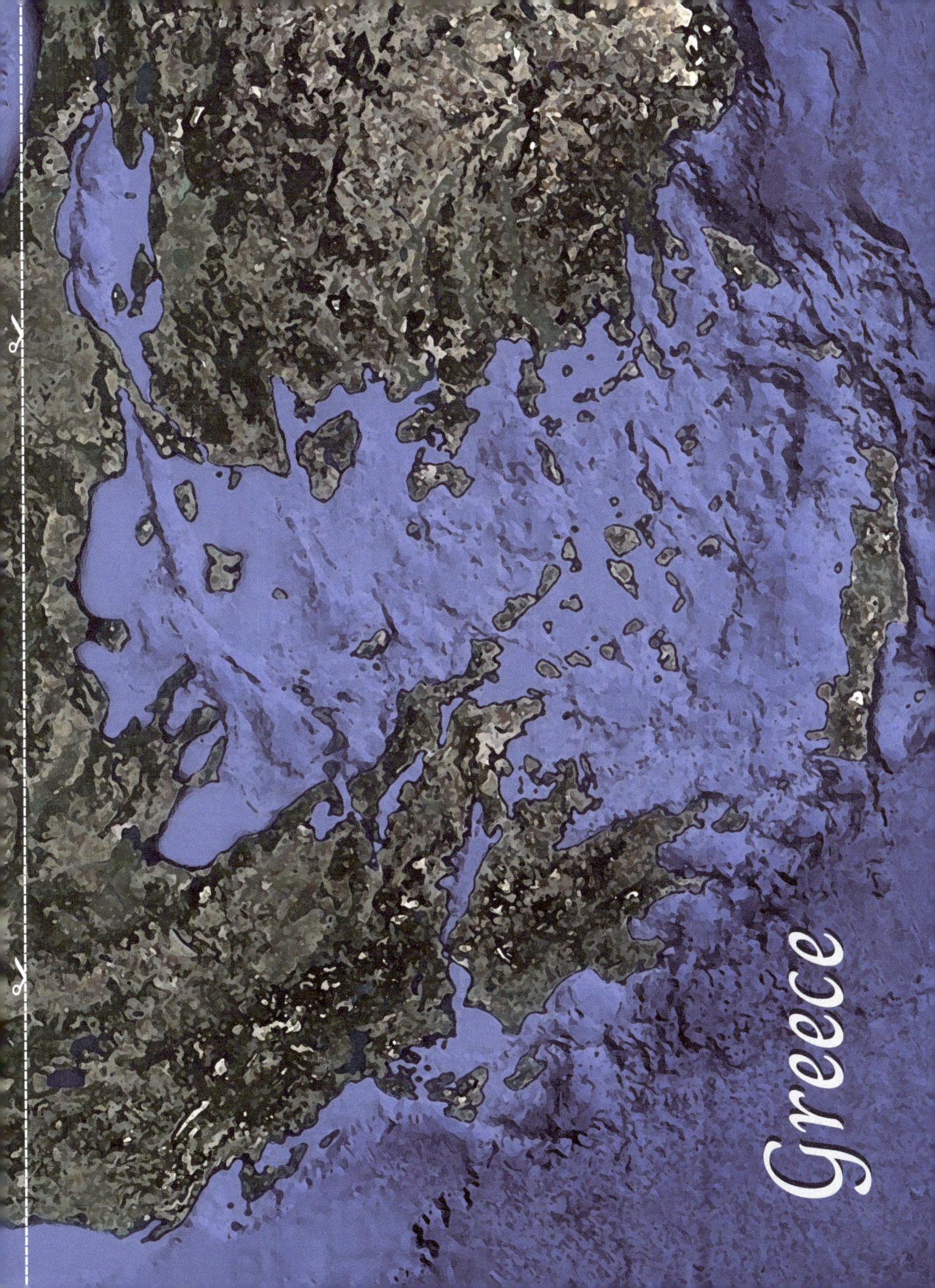

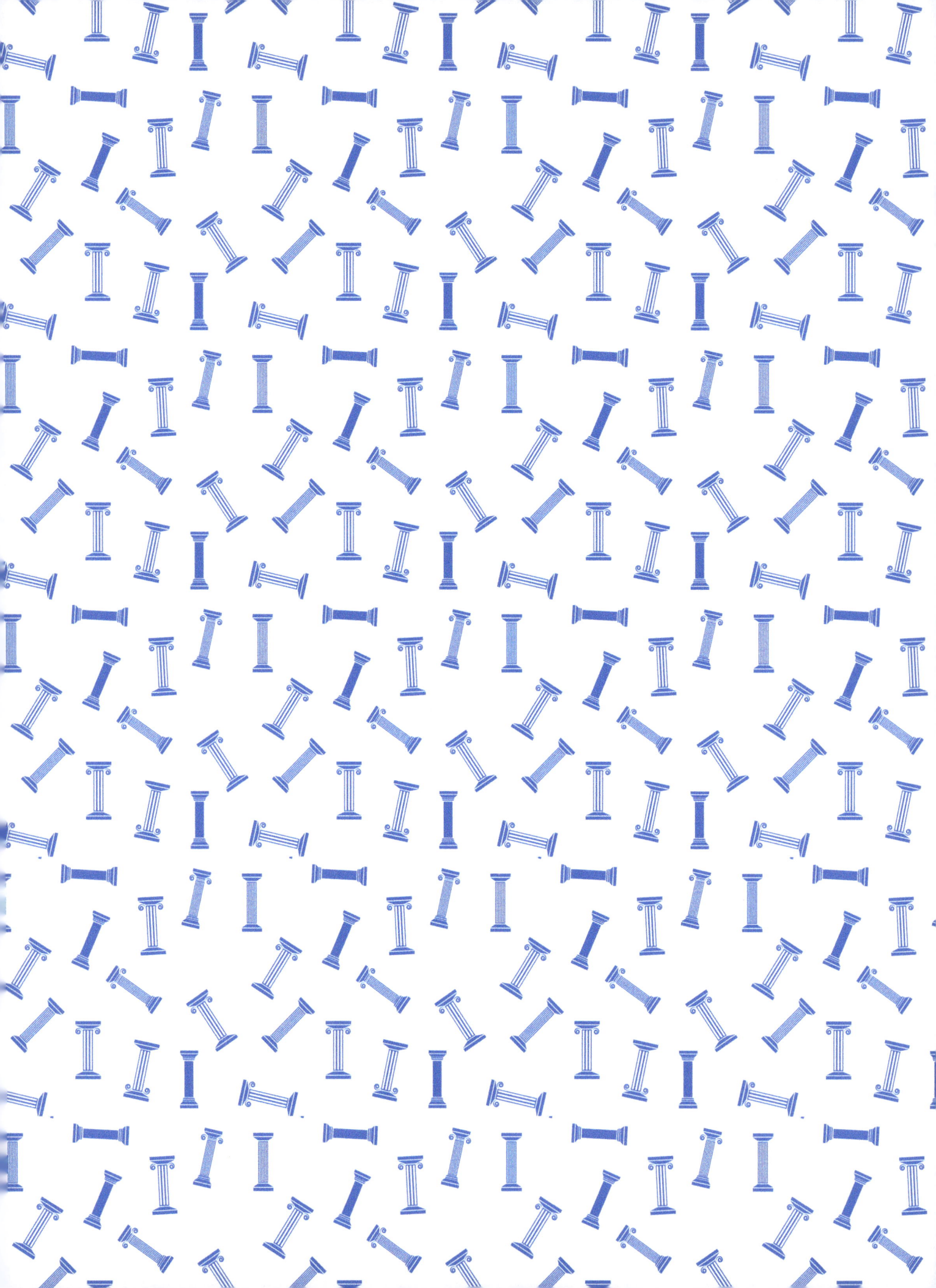

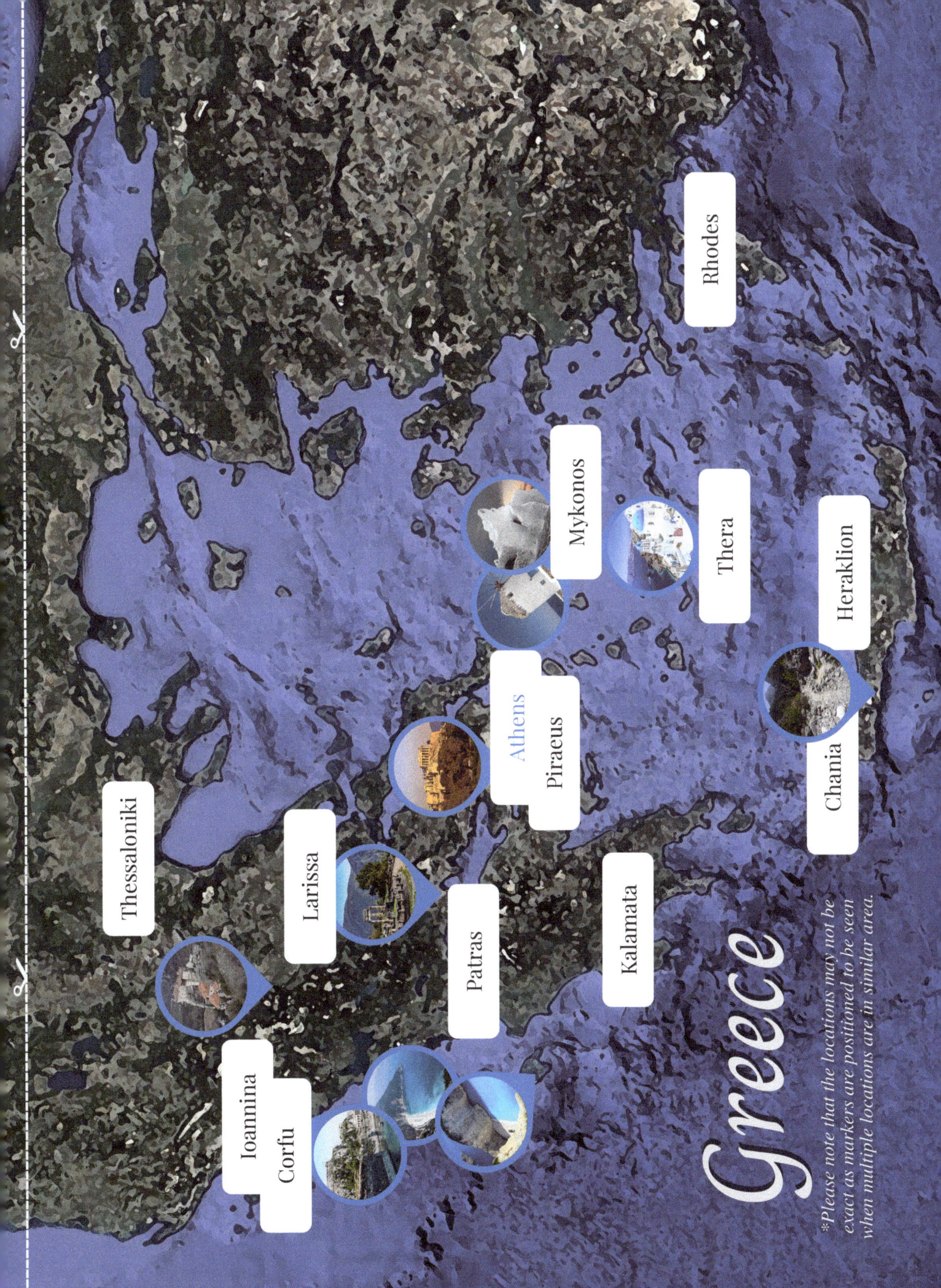

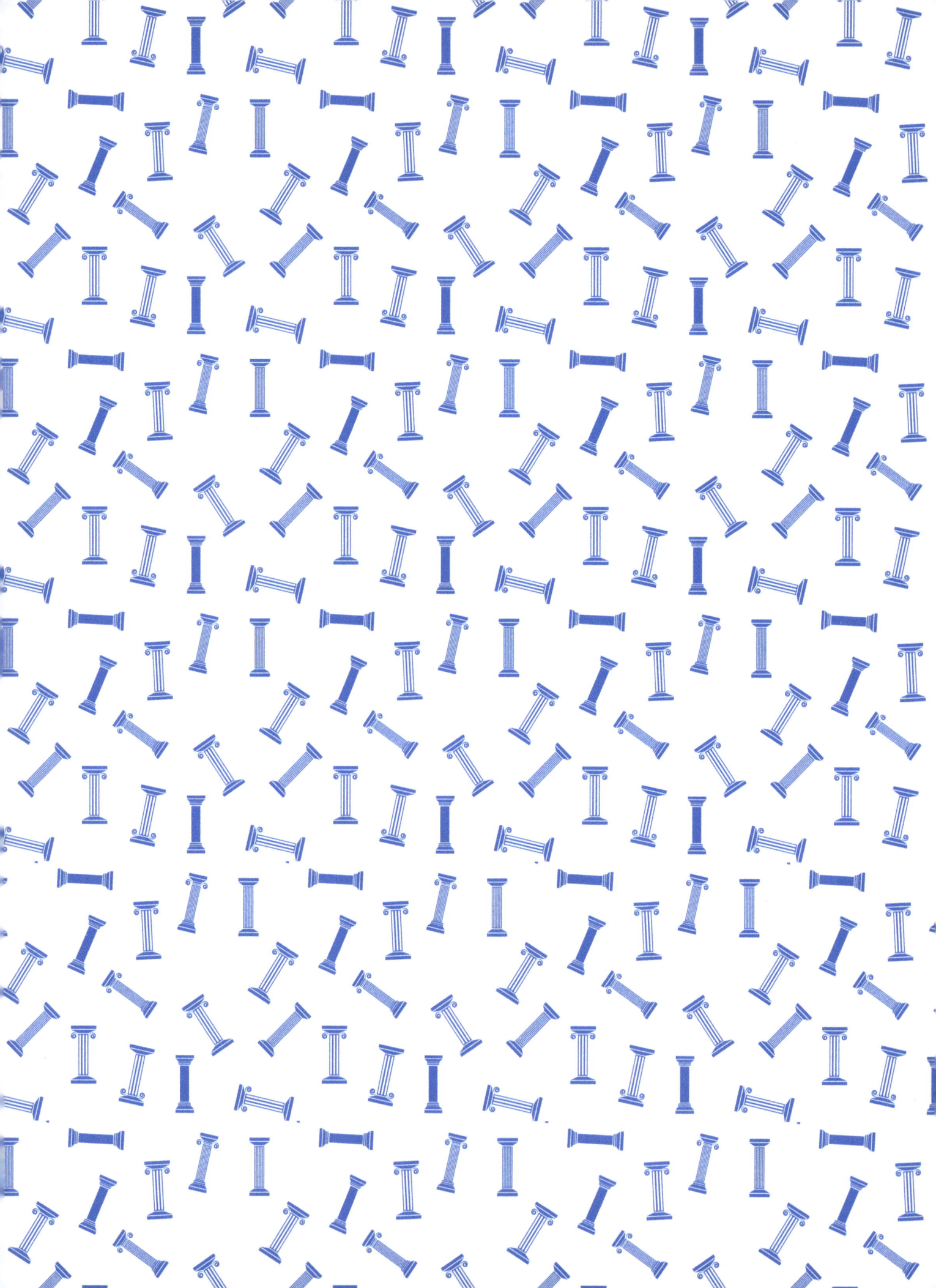

Greece

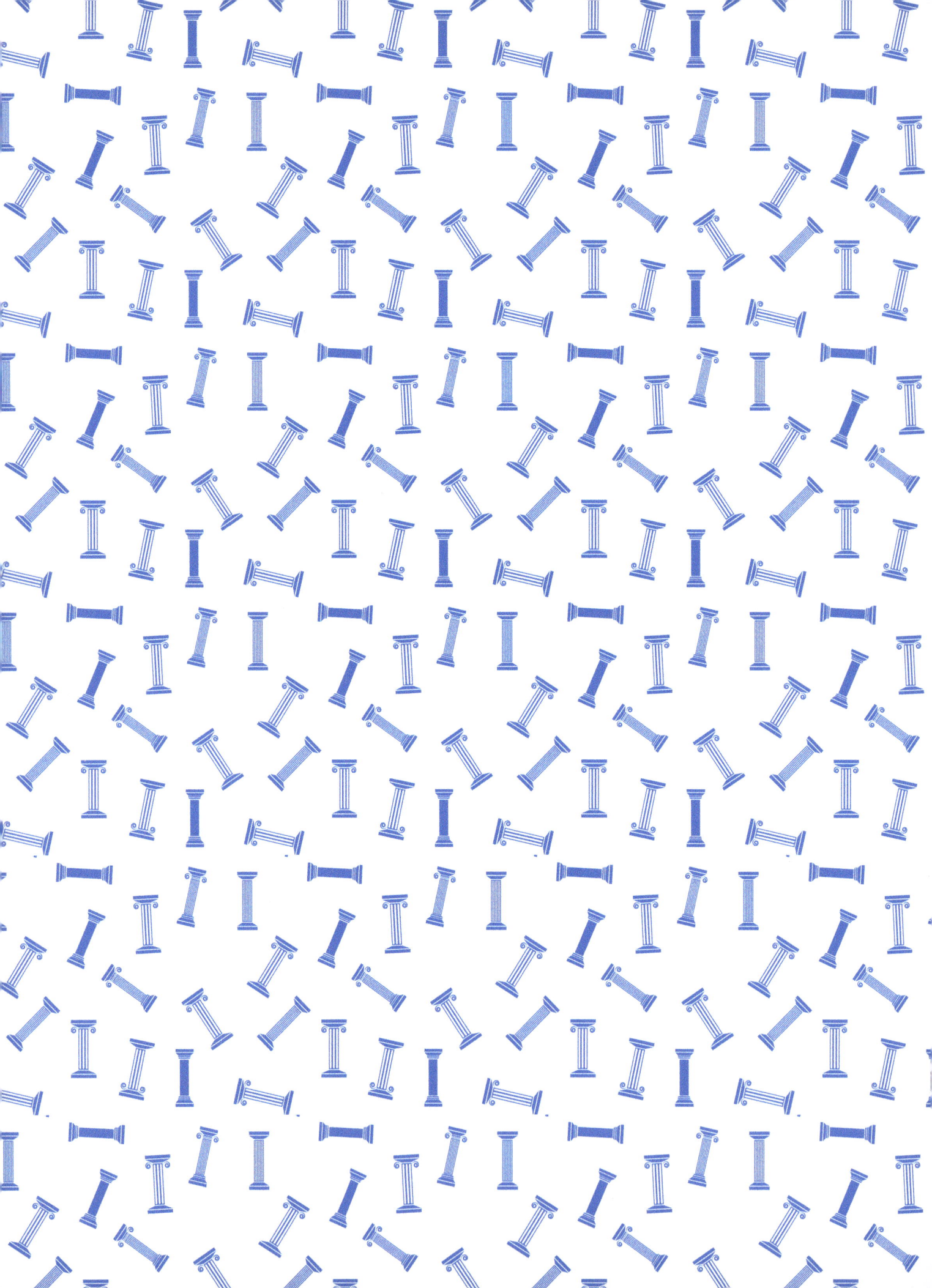

# Greece Regions
## περιφέρειες

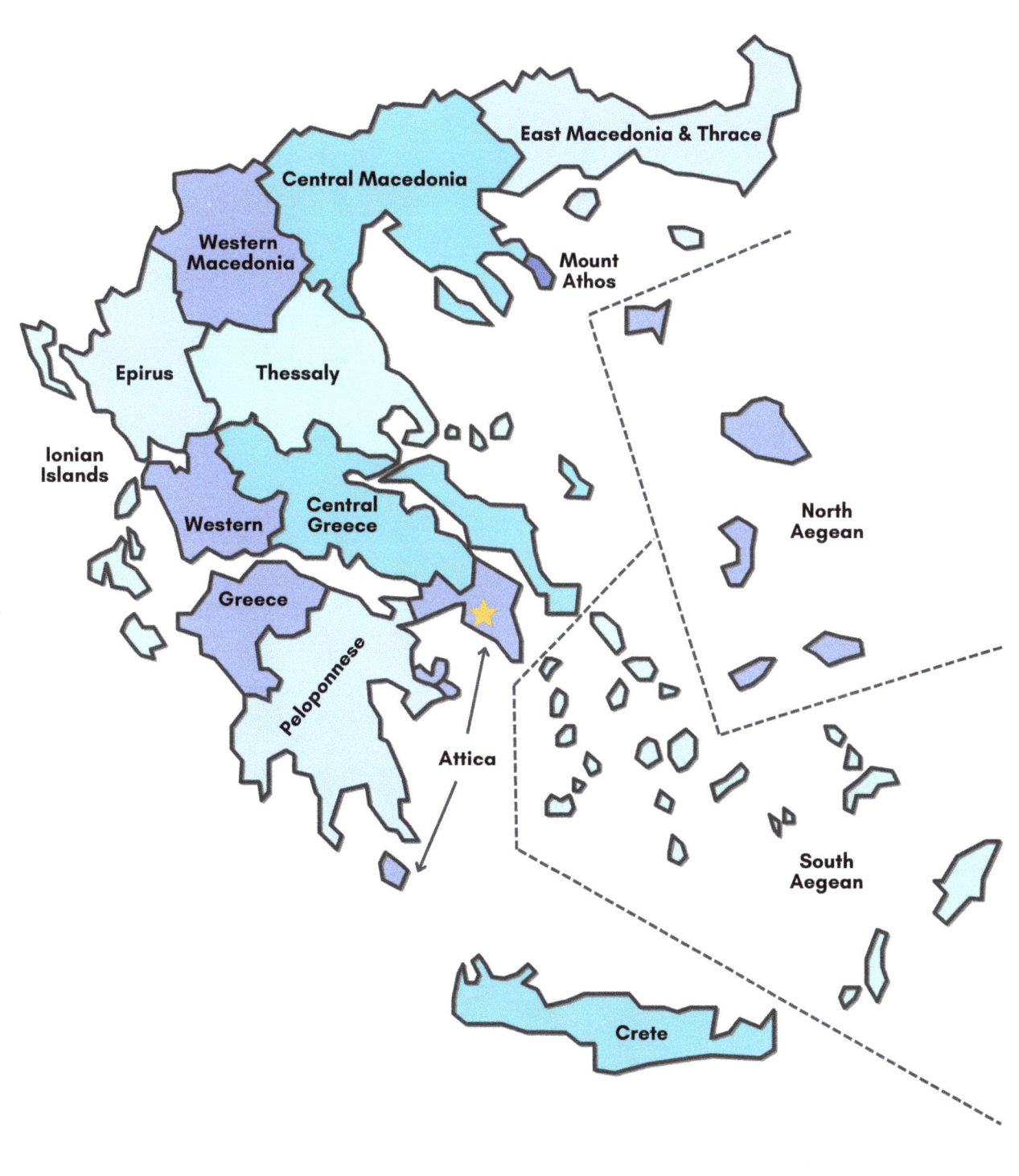

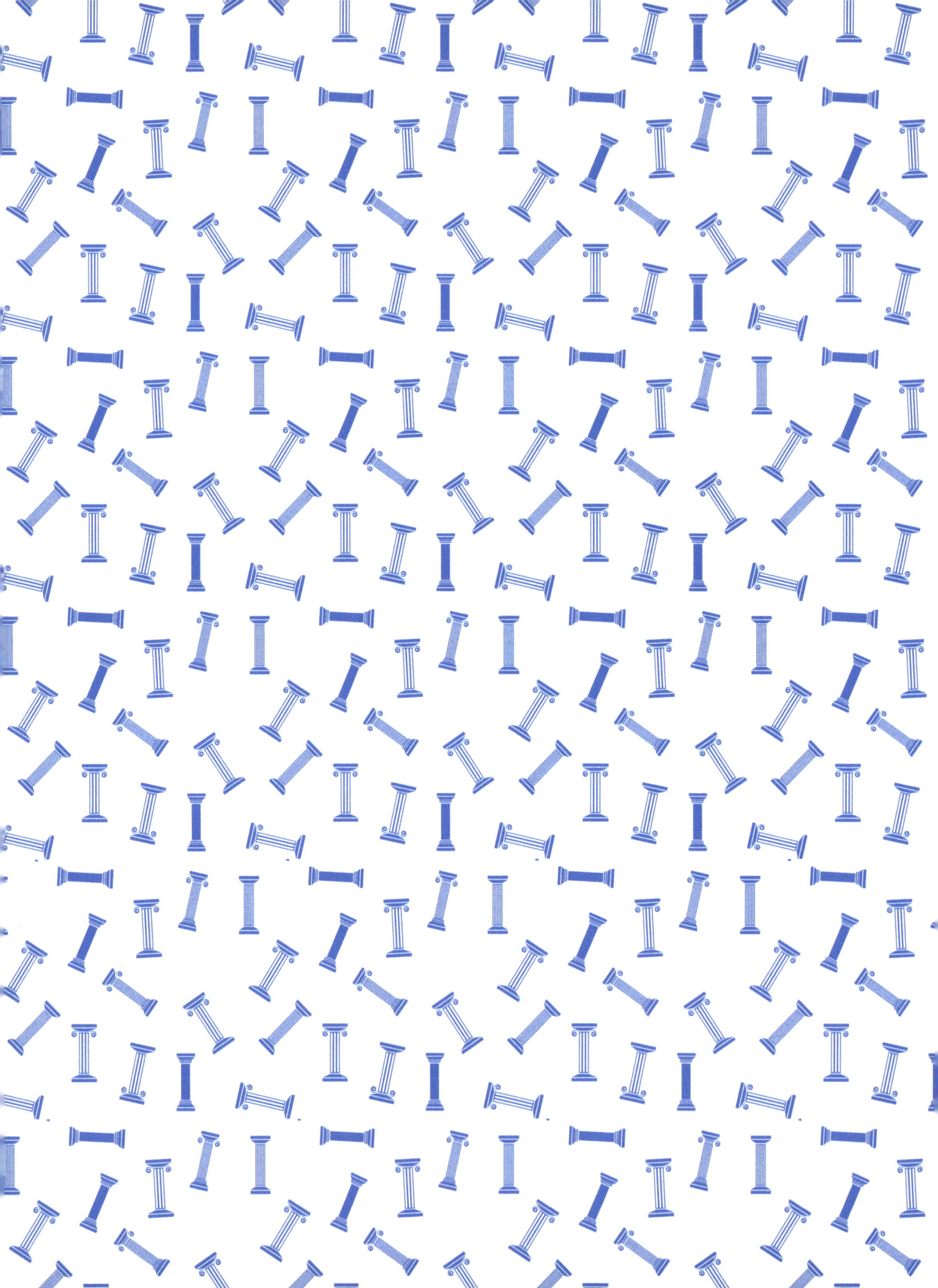

# Europe Continent: Greece

Cut out Europe continent. Glue over corkboard or cardboard. Cut out flag and glue onto toothpick or straight pin. Mark country with flag.

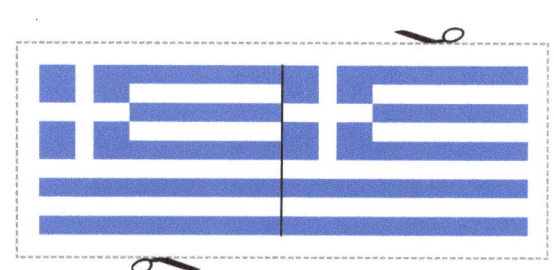

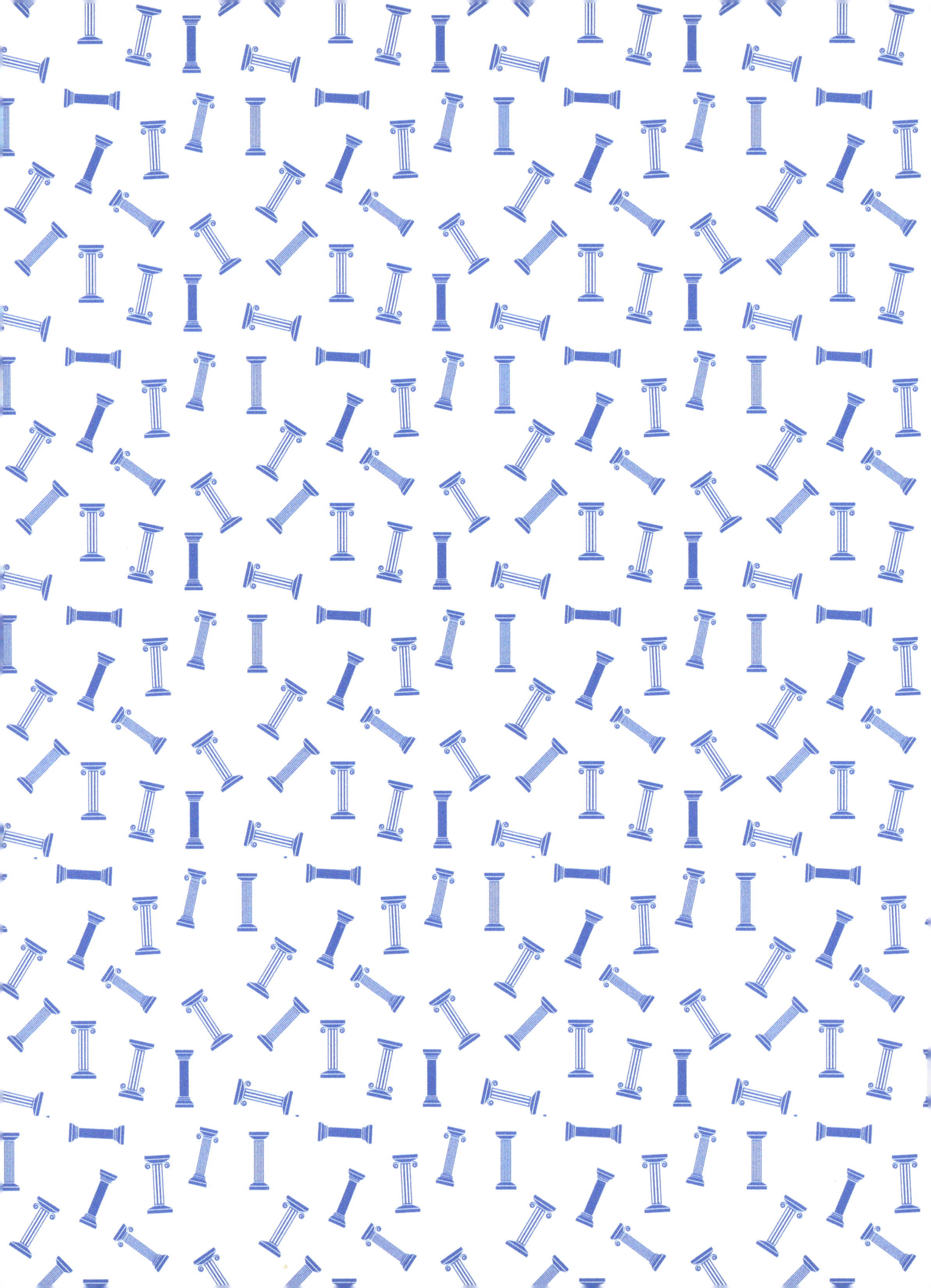

# Greece Fun Facts

Greece is made of approximately 6,000 islands, but only about 200 of them are inhabited.

More tourists visit Greece every year than the entire Greek population.

Greece is the third largest producer of olives, after Spain & Italy.

Greece is one of the most mountainous countries in Europe, with 80% of the country covered in mountains.

Greece has 18 UNESCO World Heritage Sites.

Athens has more theatres than any other city in the world.

Greece has more archaeological museums than any country in the world with more than 110.

The Olympics originated in Greece around 776 BC in honor of Zeus, the King of the Greek gods.

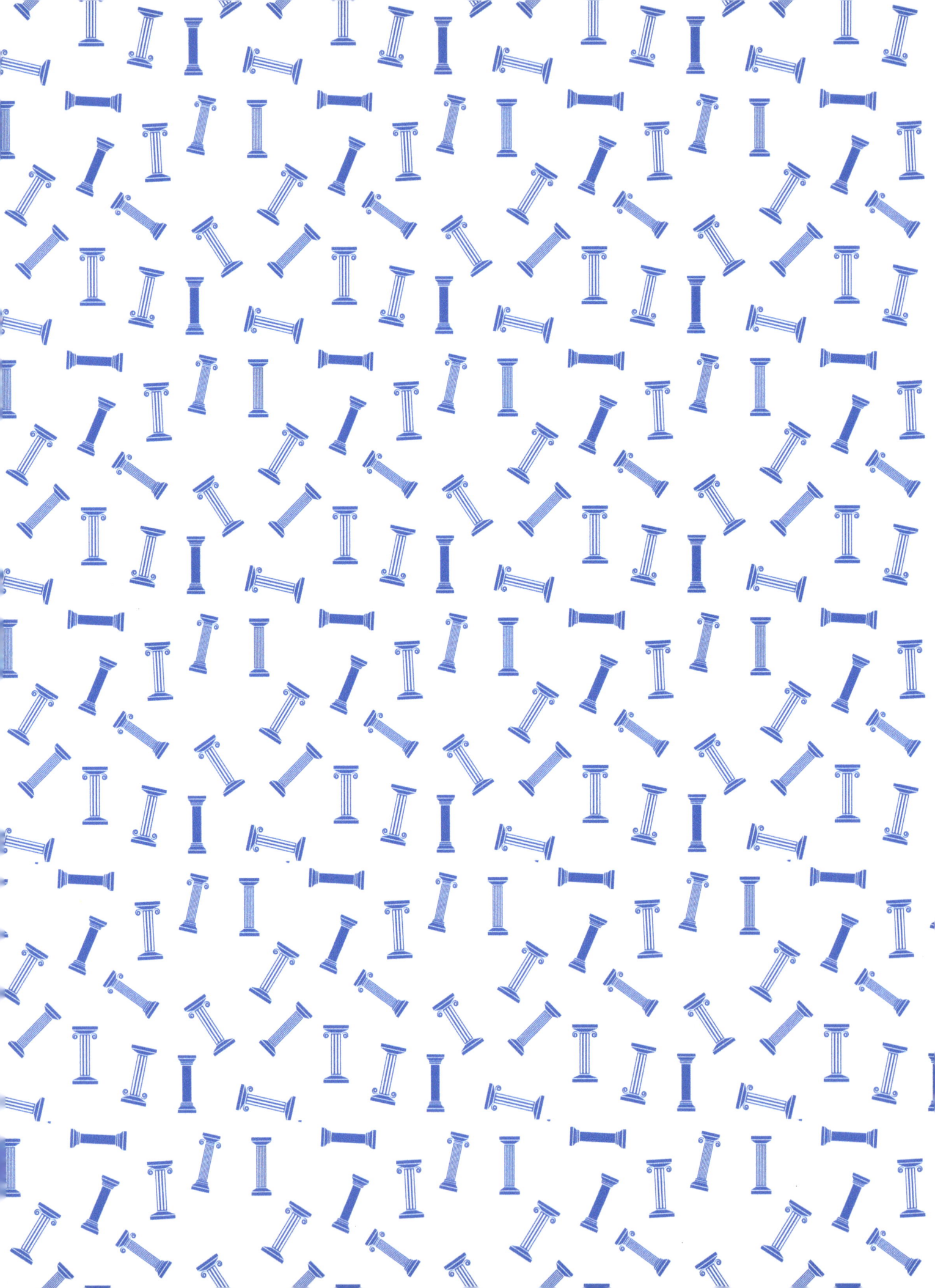

# Greece Fun Facts

Feta cheese is one of Greece's most important exports. It's nickname is "white gold".

If a baby is named after a saint, Greek parents commonly celebrate their "name day" instead of their actual birthday.

No part of Greece is more than 137 km (85 mi) away from the ocean.

Greece has several active volcanoes, located in Santorini Island (Thera), Nisyros island, Methana, and Milos island.

The official name for Greece is the Hellenic Republic, and Greeks are known as Hellenes.

There are more than 4,000 traditional dances in Greece.

The Greek language is one of the oldest written languages still in use today, influencing many other world languages.

Greece is one of the world's sunniest countries, with more than 250 sunny days or 3,000 hours of sunshine each year.

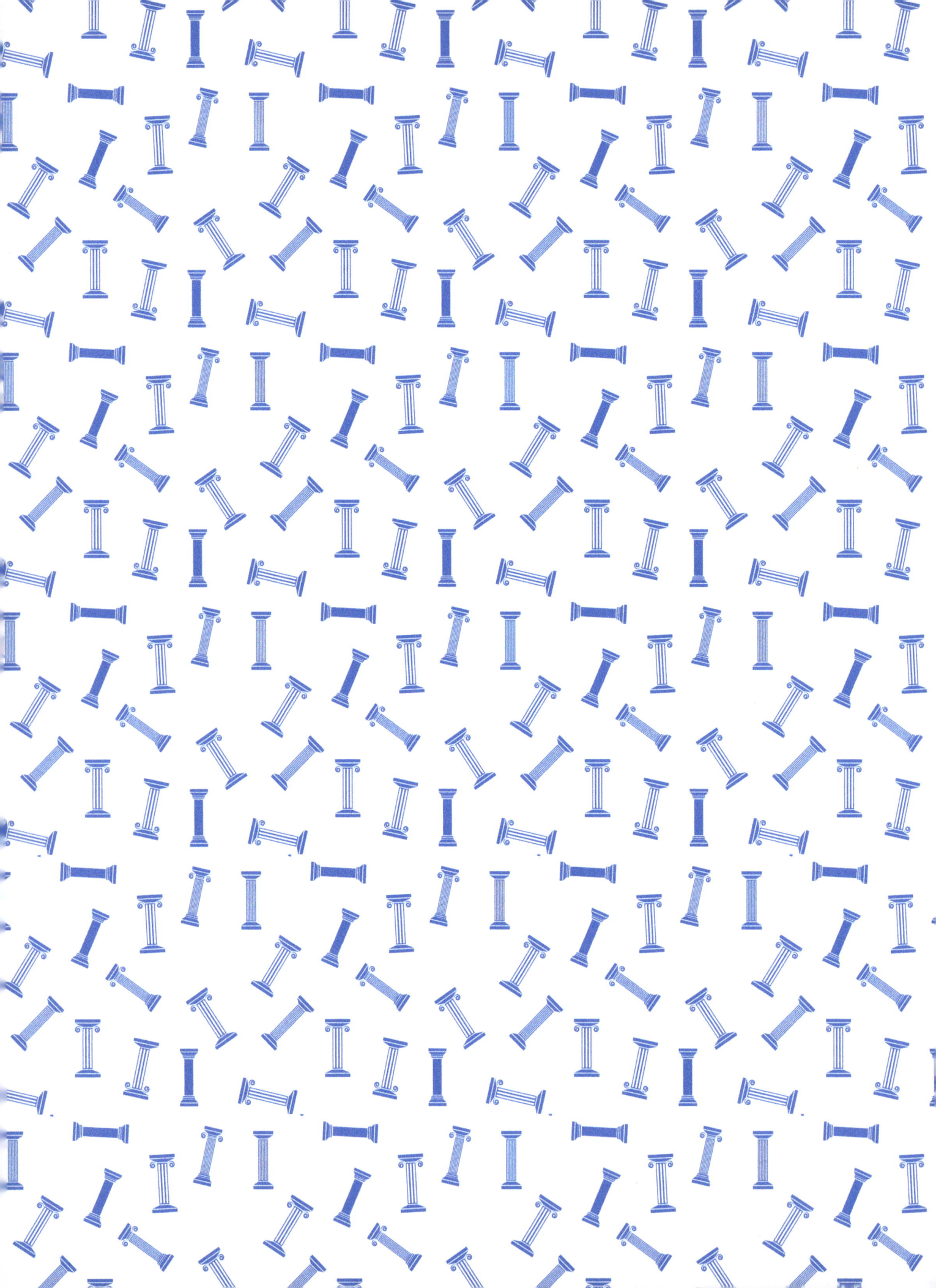

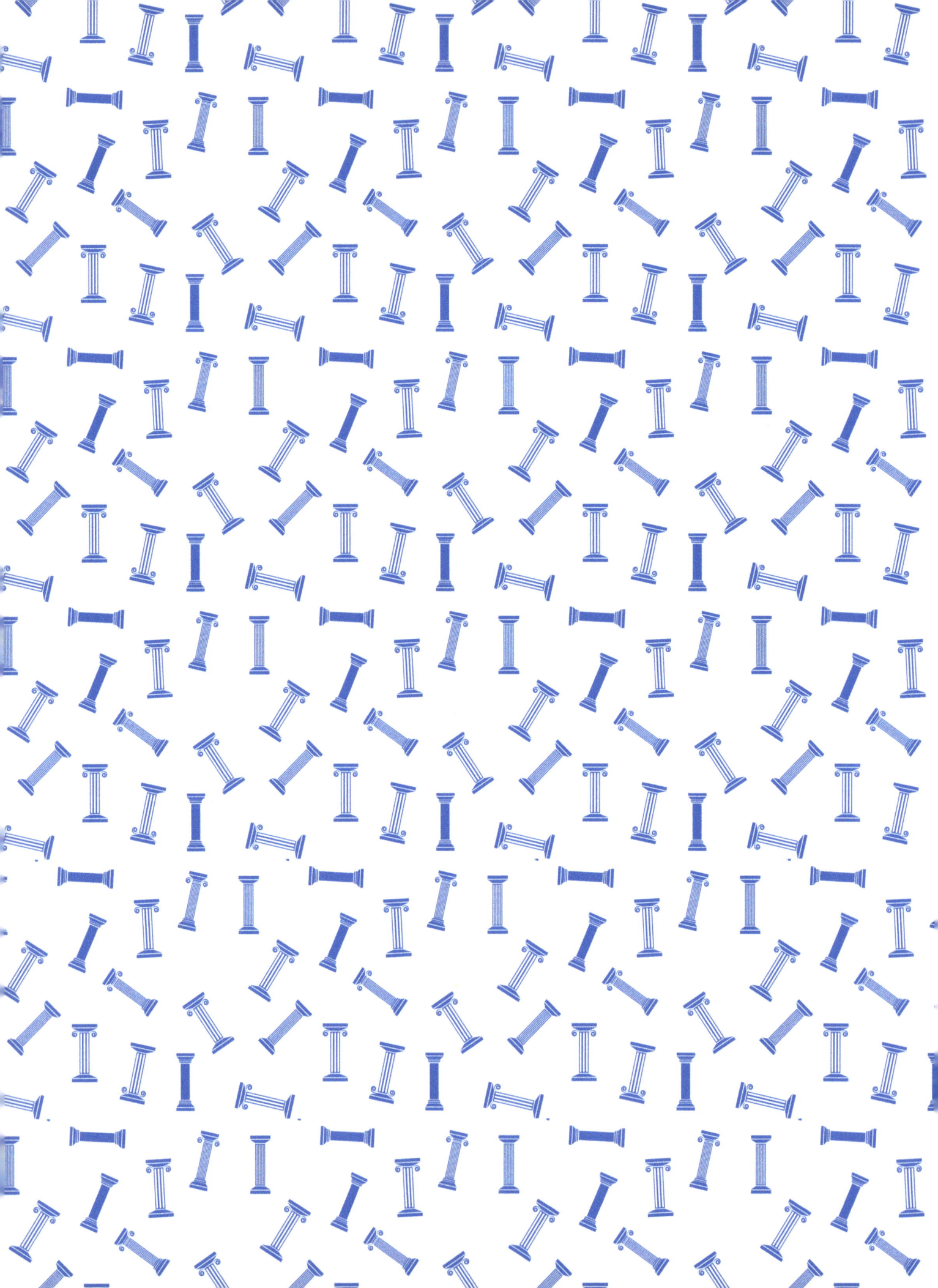

# Greek Timeline Period Cards

## Neolithic Period

Pottery, Knossos
7000 – 3200 BC

## Bronze Age

Lion Gate, Mycenae
3200 – 1100 BC

## Iron Age

Terracotta Boots
1100 – 800 BC

## Archaic Period

Temple of Apollo
800 – 490 BC

αρχή

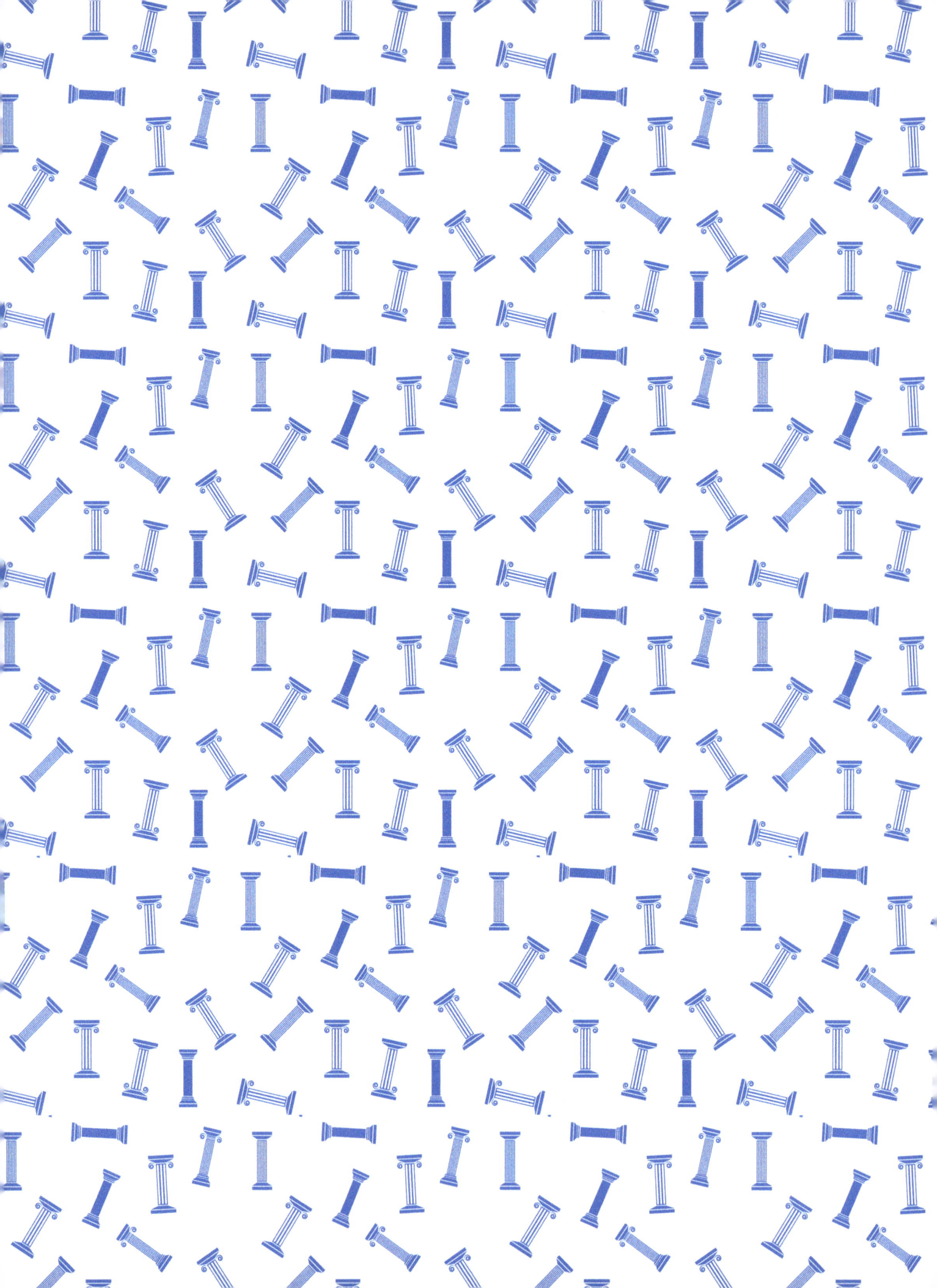

# Greek Timeline Period Cards

## Classical Period

*Parthenon, Acropolis*
490 - 323 BC

## Hellenistic Period

*Coin depicting Cassander, leader of Hellenistic Greece*
323 - 146 BC

## Roman Period

*Roman Agora*
146 BC - 324 AD

## Byzantine Greece

*Meteora Monasteries*
324 - 1453 AD

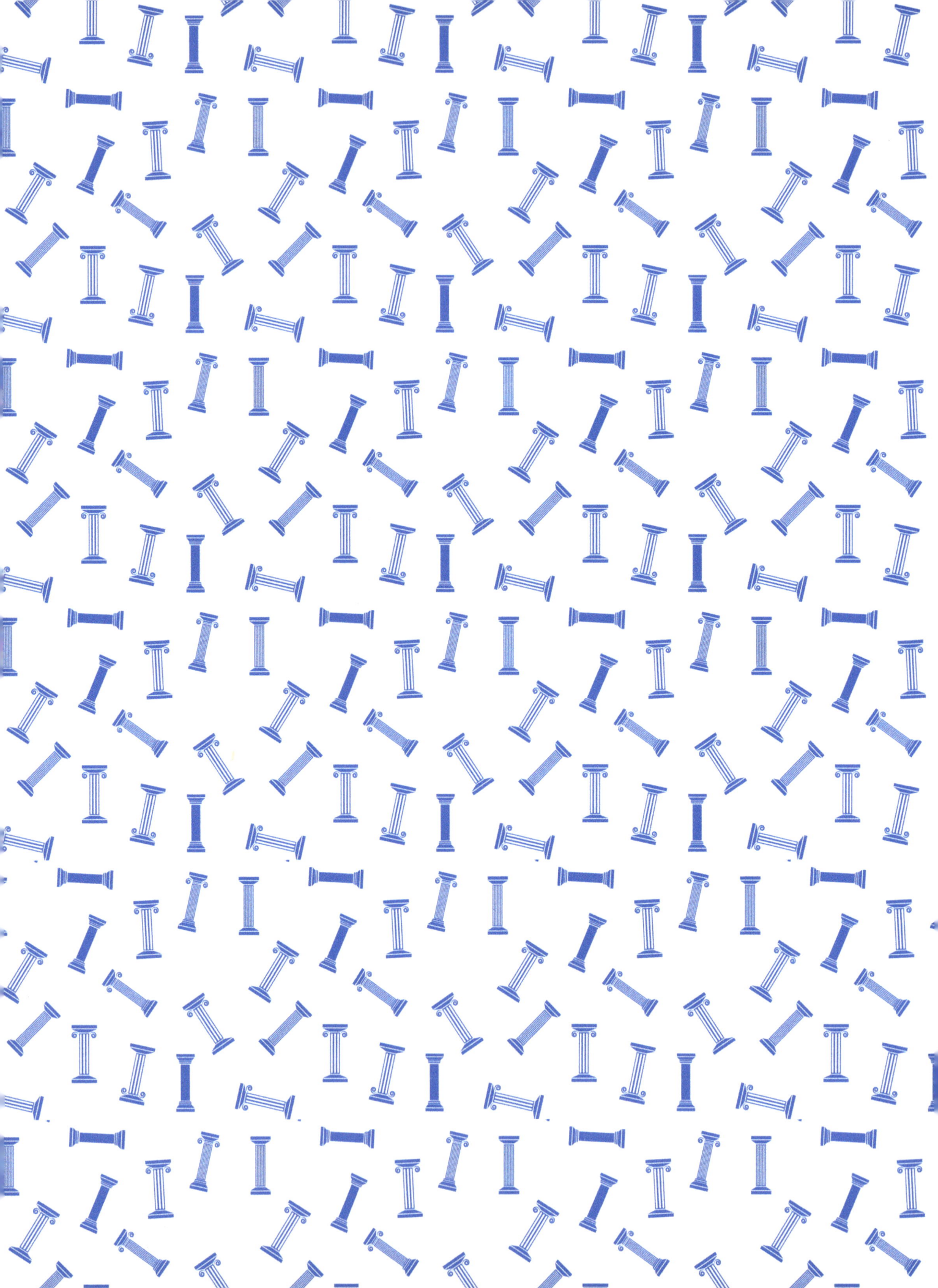

# Greek Timeline Period Cards

## Ottoman Period

*Battle of Chios*
1453 - 1821 AD

## Modern Greece

*Athens, Greece*
1821 - Current

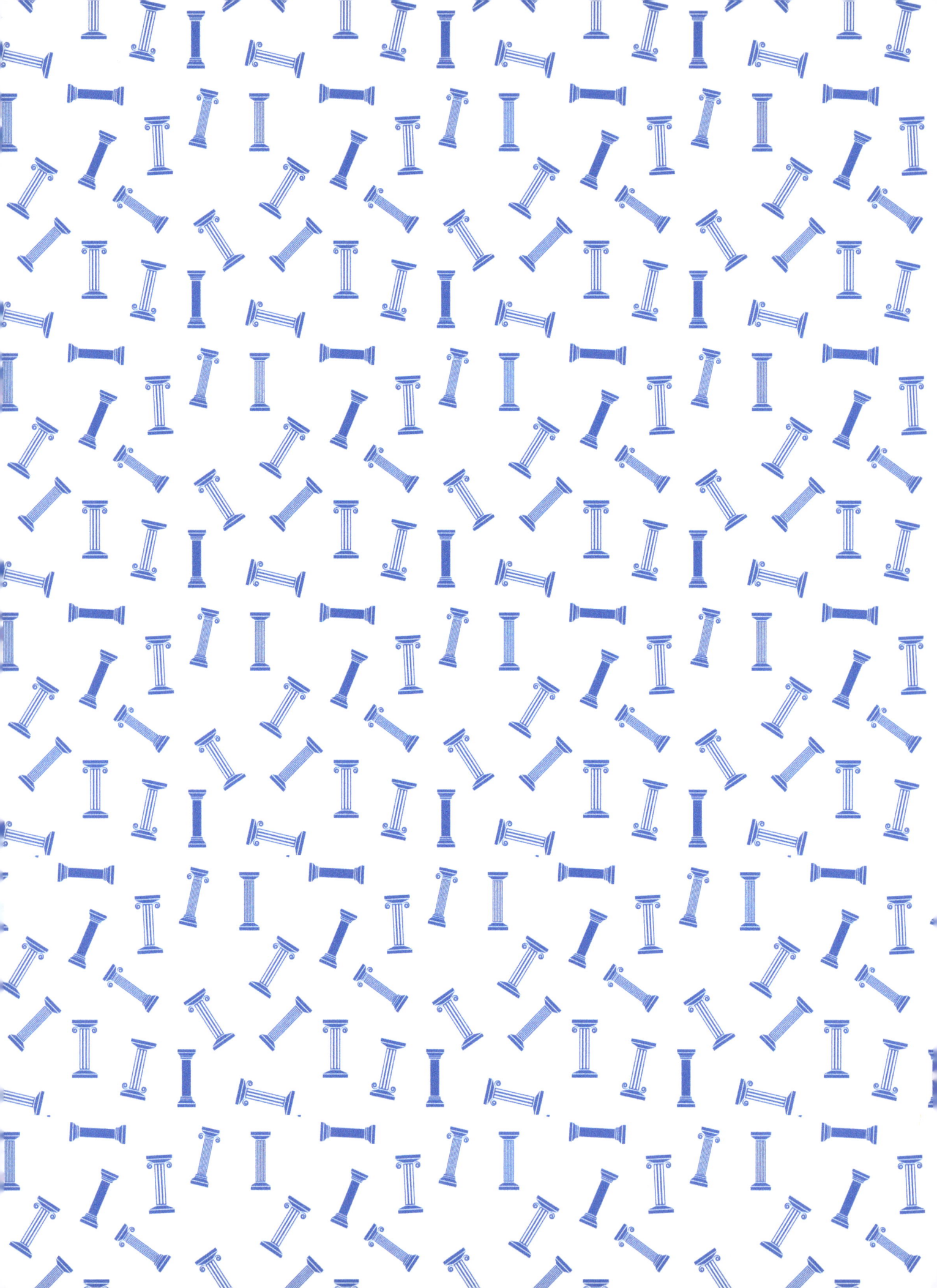

# PARTHENON MODEL

## Instructions

The Parthenon is a temple located on the Acropolis in Athens, Greece. It was dedicated to the goddess Athena, whom the people of Athens considered their patroness. Construction started in 447 BC when the Delian League was at the peak of its power. In 1687, this building was almost completely destroyed.

**Materials**
- Parthenon Template
- Scissors
- Craft Glue
- Clothespins
- Tape

Cut out each piece, paying attention to detail for more realistic final product. Glue two **Base** pieces together along center tab, matching up detail so it appears as one piece. Locate **West Side** and glue onto West side of **Base** with tab positioned underneath (hidden). Locate **Inner Columns** and **West Side Possession**; glue sides of **West Side Possession** together to form three sided structure. Fold **West Side Inner Columns** along dashed line on tabs and glue onto sides of **West Side Possession** to create two walls in front of each other, as indicated. Glue onto **Base**, just behind **West Side**, as indicated. Locate **North & South Sides**, and glue pieces together along tabs to complete full sides.

Cut slits on corners of all four side pieces as indicated, and attatch together by inserting the **West/East Sides** onto **North/South Sides**. Glue side tabs together to secure sides together at all four corners. Glue all sides to **Base** with tabs positioned underneath (hidden).

Locate **East Inner Column** and glue onto **Base** using tab just behind **East Side**. Adjust pieces and add additional glue as necessary to secure structure. Allow to dry completely before displaying.

**Discuss:** Compare Parthenon ruins to included Parthenon detail poster. Can you locate the details on the ruins, based on the illustration? What areas of the Parthenon are most damaged? What did the inside of the Parthenon look like prior to its destruction? What plans are underway to restore this iconic temple? What are other examples of this kind of architecture throughout the world? Where are they located and when were they constructed?

# Parthenon: North Side

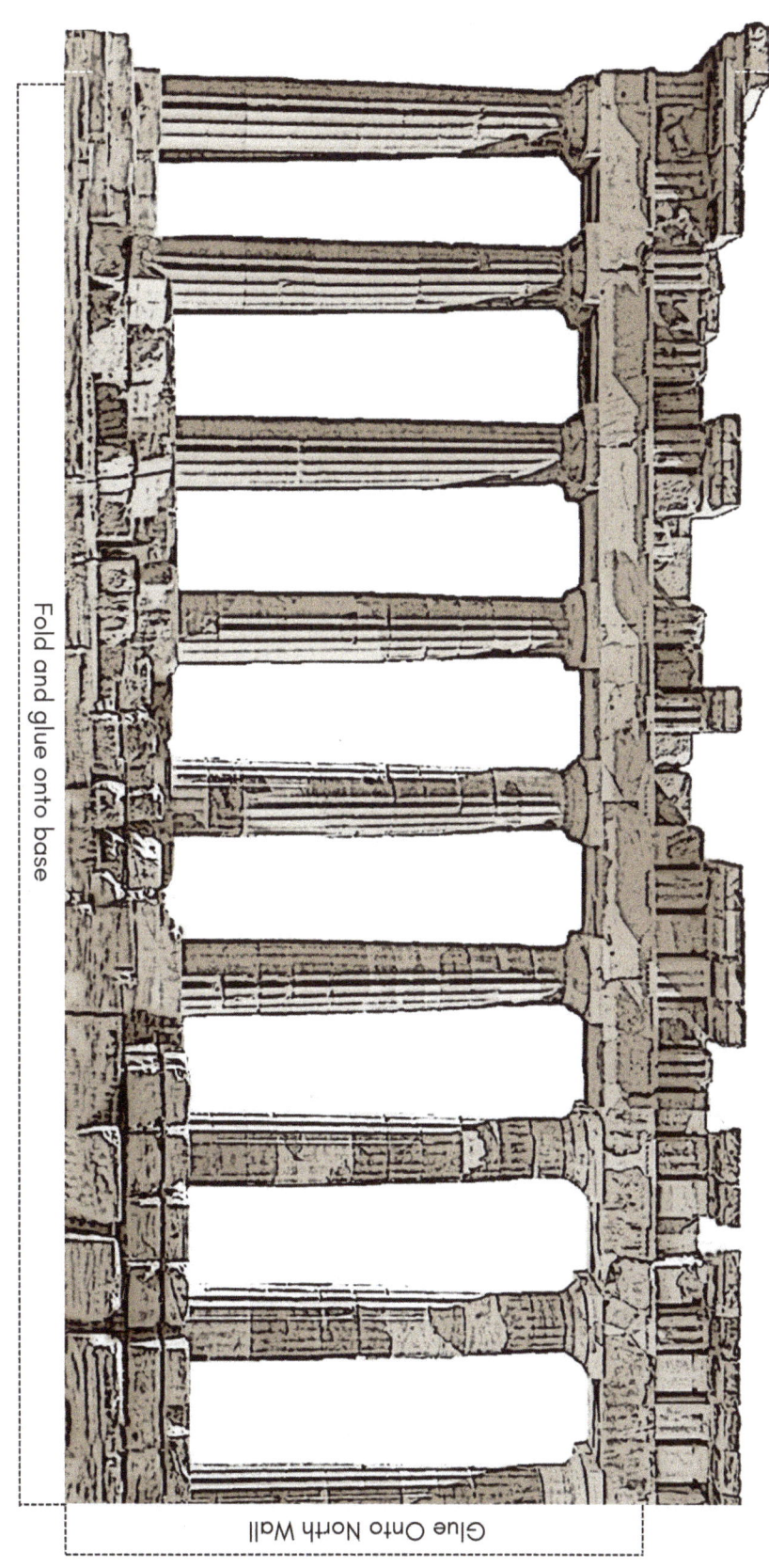

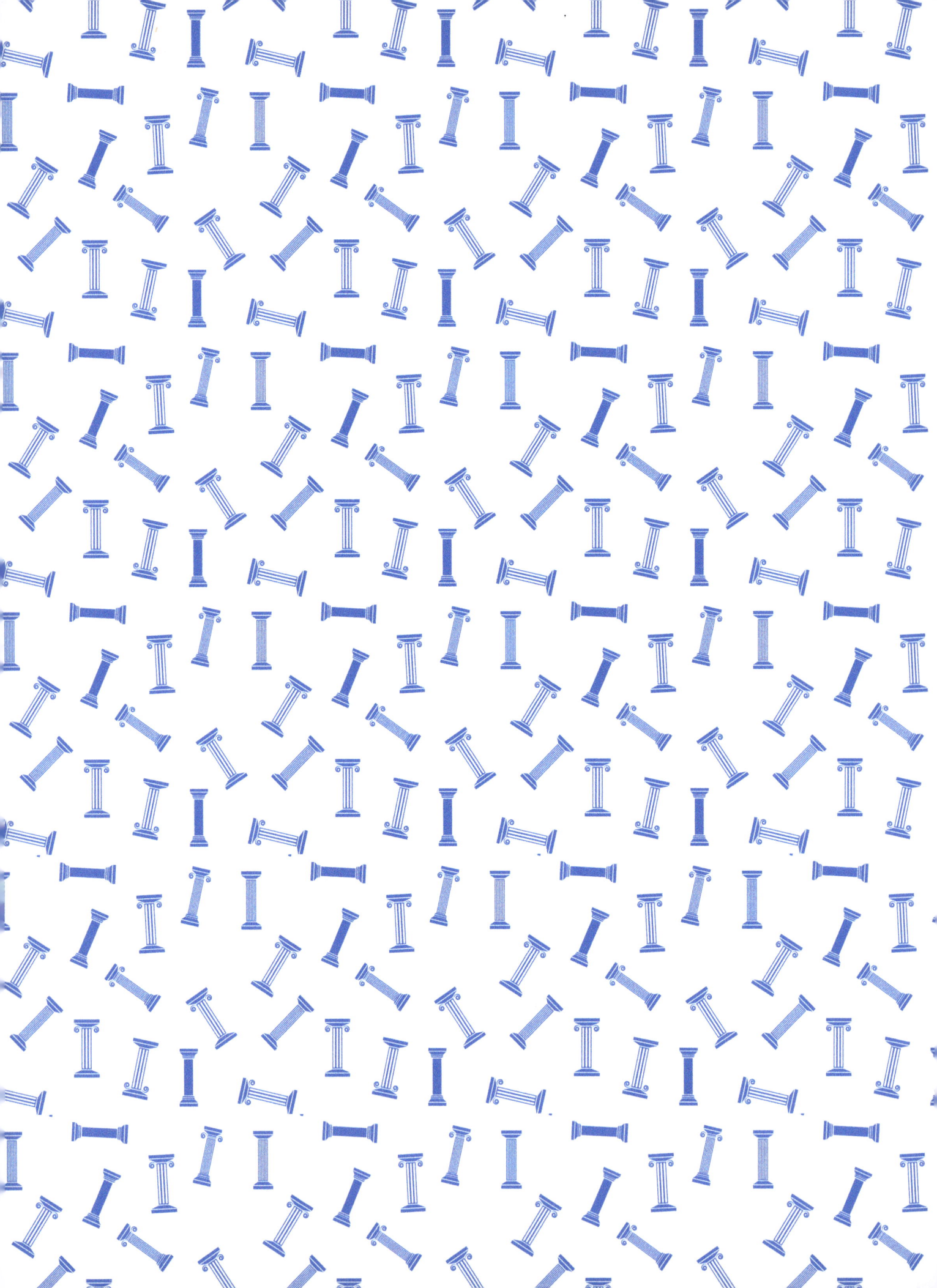

# Parthenon: North Side

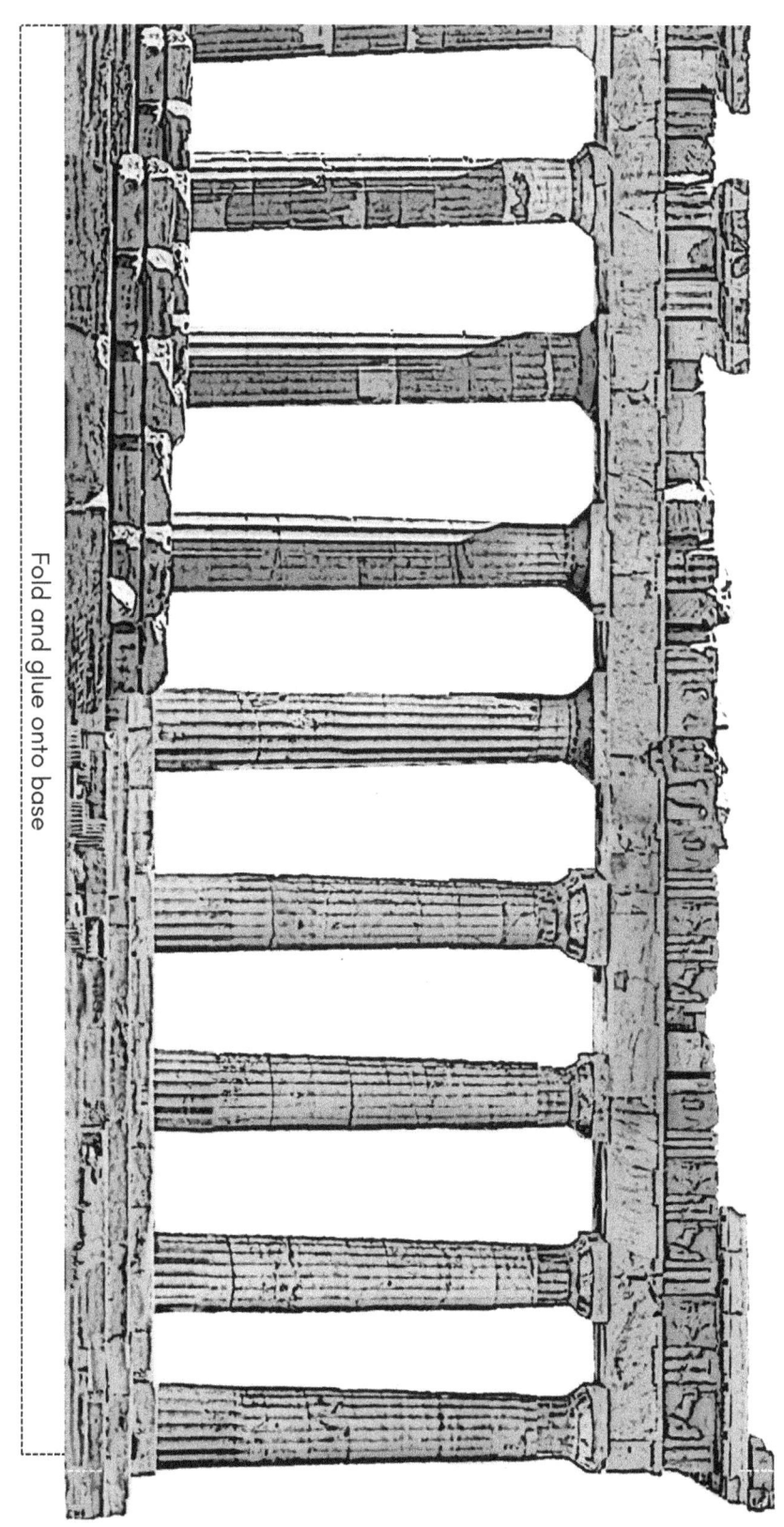

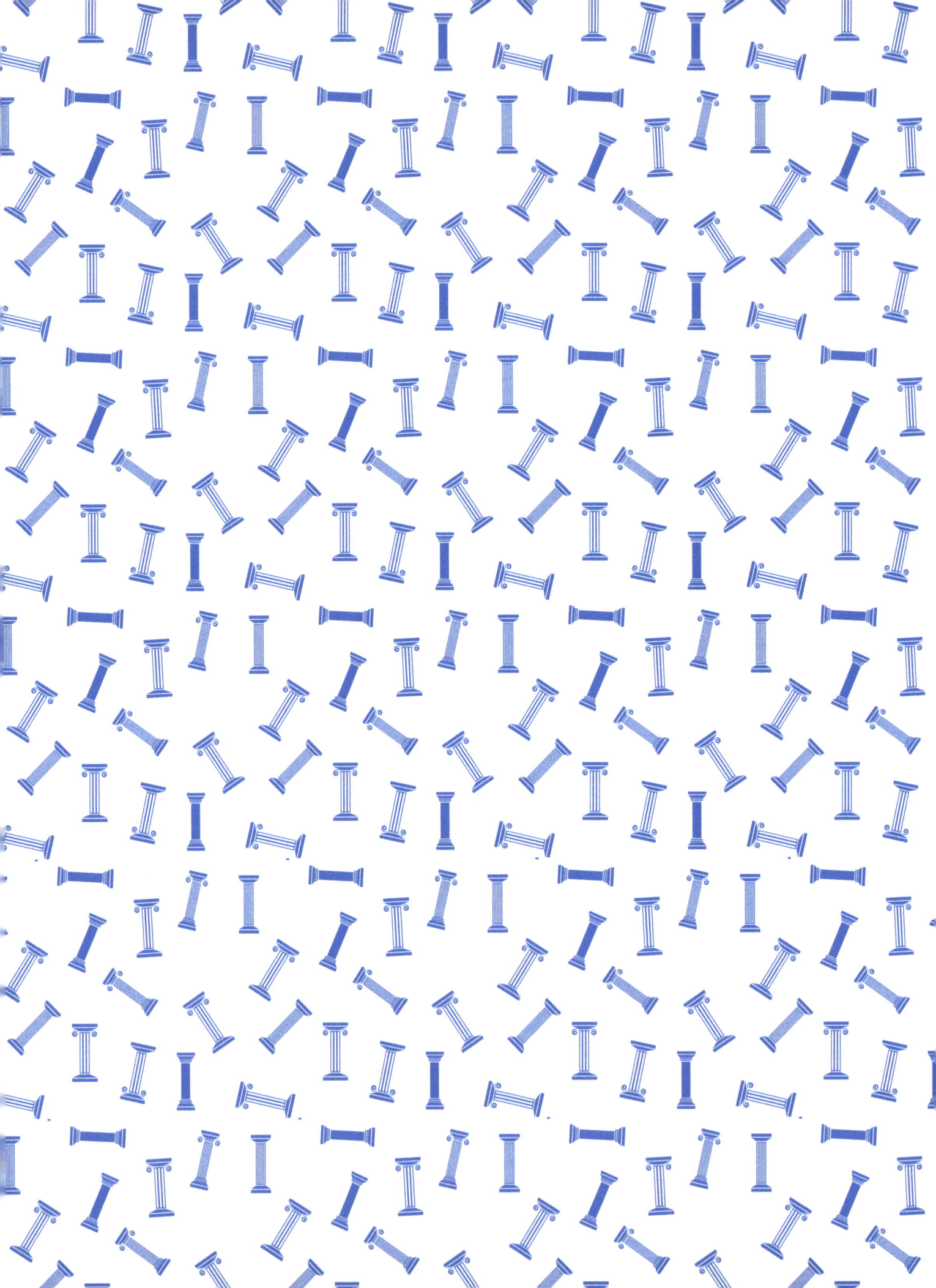

# Parthenon: South Side

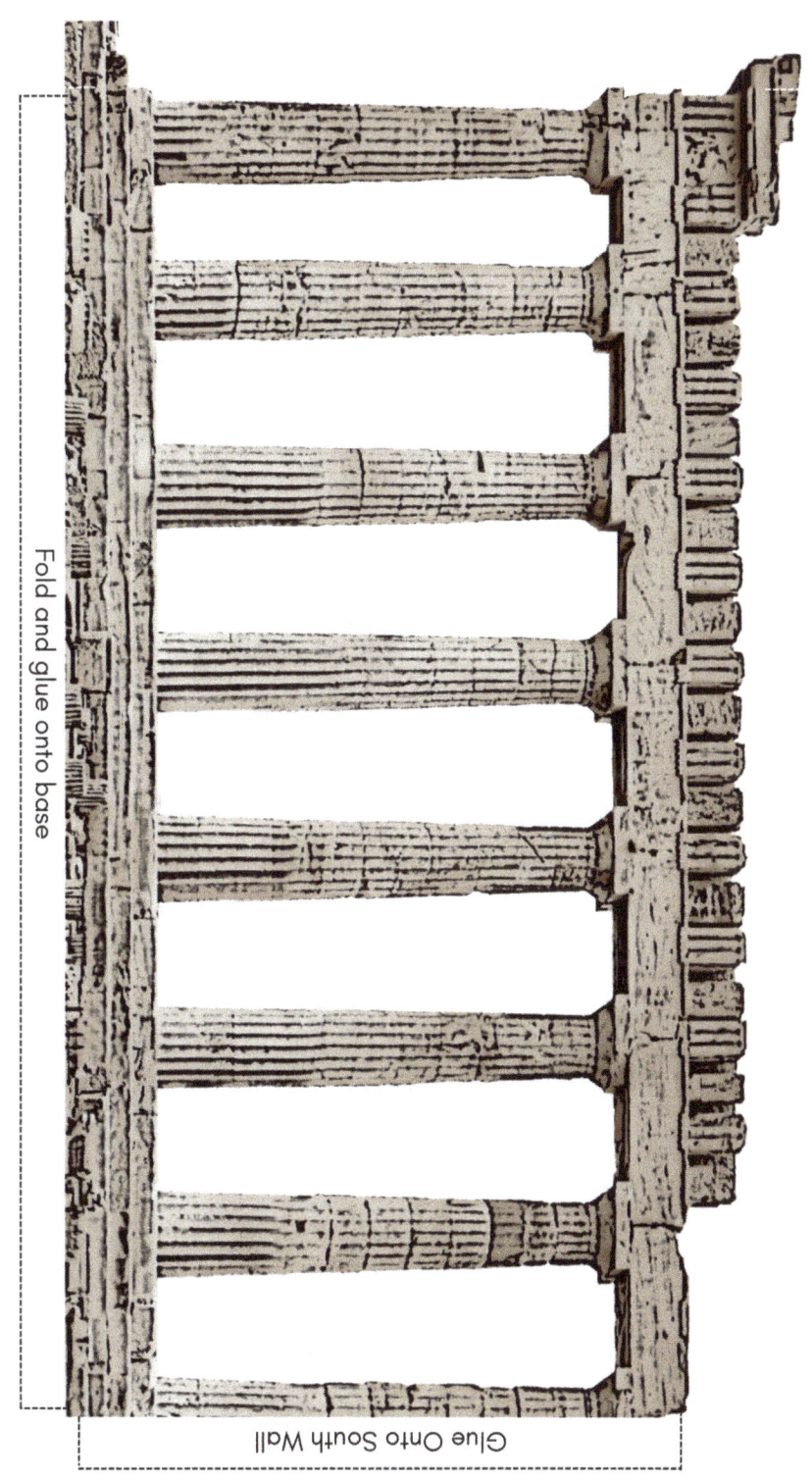

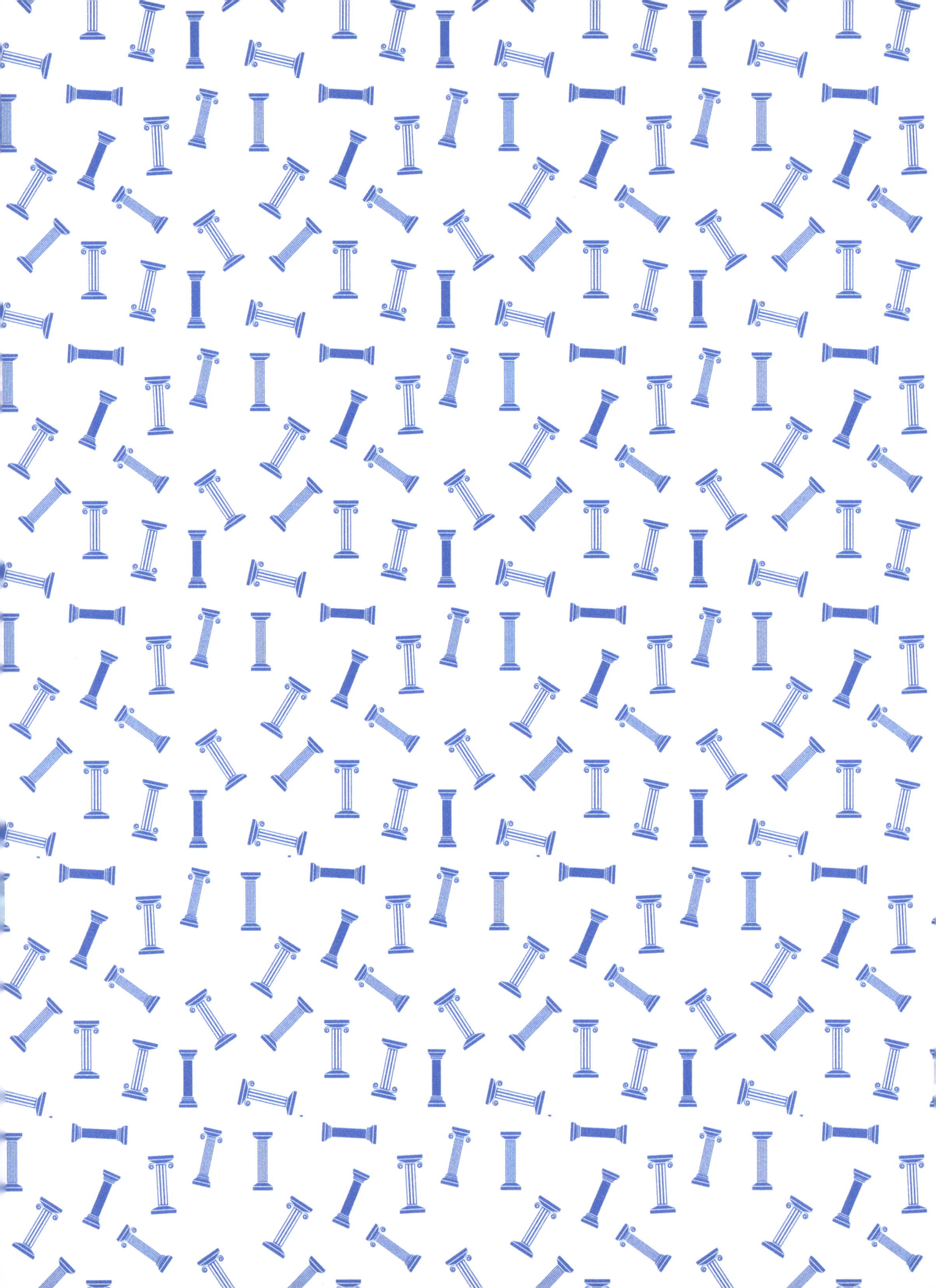

# Parthenon: South Side

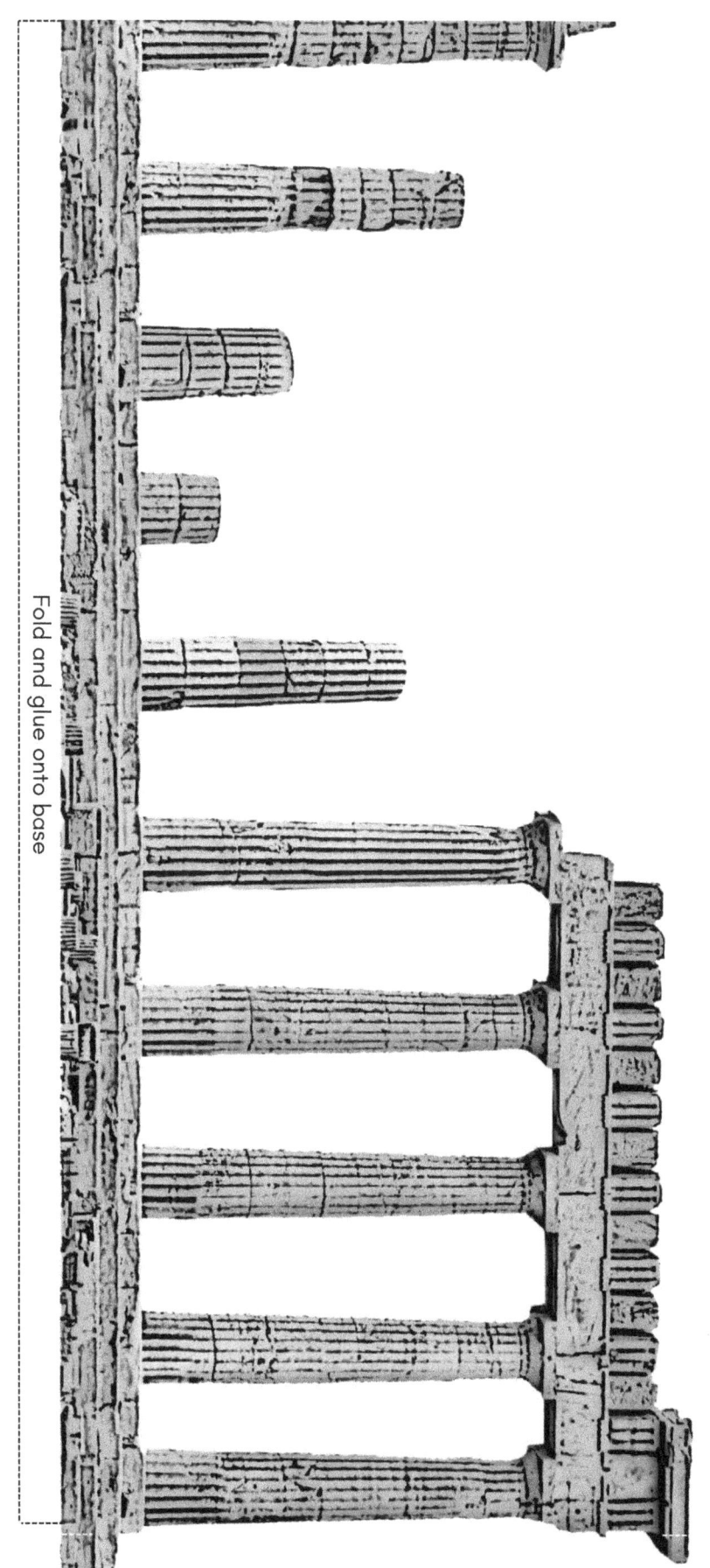

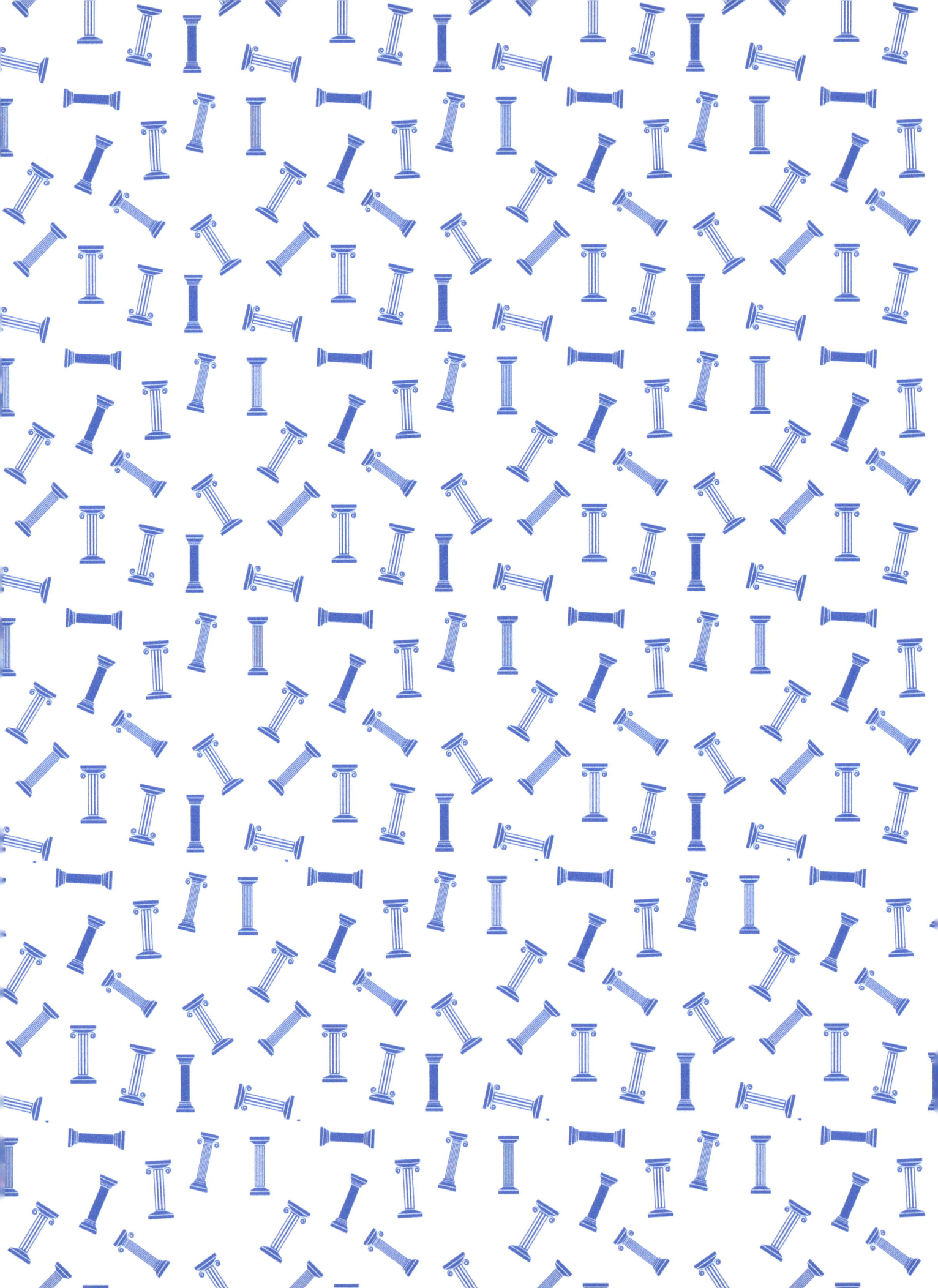

# Parthenon: West Side

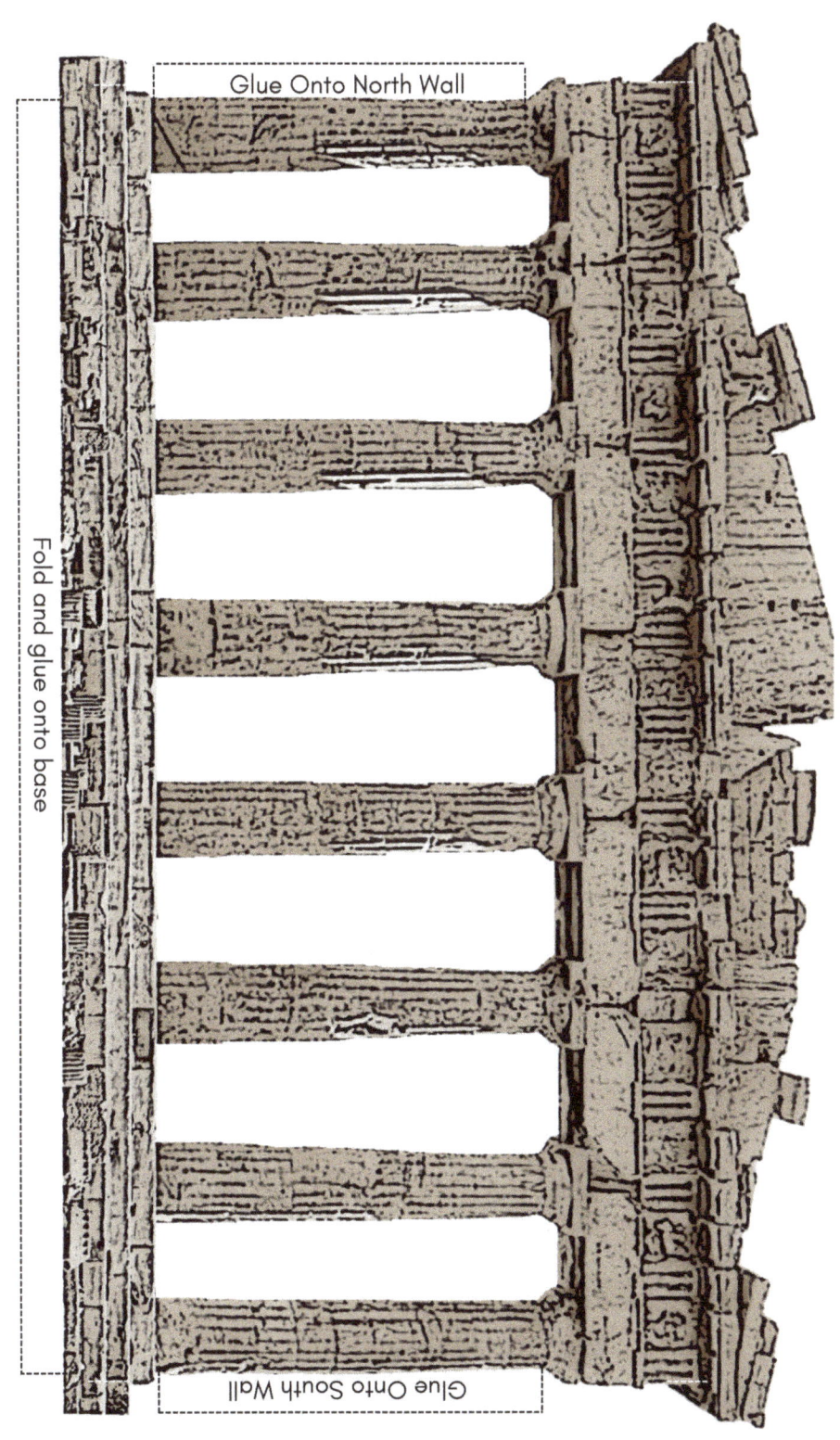

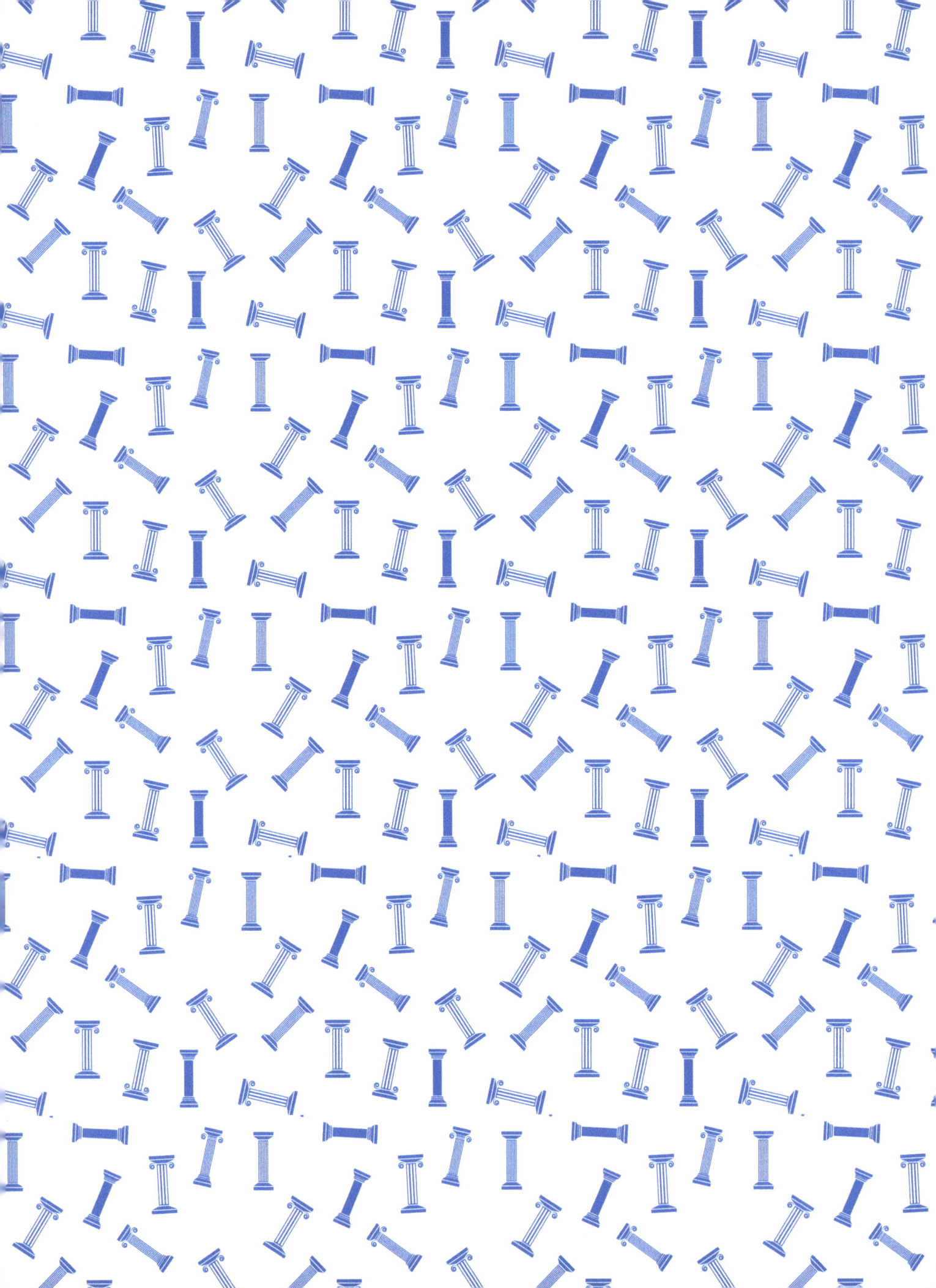

# Parthenon: East Side

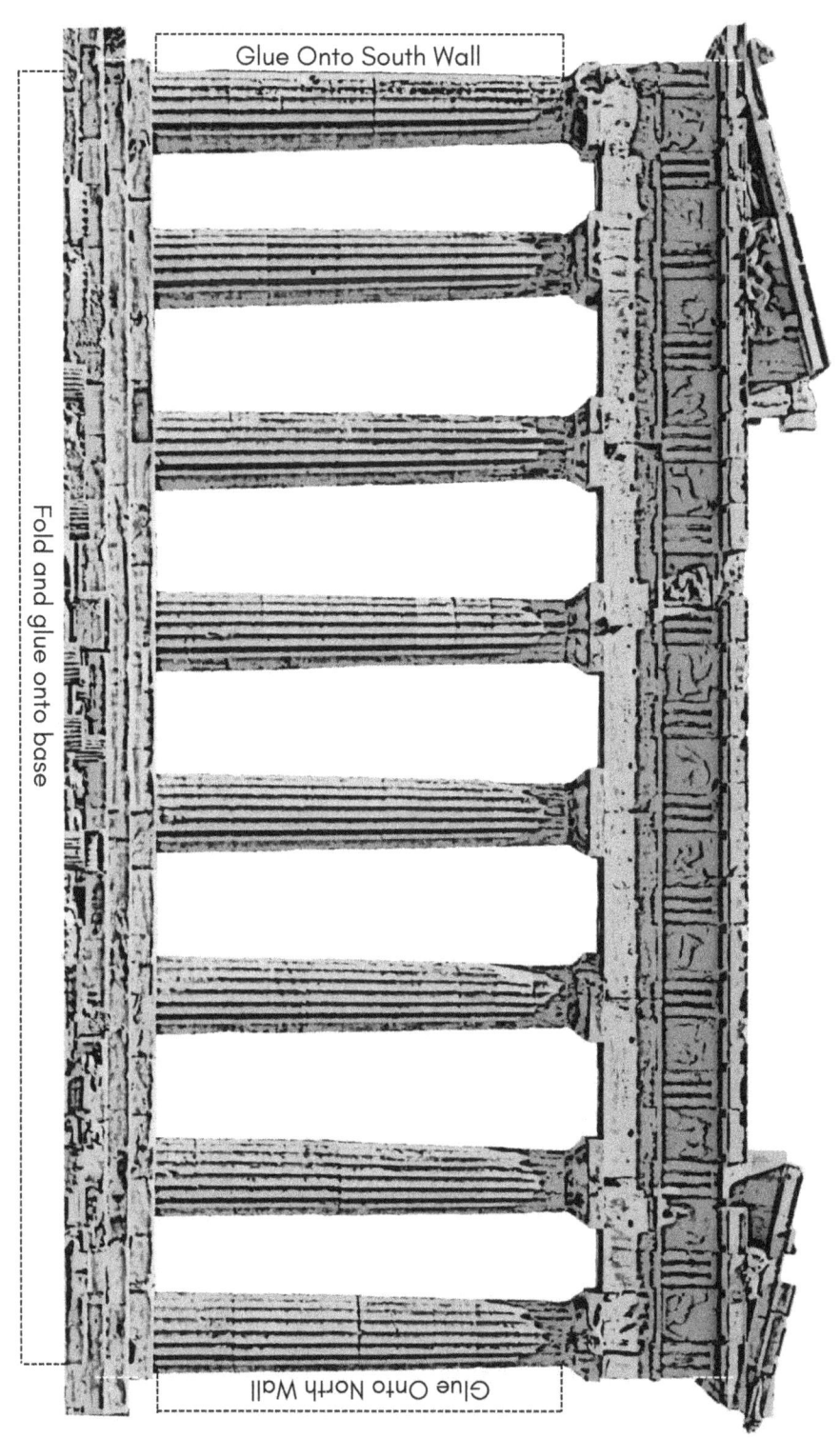

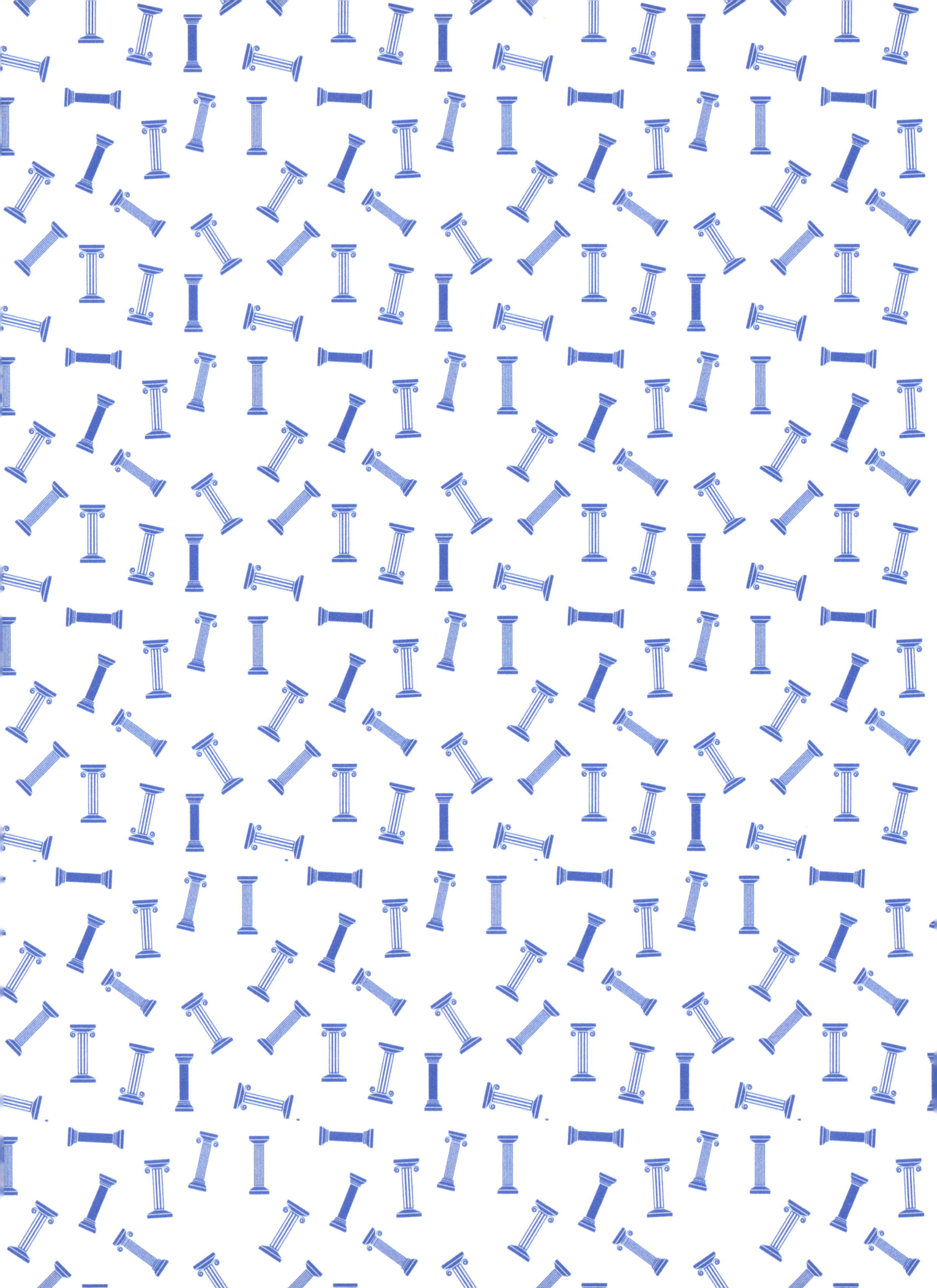

# Parthenon: Inner Columns

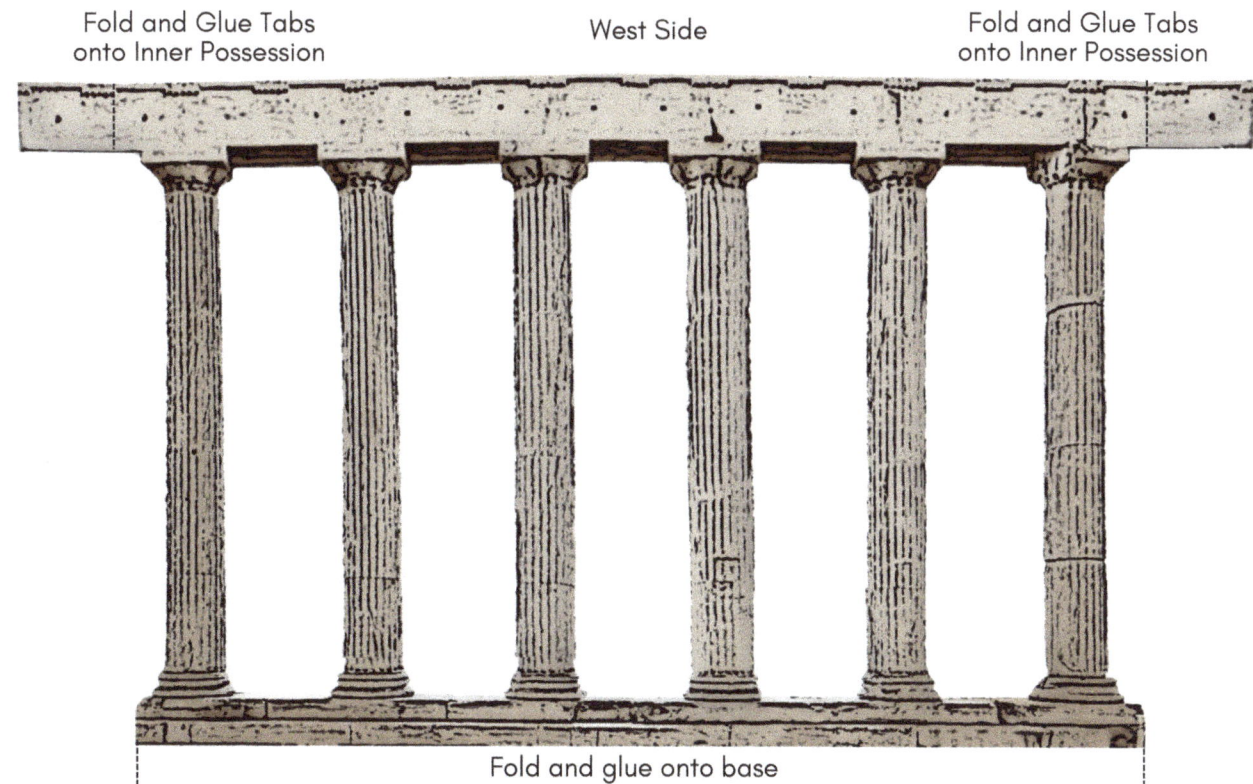

Fold and Glue Tabs onto Inner Possession    West Side    Fold and Glue Tabs onto Inner Possession

Fold and glue onto base

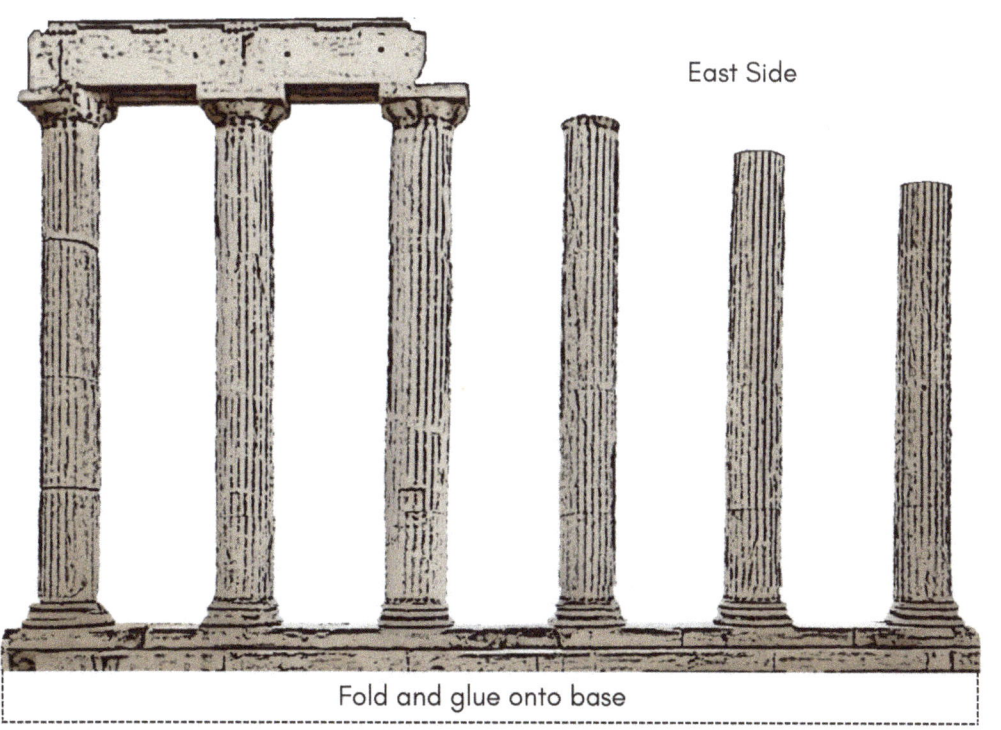

East Side

Fold and glue onto base

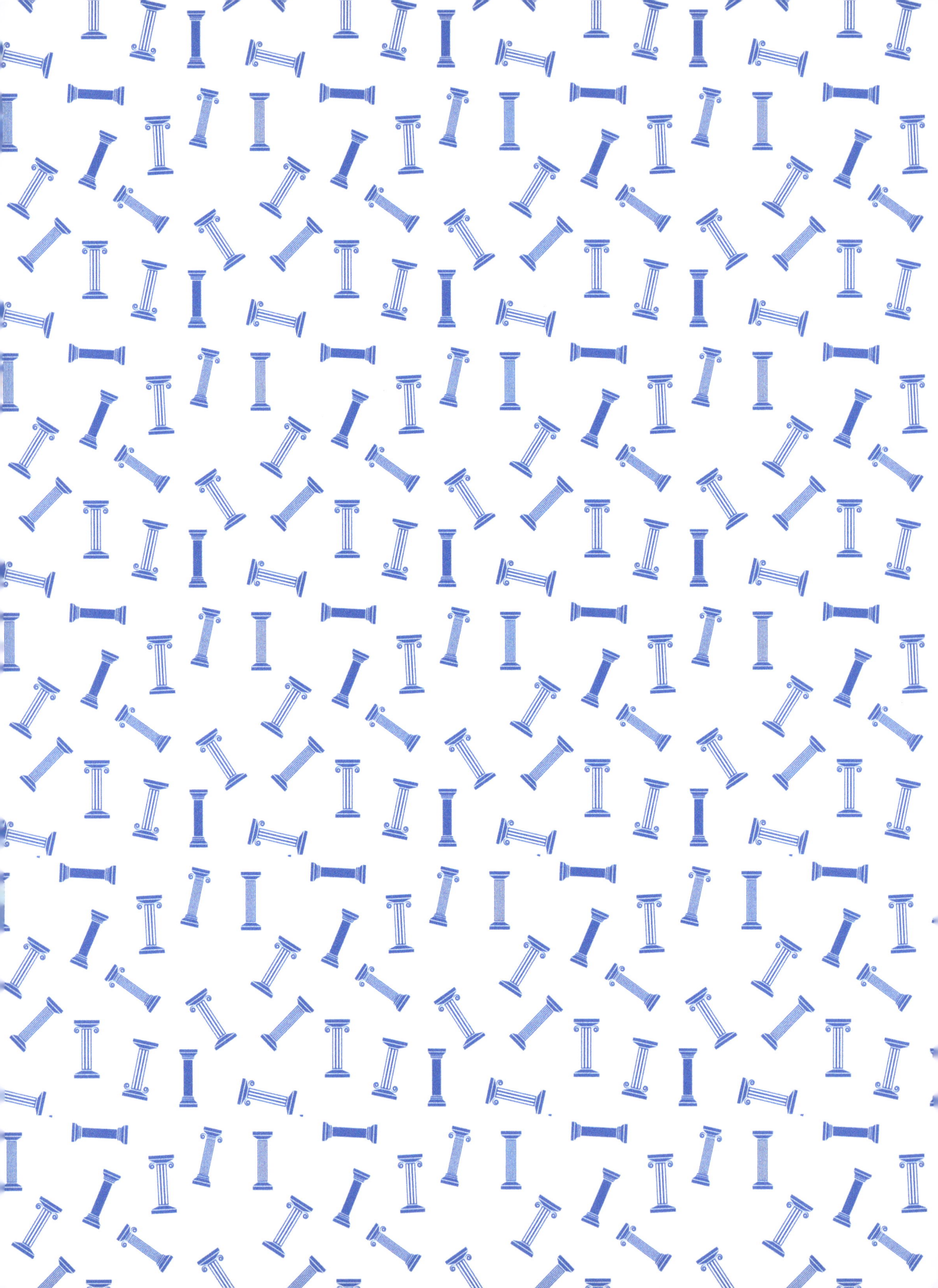

# Parthenon: West Side, Possession

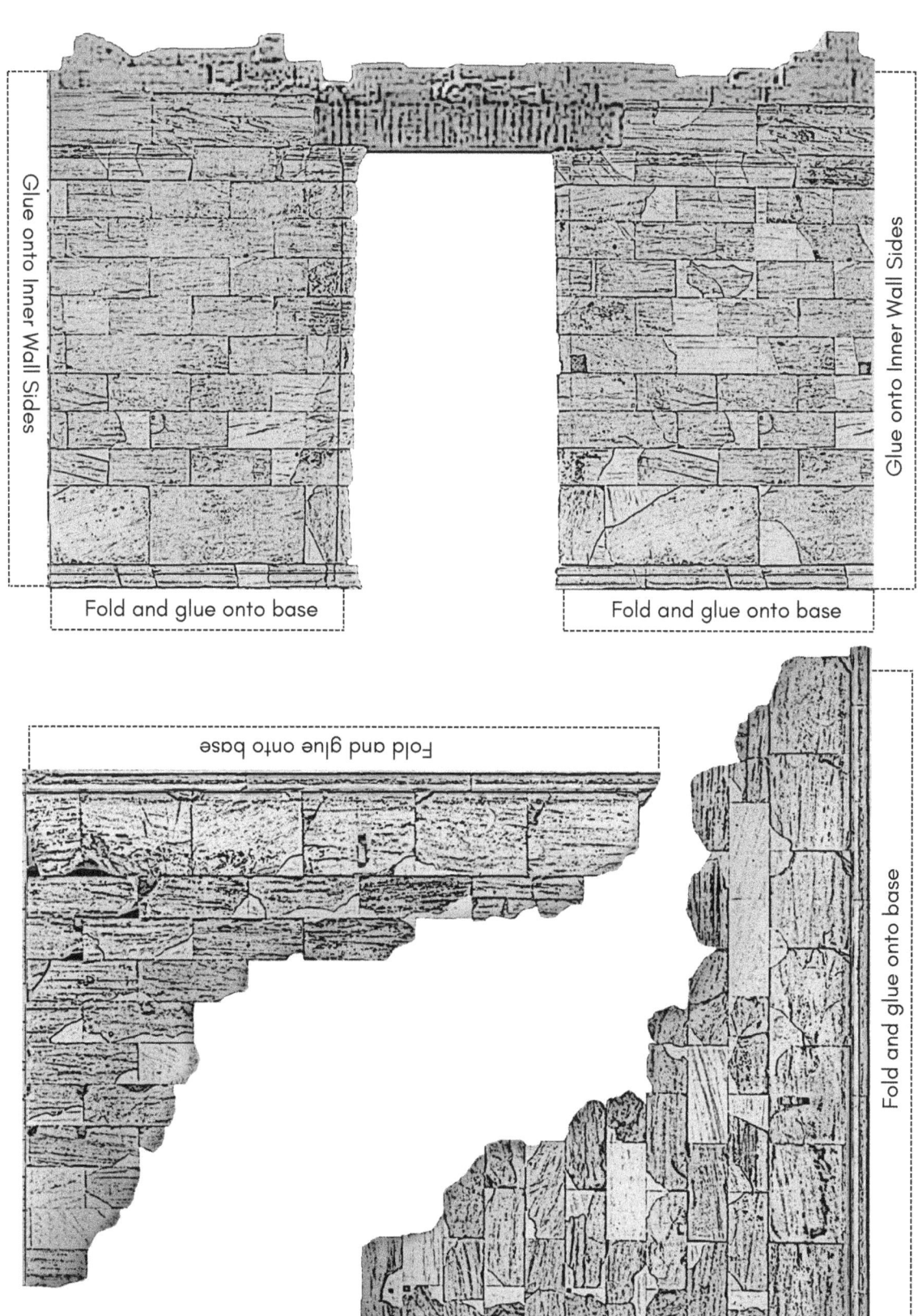

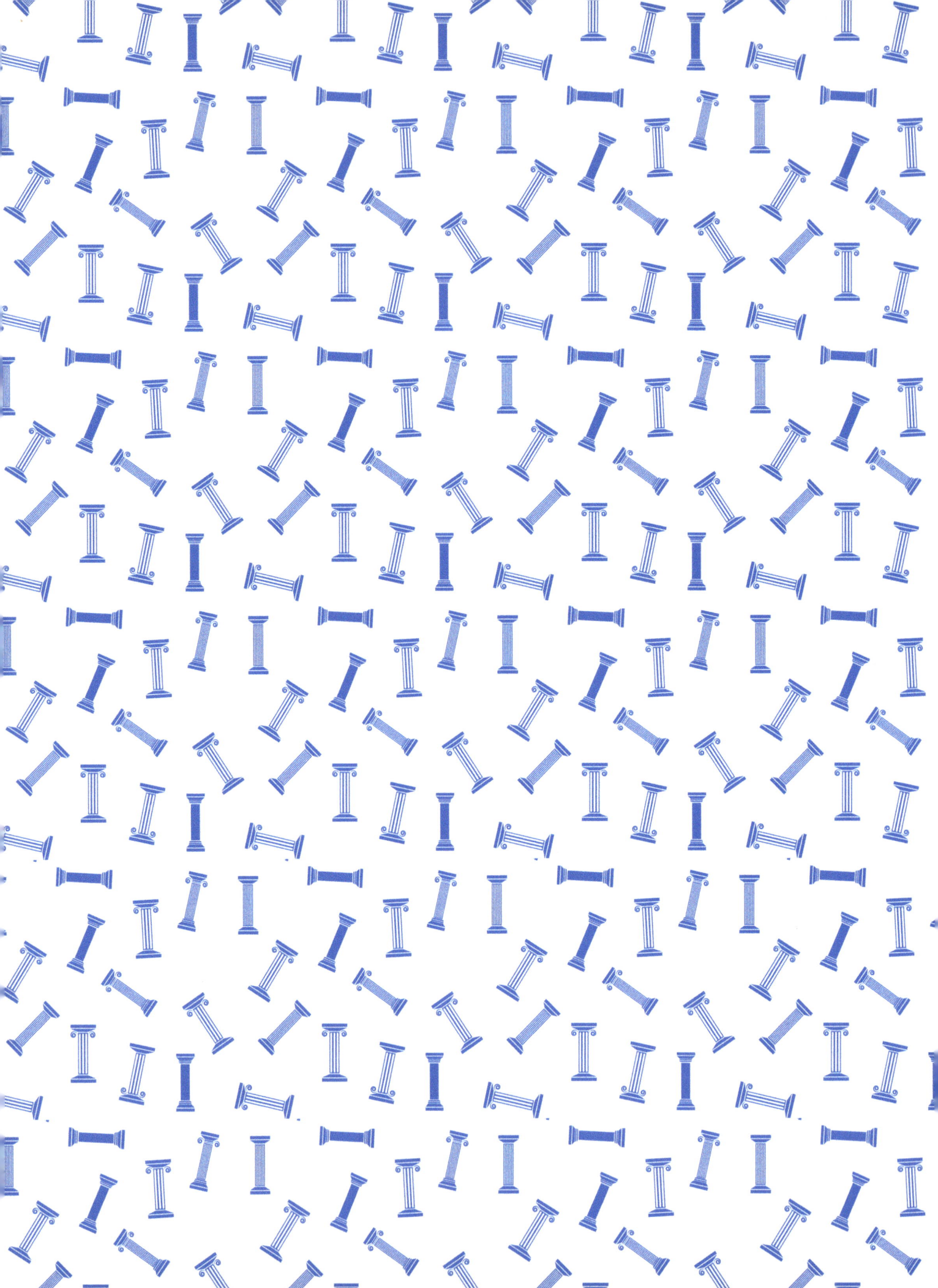

# Parthenon: Base

Glue Additional Base Piece Here

East Side

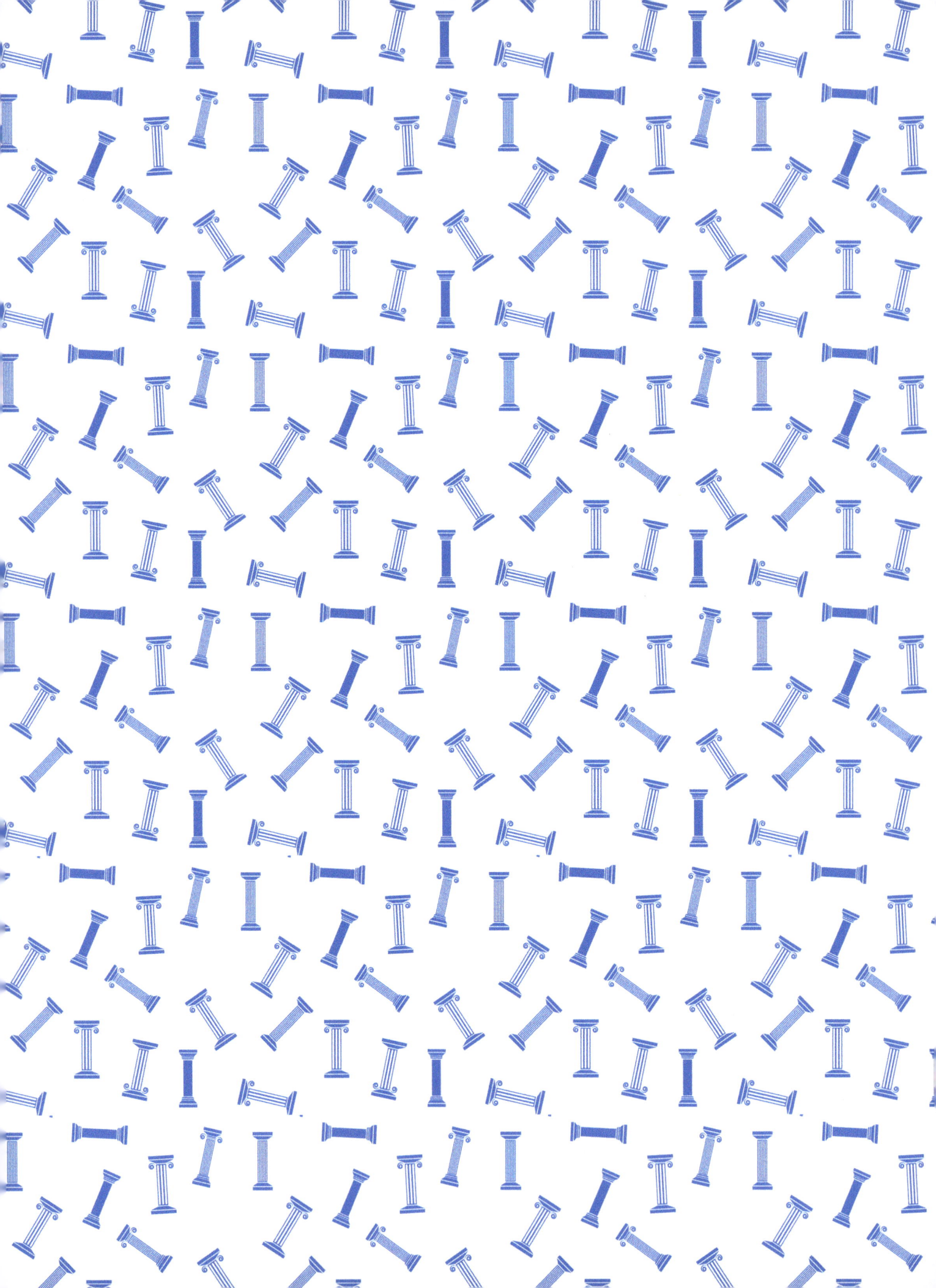

West Side

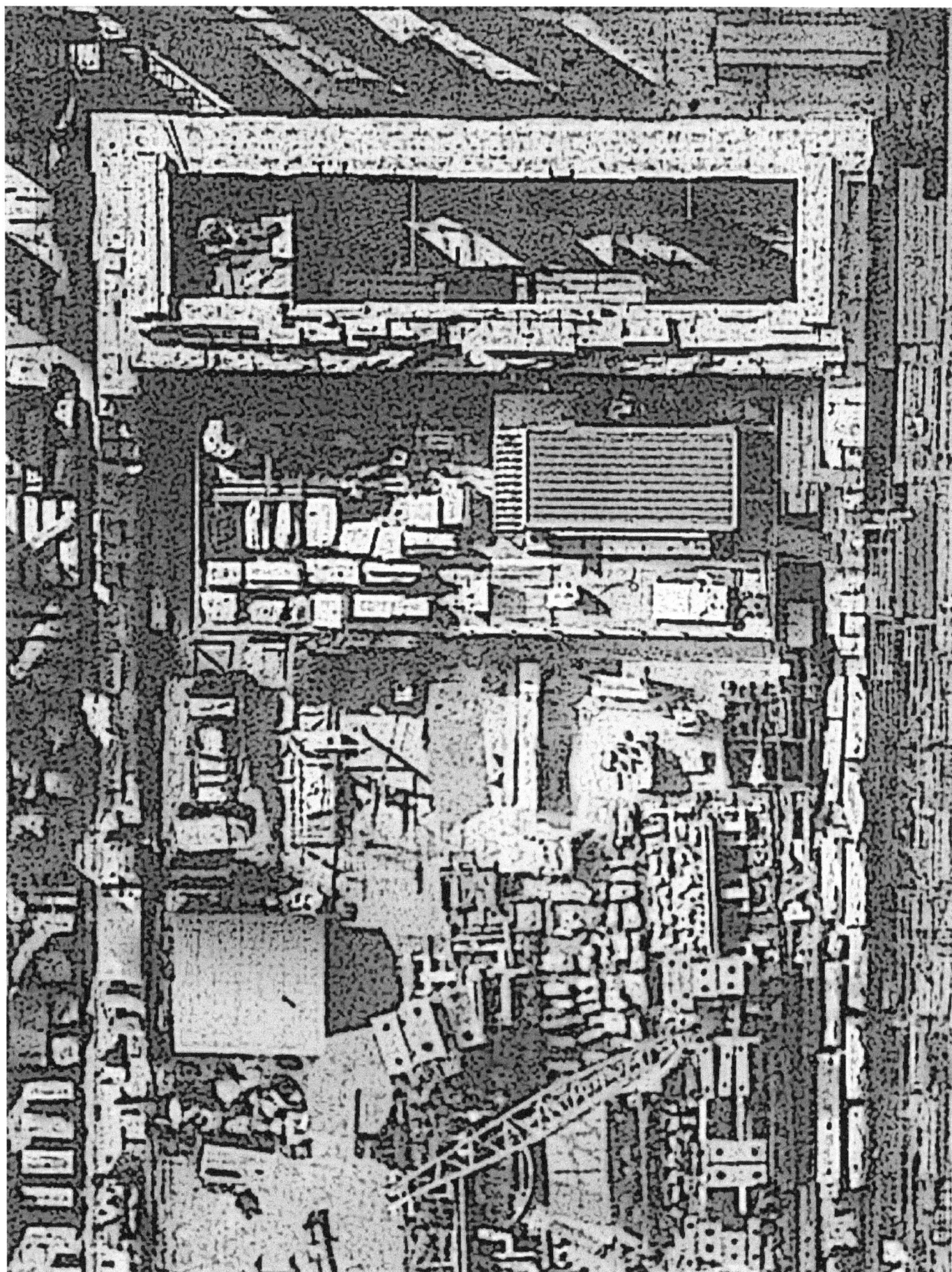

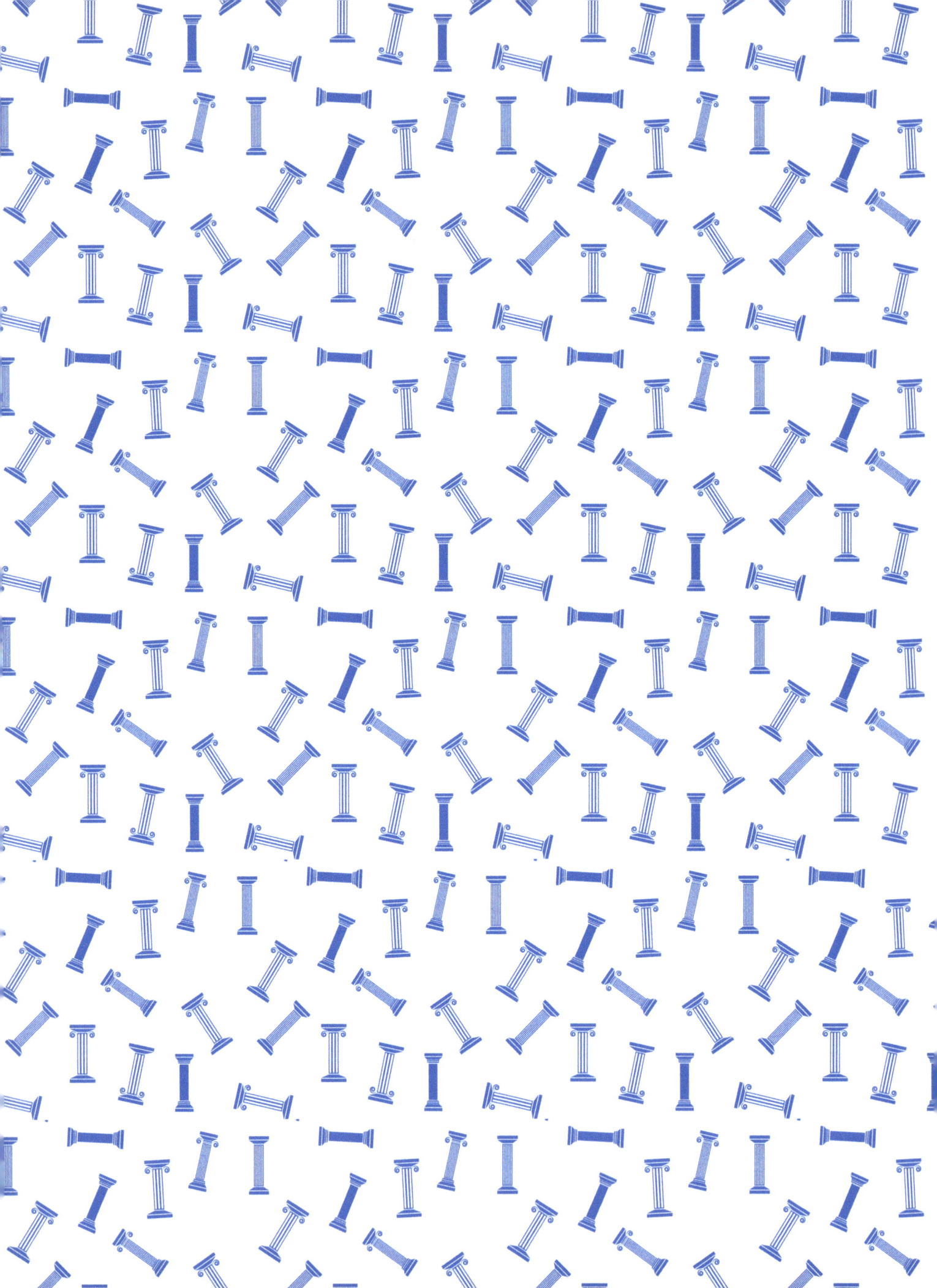

# Parts of the Parthenon

**Labels:** Fluting, Column, Capital, Architrave, Frieze, Mutules, Abacus, Echinus, Sima, Gutta, Pediment, Taenia, Cornice, Metope, Triglyph, Stylobate

The Parthenon was built using the Doric order architecture

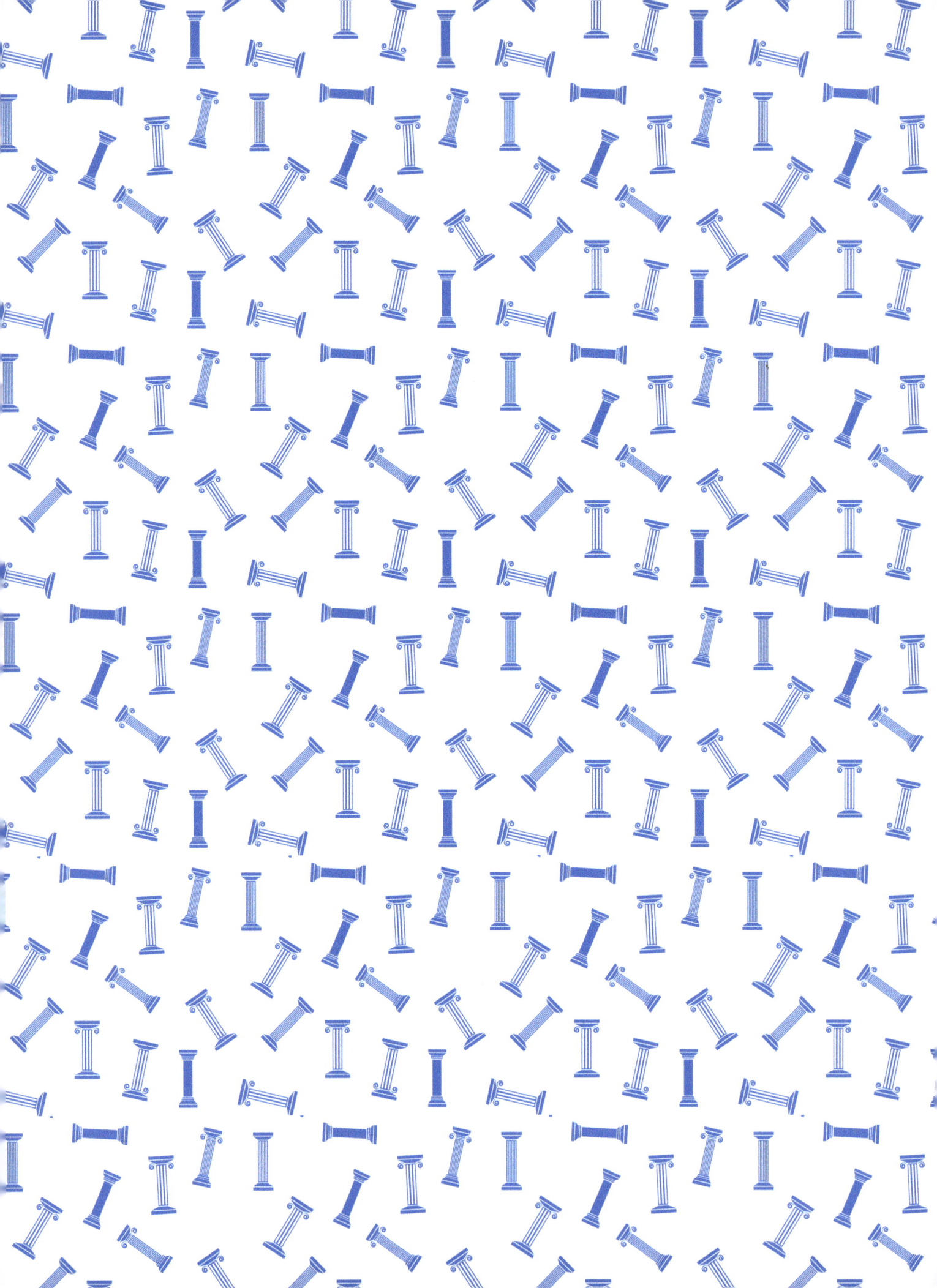

# Greek Column Matching

The ancient Greeks were incredible architects. They invented three types of columns to support their buildings. There was the stylish Doric, the Ionic with its scrolls, and the fancy Corinthian.

The **Doric Order** was first seen towards the beginning of the 7th century BC. Doric columns were stouter than those of the Ionic or Corinthian orders. The most iconic example of Doric columns is the Parthenon, which was built in the 5th century BCE to honor the Greek goddess, Athena.

The **Ionic Order** originated in Ionia, a coastal region of what is now called Turkey, and is characterized mainly by the scroll-like ornaments that appear on Ionic column capitals known as volutes, as well as the column base supports that are not featured on Doric columns. Developed during the mid-sixth century BC, Ionic columns made their way to mainland Greece the following century.

The **Corinthian Order** grew directly out of the Ionic Order in the mid-5th century BC. Taking its name from the city of Corinth, the Corinthian Order can be distinguished from the Ionic Order by its more ornate capitals carved with stylized acanthus leaves.

Match the included examples of columns with the correct order type.

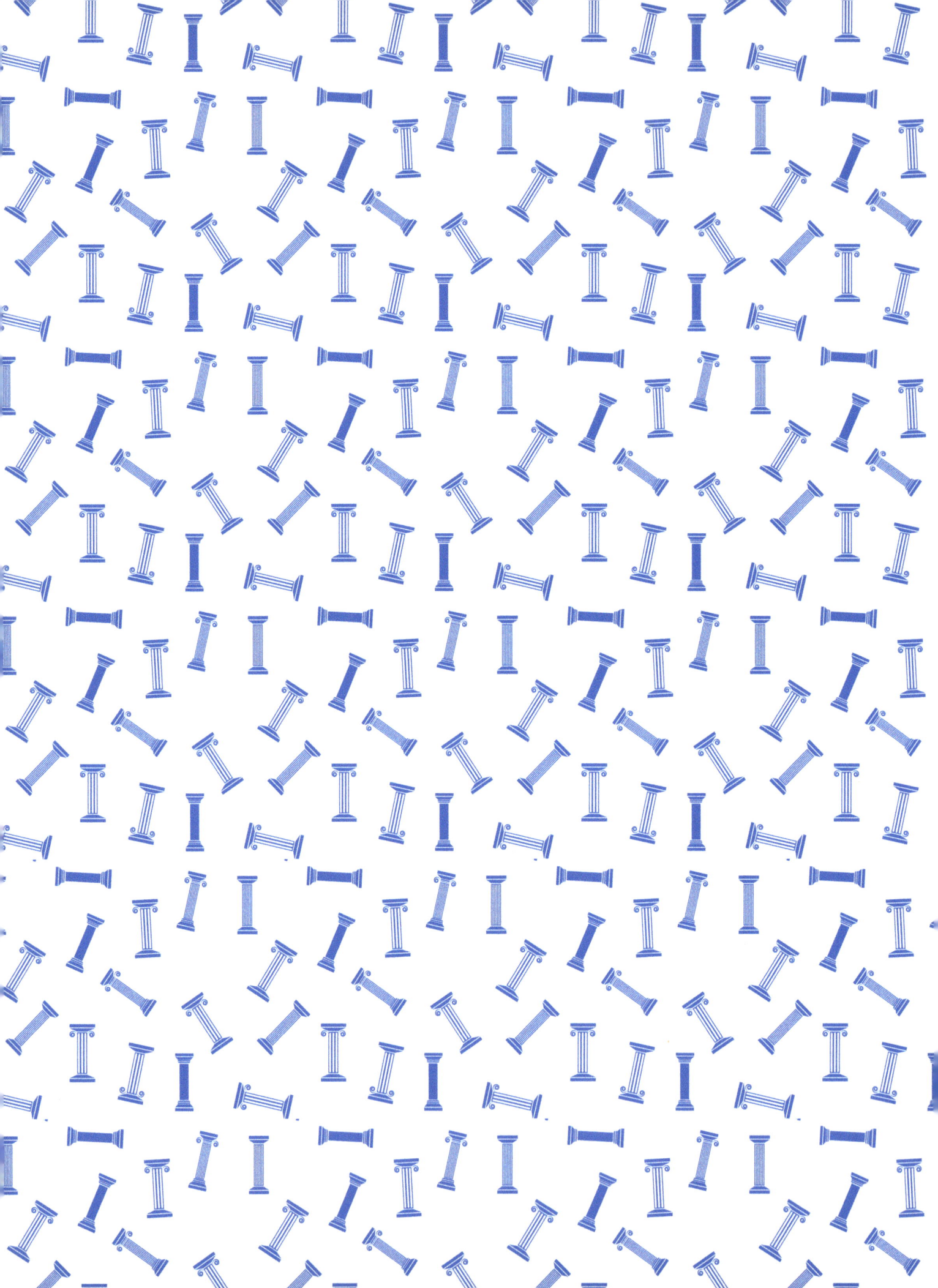

# Ionic

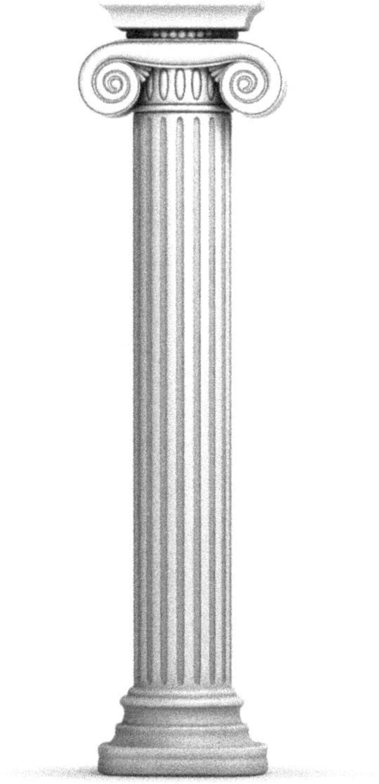

# Corinthian

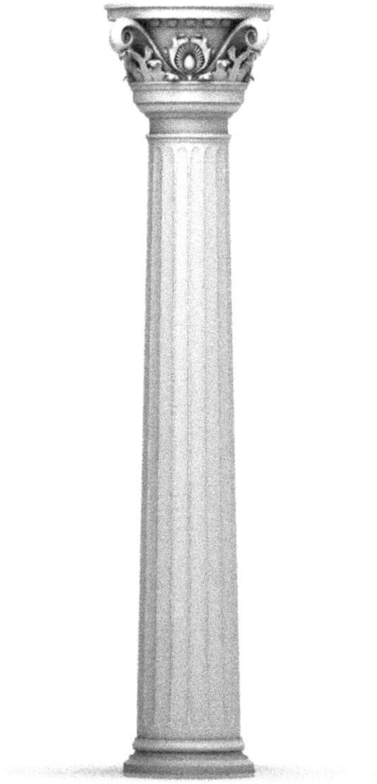

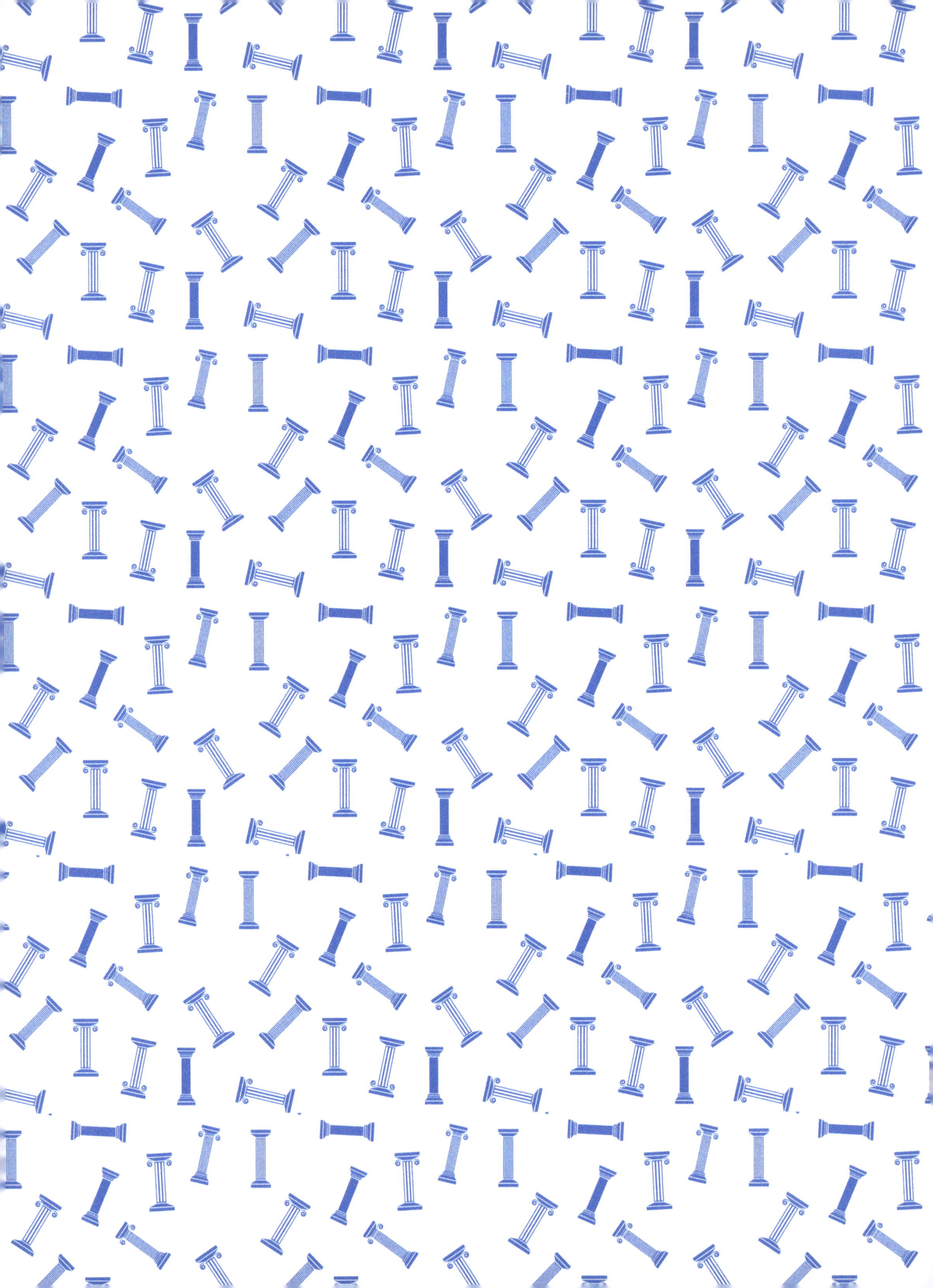

# Greek Column Design Match

Doric

Ionic

Corinthian

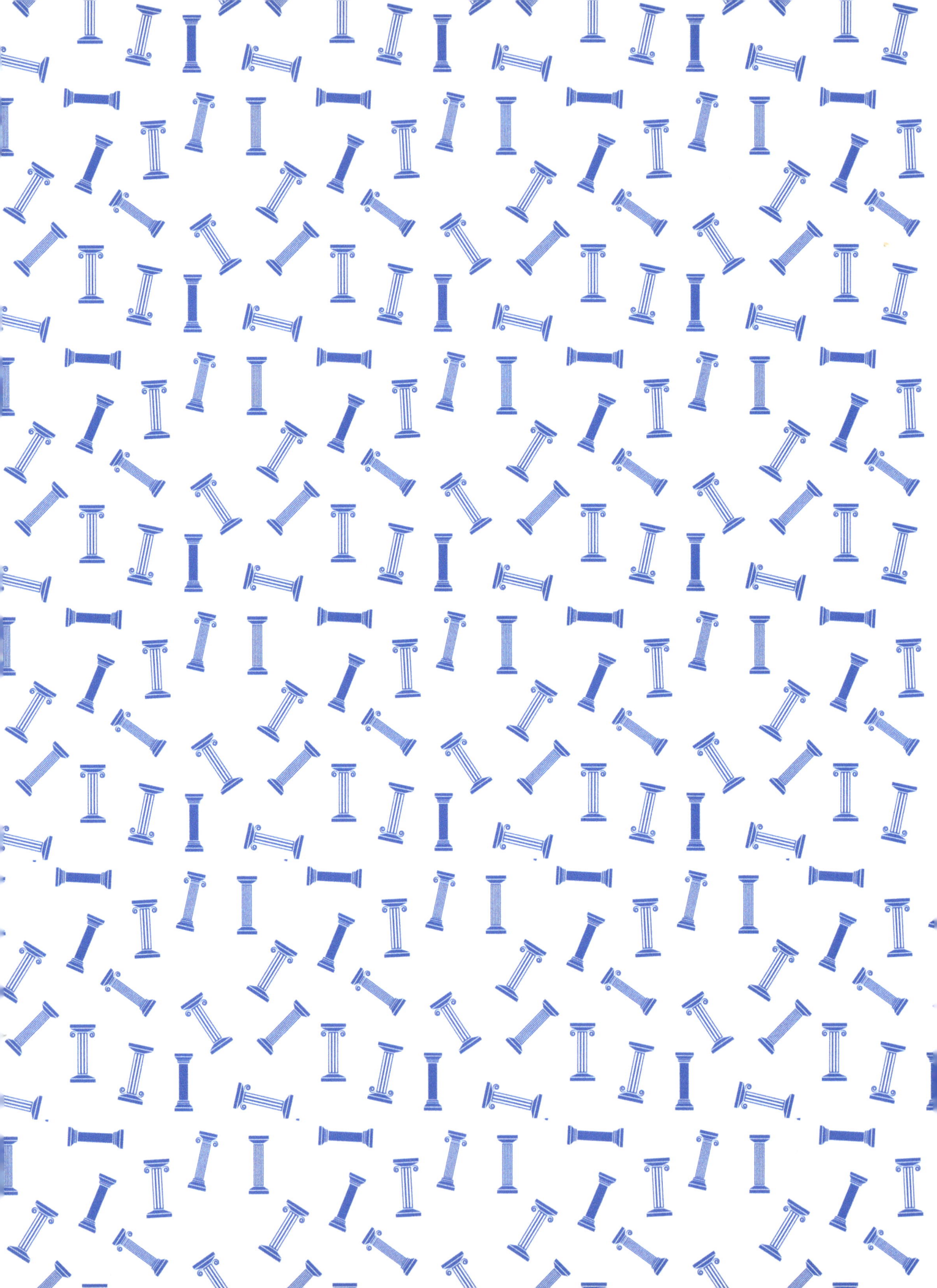

# Ancient Greek Persons

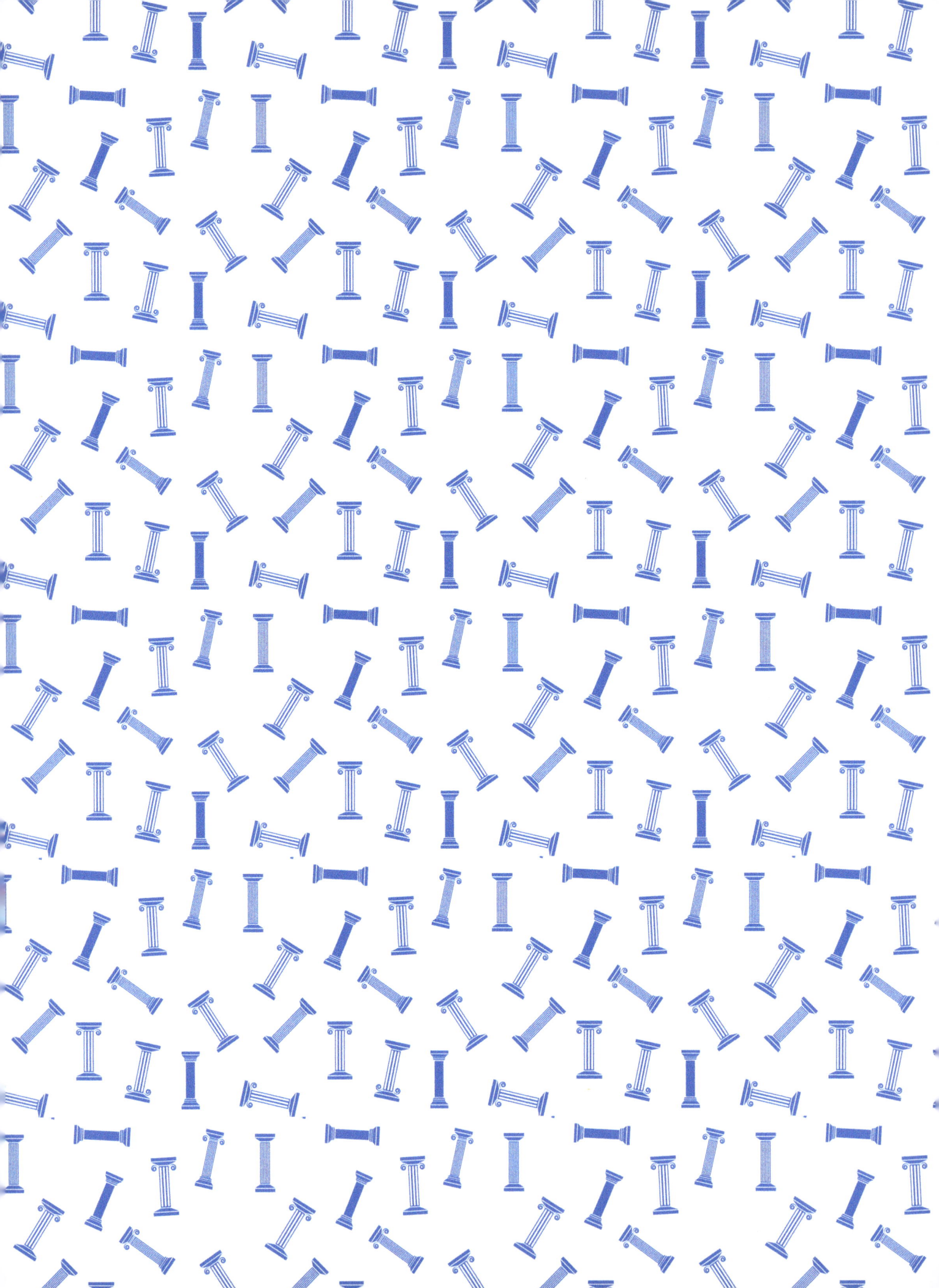

# THEATER MASKS

## Instructions

Theater masks first made their debut in Athens, Greece around 535 BC. The city had just built the first theater in the world — the iconic Theater of Dionysus. The actors stepped on stage wearing masks made of stiffened linen. The masks represented different characters in the play with exaggerated emotions. Over time these masks evolved into the comedy and tragedy genres that expressed the range of human emotions.

Cut out included theater mask templates. Laminate for additional durability. Glue large popsicle sticks to bottom or punch holes on side and add elastic to secure onto face. Allow to dry thoroughly. Perform an impromptu play - what type of role would a comedy character play? What role would a tragedy character play? Discuss real life examples of both comedy and tragedy.

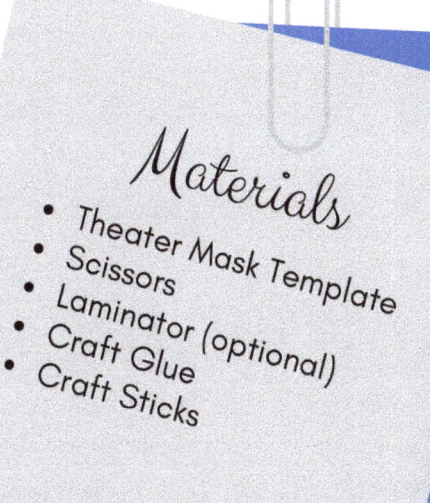

**Materials**
- Theater Mask Template
- Scissors
- Laminator (optional)
- Craft Glue
- Craft Sticks

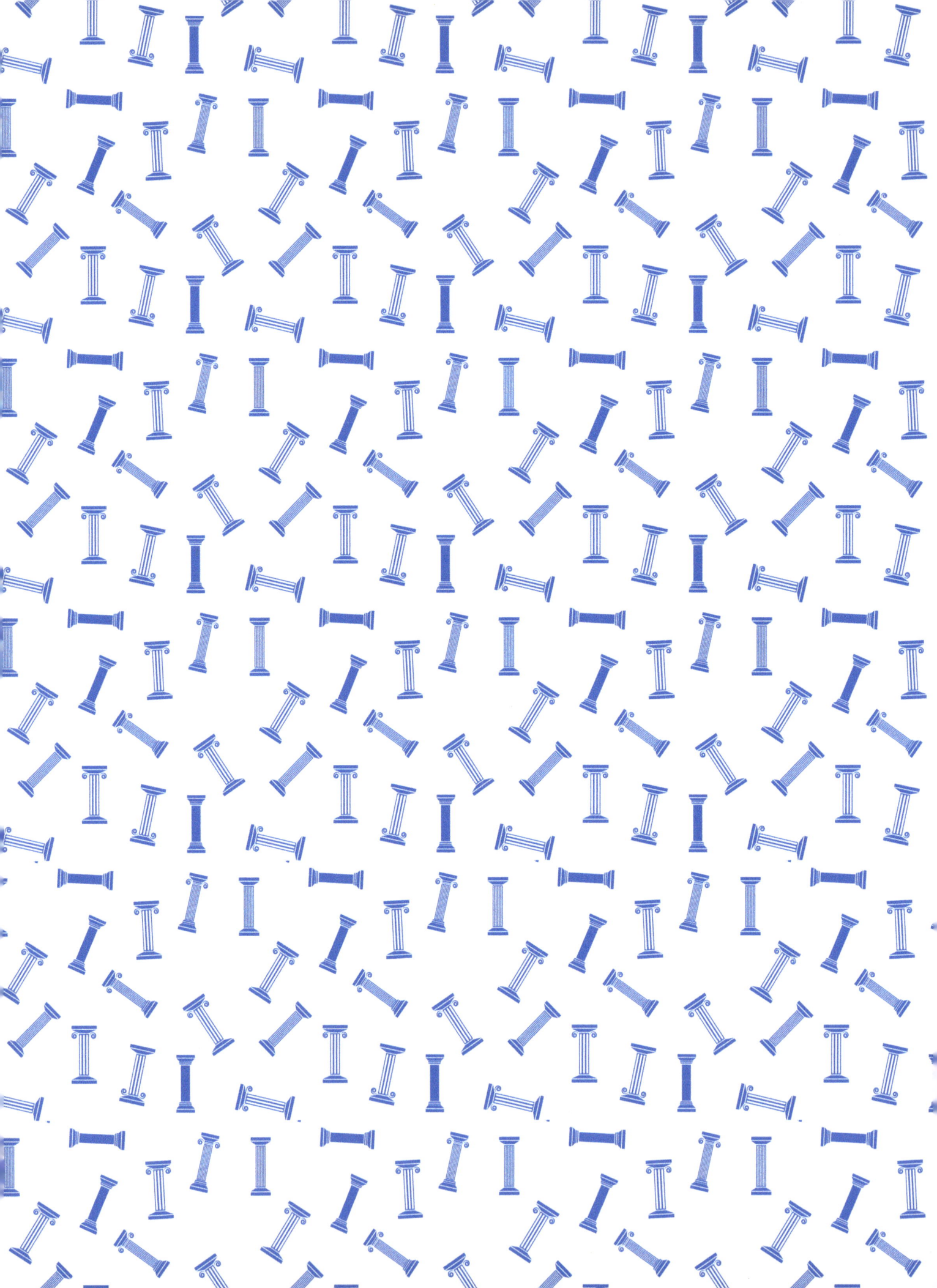

# Theater Mask: Comedy

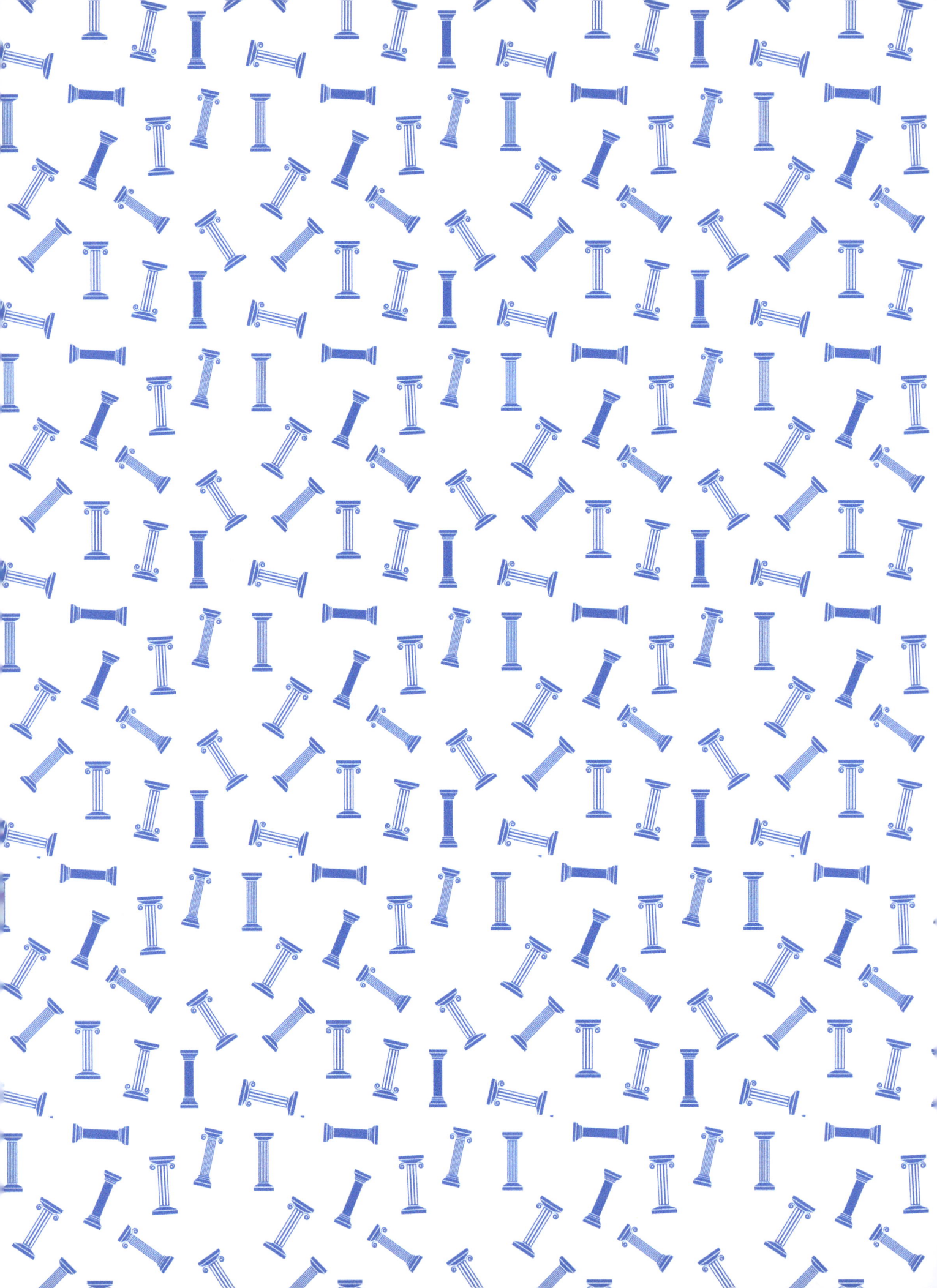

# Theater Mask: Tragedy

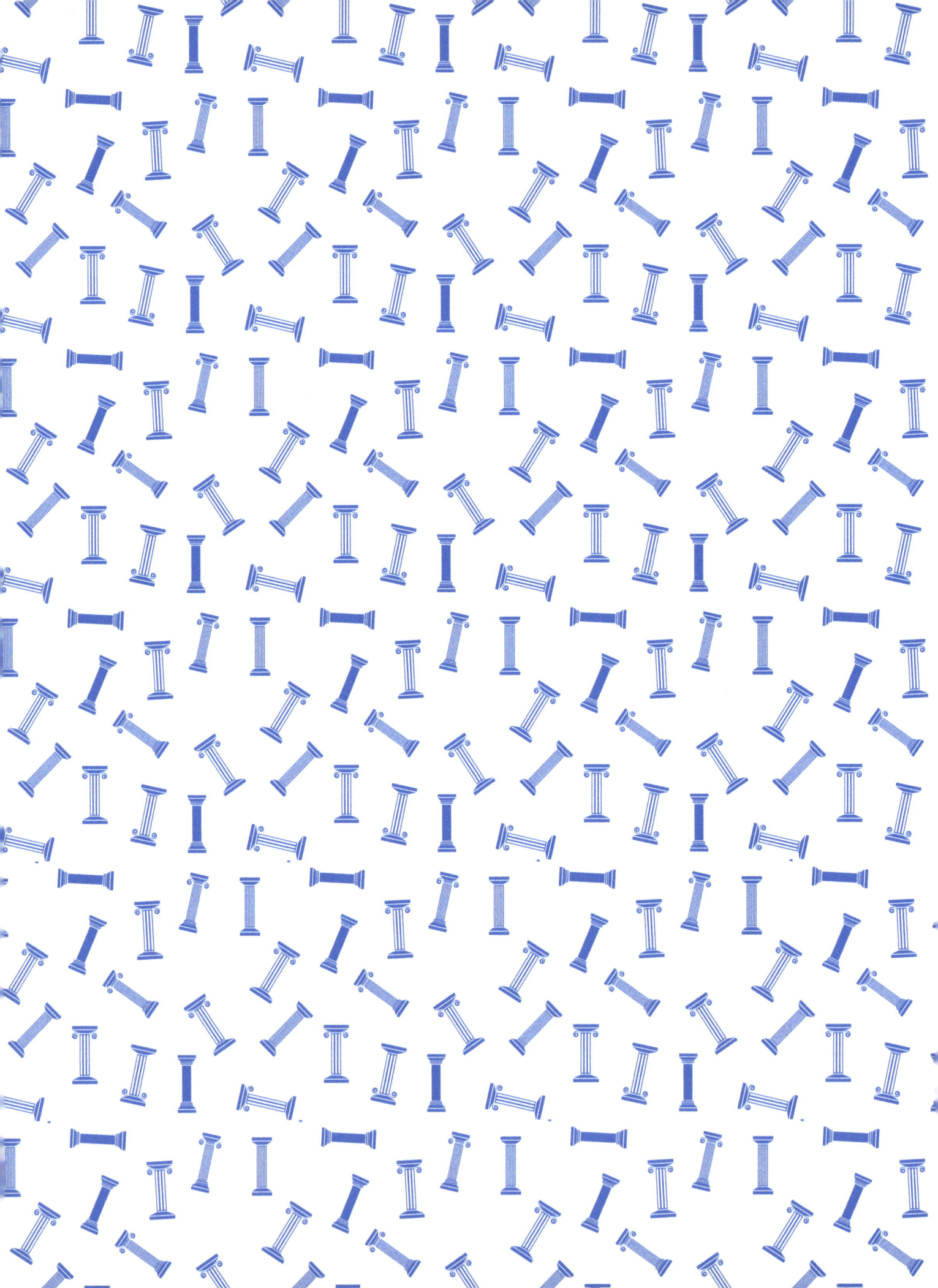

# ANCIENT GREEK POTTERY ART

### Materials
- Pottery Templates
- Greek Geometric Patterns
- Kraft Paper
- Scissors
- Black Marker(s)

## Instructions

Ancient Greek pottery developed from a Mycenaean tradition. The earliest stylistic period is the Geometric, lasting from about 1000 to 700 BC. In this period the surface of the pot was completely covered with a network of fine patterns.

Cut out included pottery templates. Trace on folded kraft paper along fold. Cut out tracing to create a full pottery design. Flatten paper either by ironing or pressing under a weight if necessary. Provide child with pattern ideas and pottery cutout. Copy designs onto pottery cutout - alternate designs and be creative with size and pattern. Continue until pottery design is complete. Compare with examples of ancient pottery - how do these designs compare. What patterns are the most difficult to reproduce?

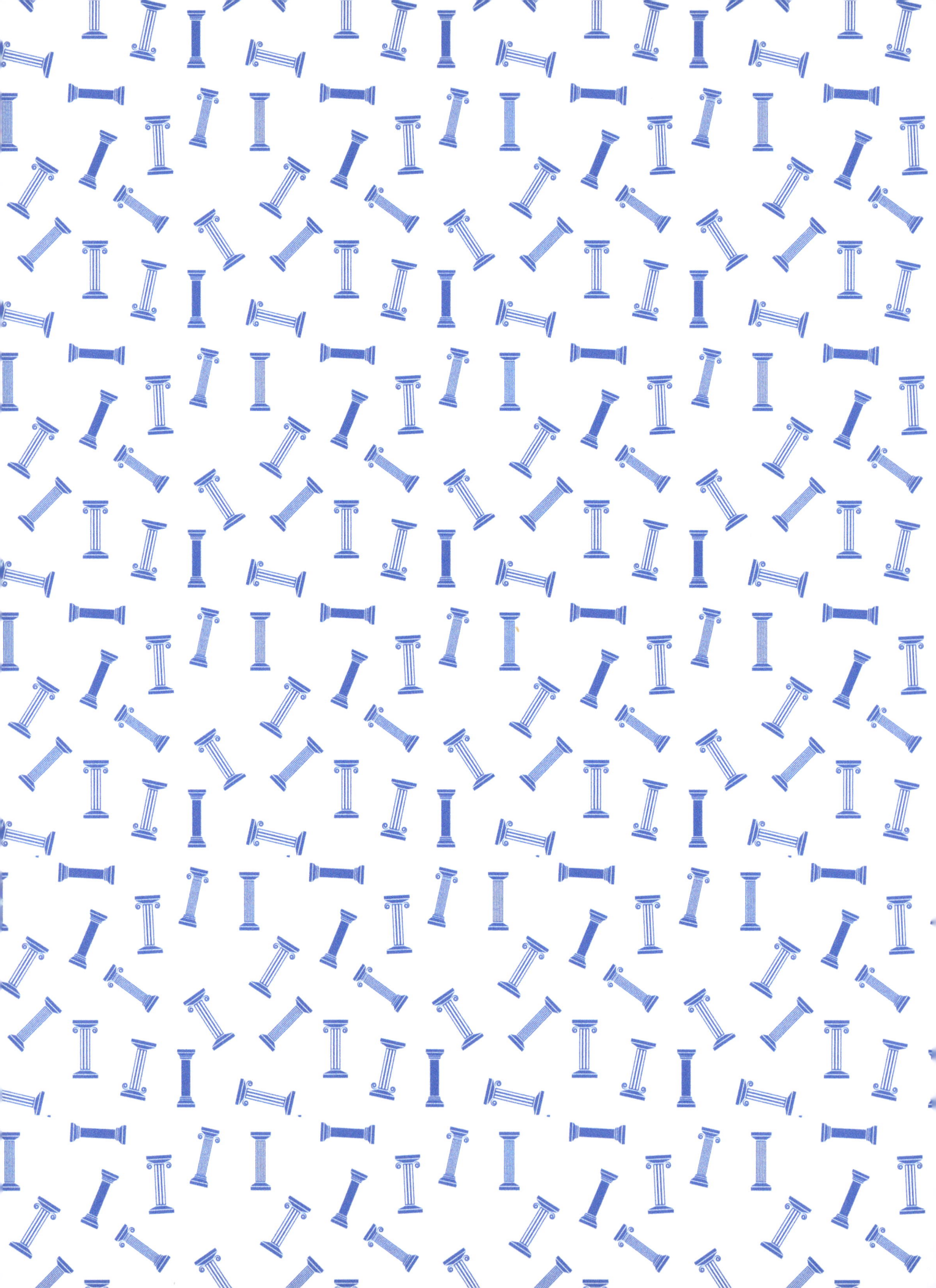

# Pottery Outlines

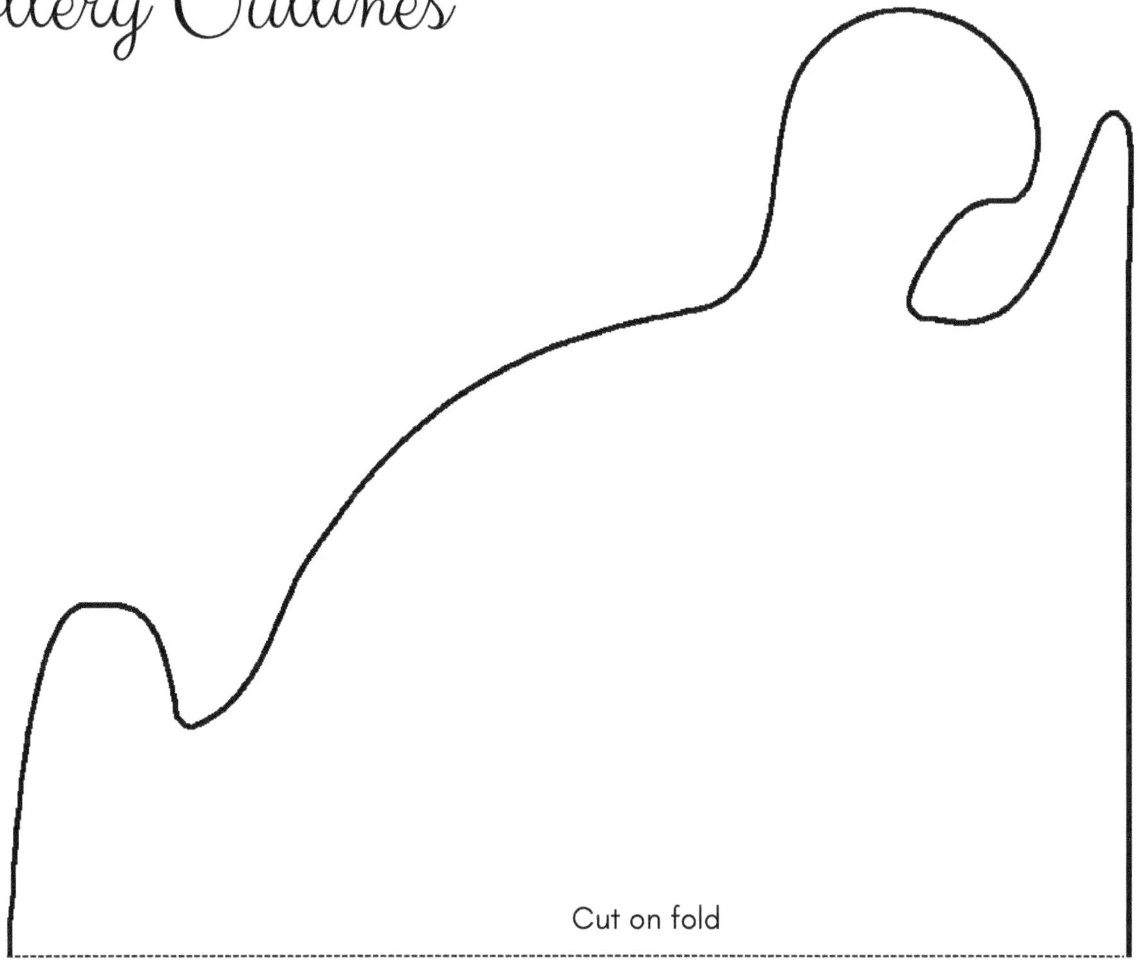

Cut on fold

Cut on fold

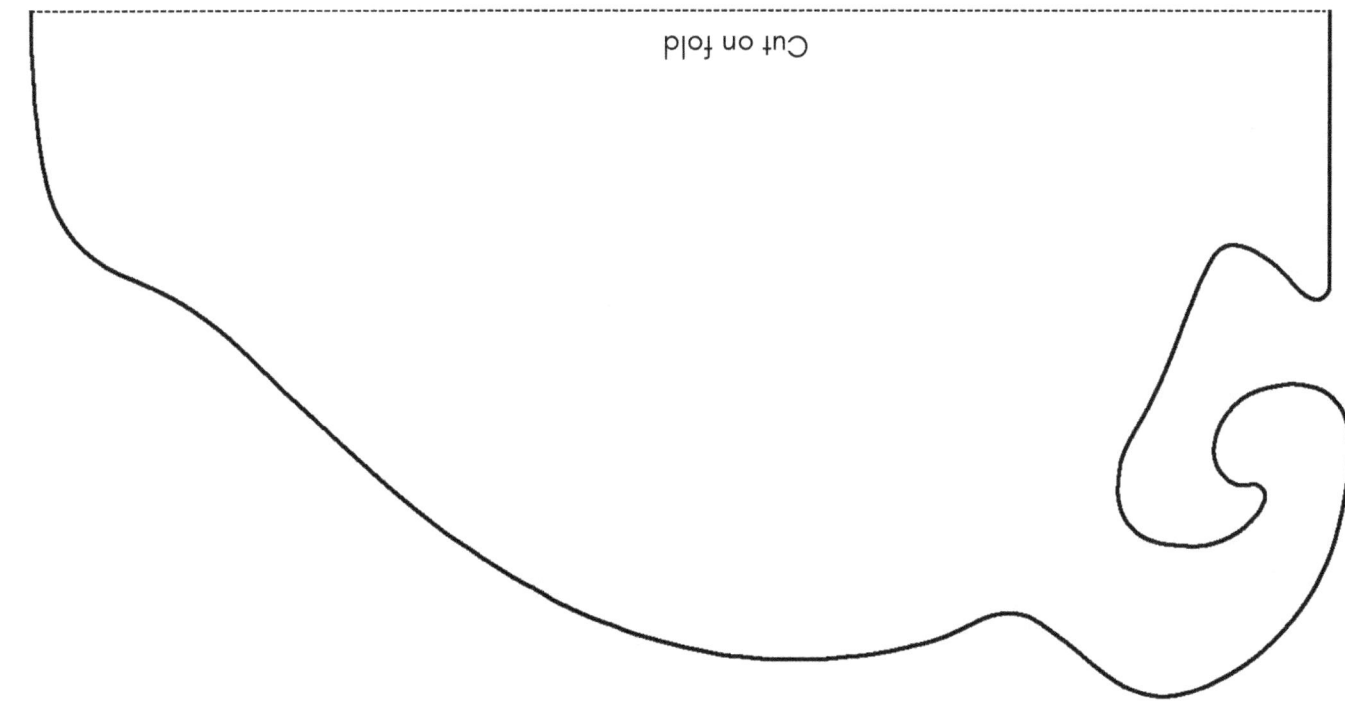

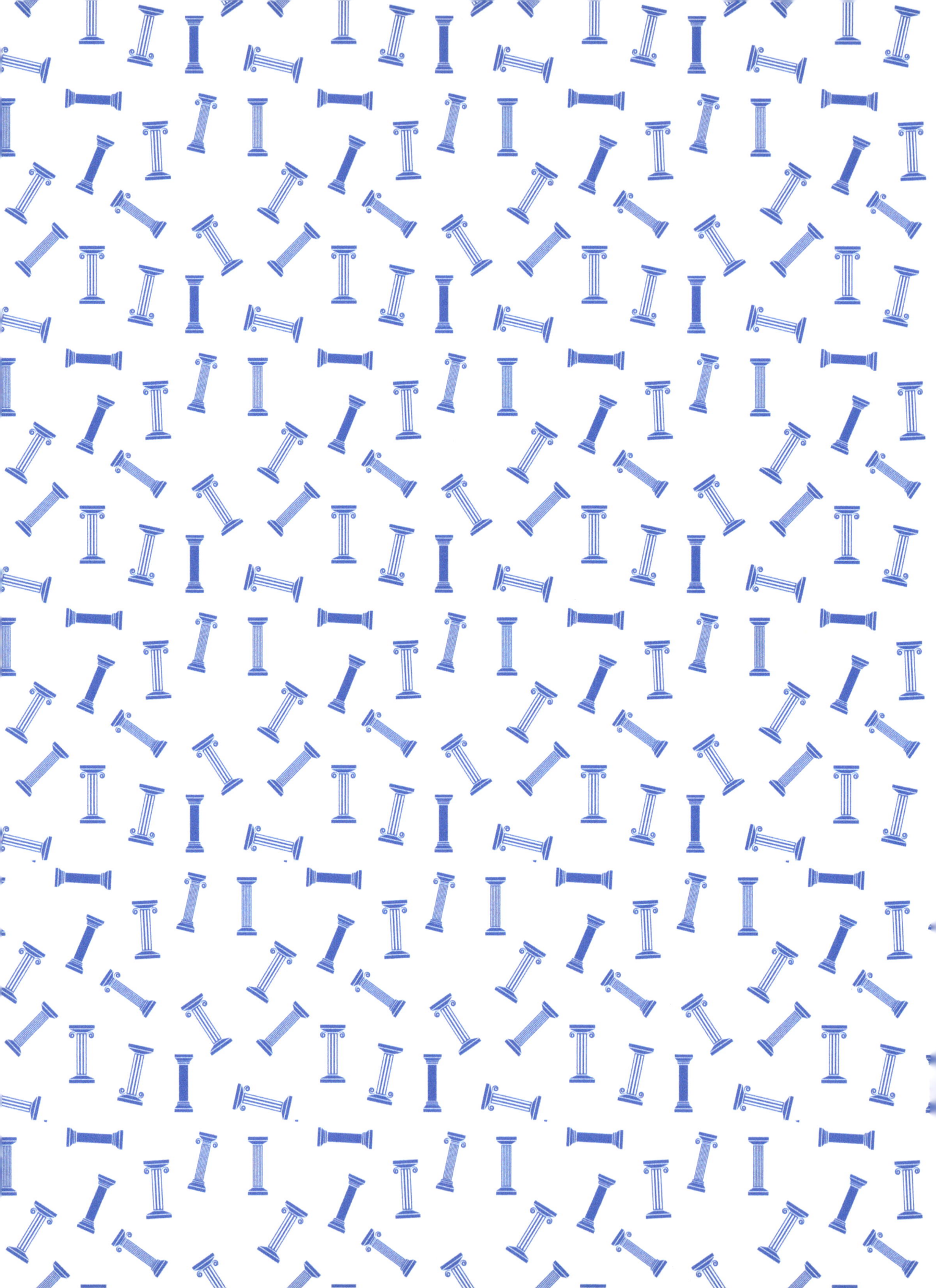

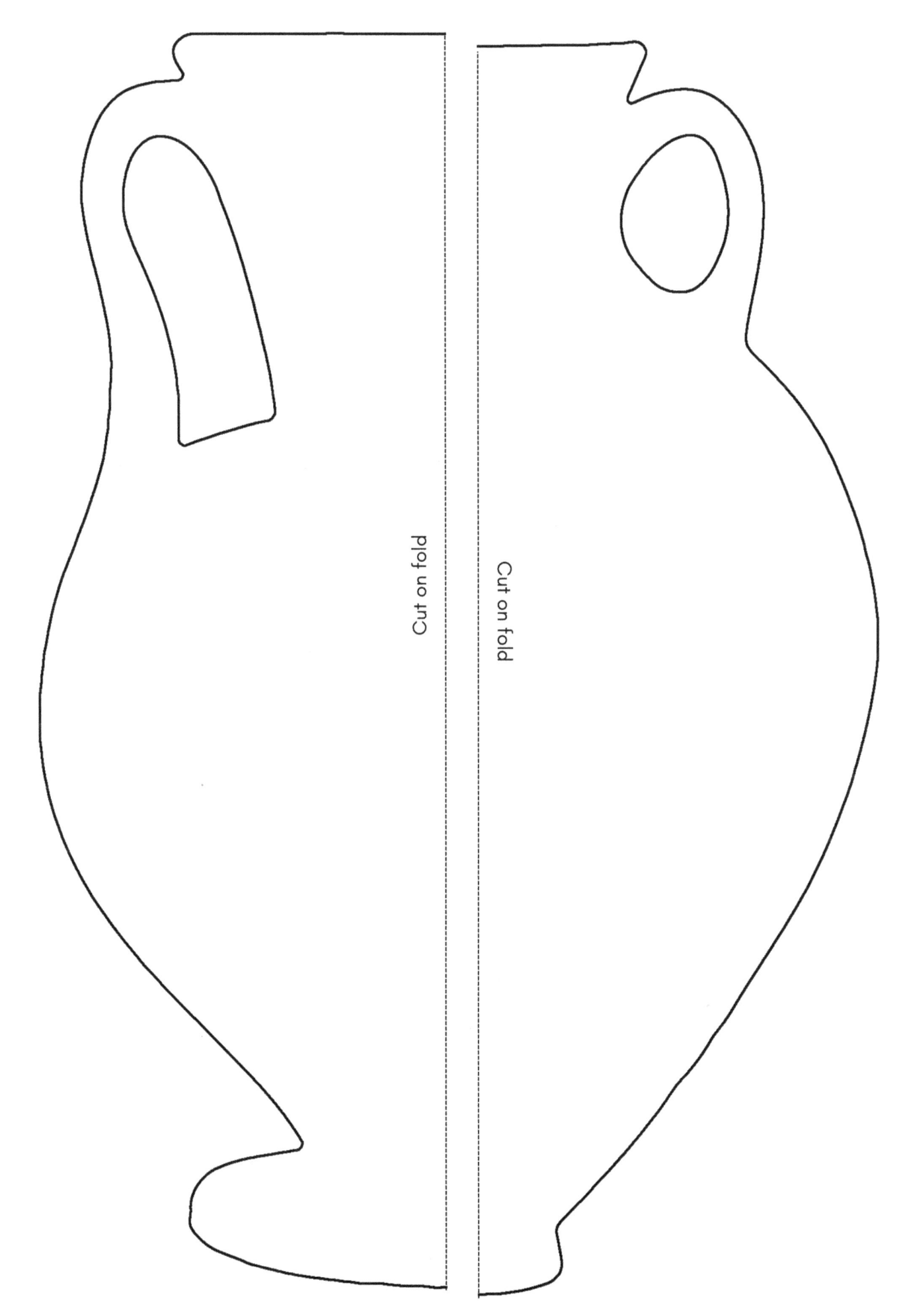

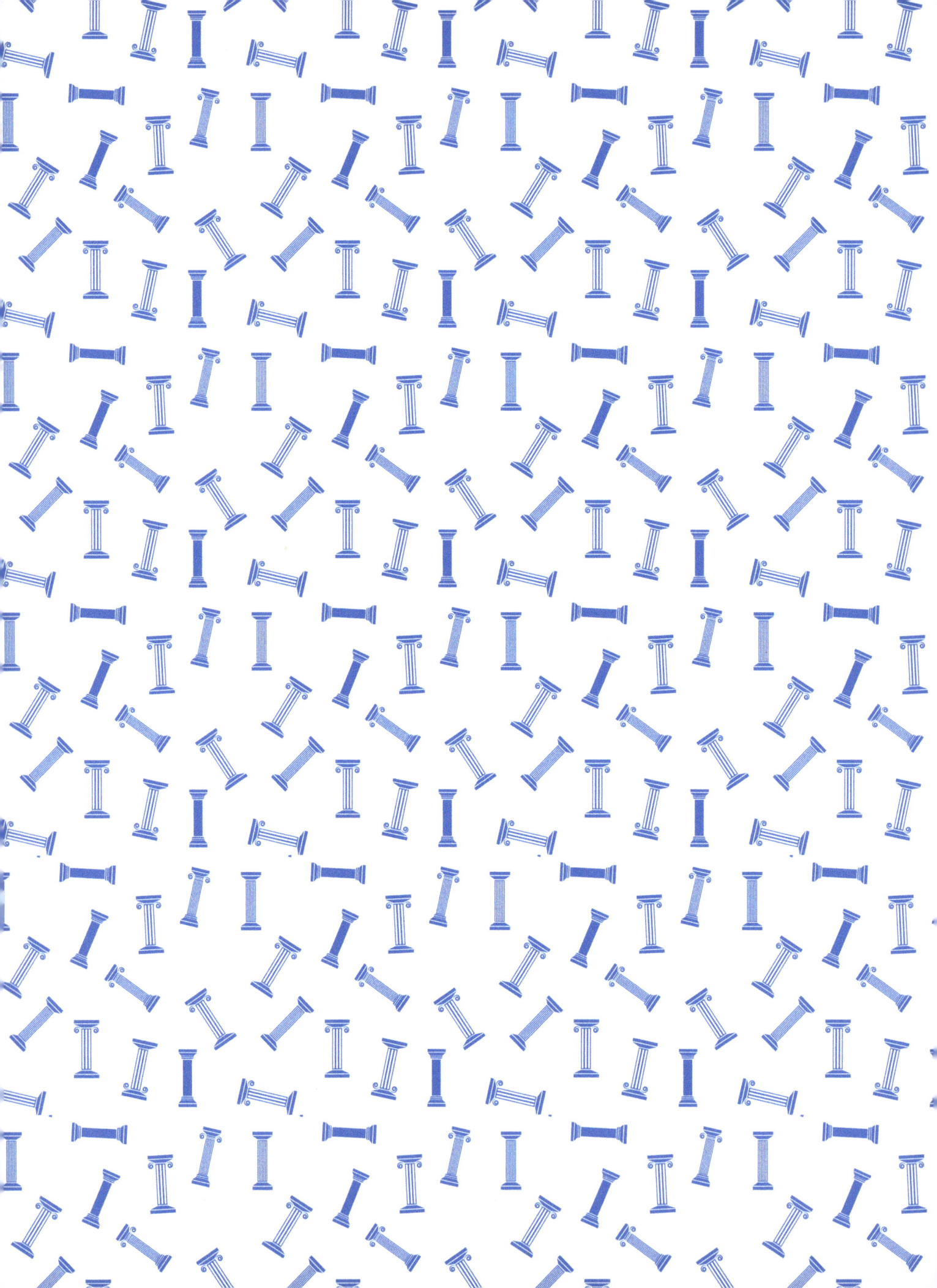

# Greek Geometric Patterns

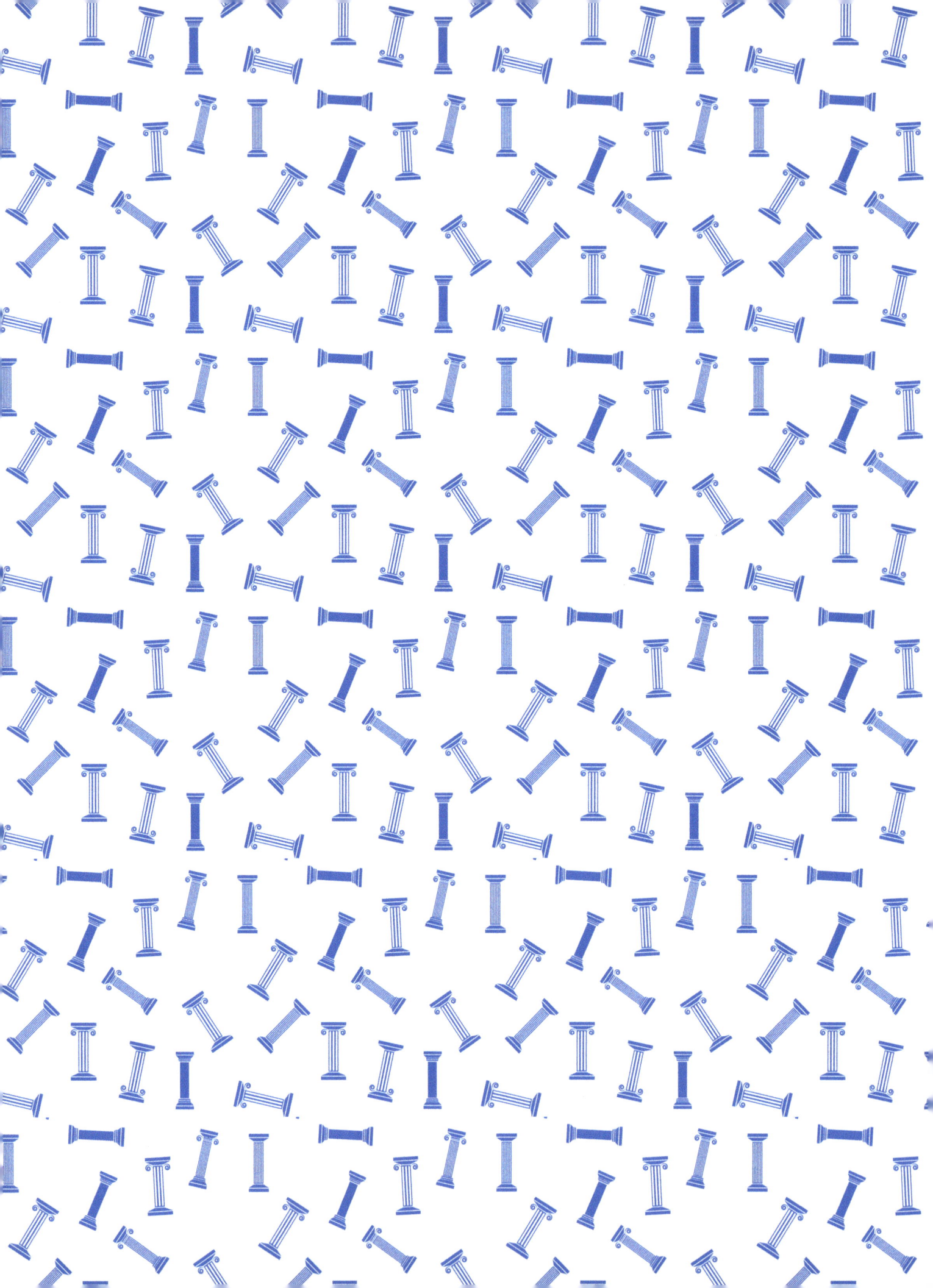

# Olympians: Greek Mythical Gods

## Poseidon

Poseidon was the god of the seas, water, storms, hurricanes, earthquakes, and horses. He was also the brother of Zeus and Hades. It was initially a toss-up between Poseidon and his brother Hades as to who would be the god of the seas and who would be the god of the underworld. Neither cared much about which realm they ruled over but were extremely competitive and wanted desperately to one-up the other.

## Hera

Hera was Queen of the gods and the goddess of marriage, women, childbirth, and family. She was the wife of Zeus. Zeus had many affairs throughout their marriage, both with other goddesses and mortals. This, infuriated Hera, not only because she was his wife, but also because she was the goddess of marriage. In her fury, she frequently attempted to get revenge on Zeus' lovers and their children.

## Zeus

Zeus was the King of the gods and the ruler of Mount Olympus, so he was extremely powerful. It was he that led the 10-year war of the gods against the previous rulers of Mount Olympus, the Titans. As a ruler, Zeus was the god of law, order, and justice, as well as being the god of the sky, lightning, and thunder.

## Hephaestus

Hephaestus was a master blacksmith and craftsman and the god of the forge, craftsmanship, invention, fire, and volcanoes. His mother was Hera, but it was disputed as to whether Hephaestus was the son of Zeus or through parthenogenesis, which requires no male involvement at all. Hephaestus was married to Aphrodite.

## Apollo

Apollo was very busy being the god of many things. Amidst his long list of titles, was the god of light, the Sun, prophecy, philosophy, archery, truth, inspiration, poetry, music, arts, manly beauty, medicine, healing, and plague. Apollo was also the son of Zeus and the twin brother of Artemis.

## Athena

Athena was the goddess of wisdom, handicraft, and warfare. She was viewed as the patron and protector of many cities in Greece, most notably in Athens, which is thought to be where she gained her name. Athena was the daughter of Zeus and said to have risen from his head fully grown and dressed in armor.

## Demeter

Demeter was the goddess of the harvest, fertility, agriculture, nature, and the seasons. As part of her title, Demeter ruled and watched over the grains and the fertility of the earth. She was also both the lover of Zeus and the mother of Persephone, Despoine, and Arion.

## Dionysus

Dionysus was the god of wine, the grapevine, fertility, festivity, ecstasy, madness, and resurrection. He was also the patron of the art of theatre. Dionysus was the son of Zeus and was the youngest Olympian god and the only one to have been born of a mortal mother. Moreover, he was married to Ariadne, who was a Cretan princess.

# Olympians: Greek Mythical Gods

## Ares

Ares was also the son of Zeus and Hera, and was the god of war, violence, bloodshed and manly virtues. He was known for his mindless anger and brutality and, as a result, was despised by all of the gods except Aphrodite.

## Artemis

Artemis was the daughter of Zeus and the twin sister of Apollo. She was the goddess of many things, including, the hunt, the wilderness, virginity, the Moon, archery, childbirth, protection, and plague.

## Hermes

Hermes was the son of Zeus and was the second-youngest Olympian. Hermes was the messenger of the gods and the god of travel, commerce, communication, borders, eloquence, diplomacy, thieves, and games. Hermes also held the responsibility of guiding the souls of the dead.

## Aphrodite

Aphrodite was the goddess of love, pleasure, passion, procreation, fertility, beauty, and desire. There is some speculation around Aphrodite's birth, but many believe she was the daughter of Zeus. Aphrodite was married to Hephaestus, but had many affairs, most famously with Ares, the god of war.

# String the Lyre

The lyre was an ancient Greek instrument. Cut out illustration and punch holes as indicated. Have child string through holes to complete the lyre.

Cut Out

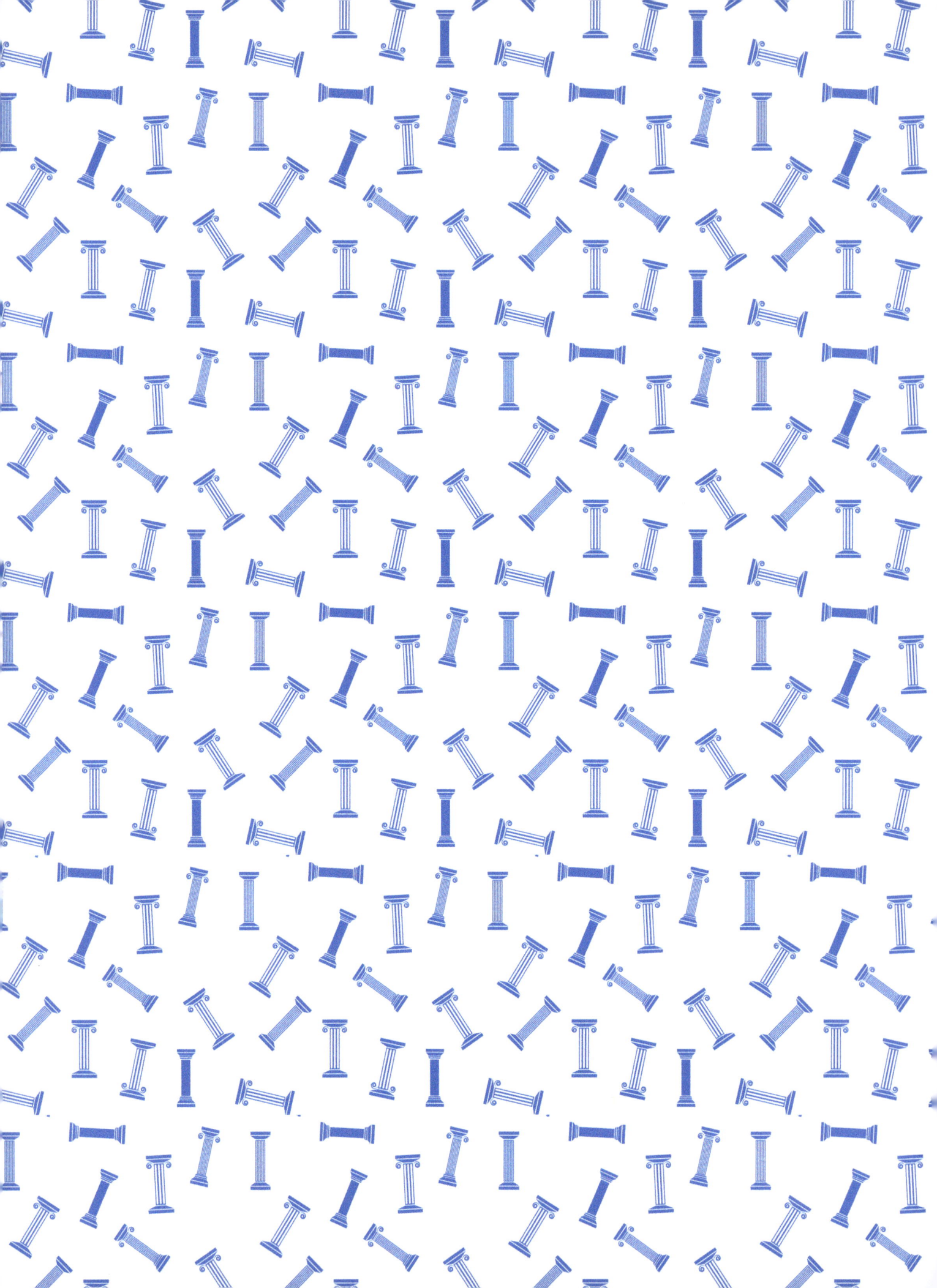

# IYNX WHEEL

## Instructions

The iynx is a simple toy commonly known as a buzzer or whirligig today. The iynx has strong connections to ancient Greece as both a toy and a religious ritual device. The word iynx comes from the Greek name for the wryneck bird; a well-balanced iynx wheel makes a repetitive whirring sound, which somewhat resembles the pulsing call of the iynx bird in the wild. The design is simple - at the center is a small disc that is threaded with string. By twirling the ends of the strings, you spin the disc and wind the strings together. If you now pull the strings outwards, they unwind and rapidly spin the disc in the opposite direction. Ancient Greeks often made these from pottery and stone.

Cut out wheel template. Laminate for additional durability. Punch holes as indicated and thread string through the holes and tie securely. Twirl the end of the strings to create tension and pull outward to release and watch the disc spin.

### Materials

- Iynx Template
- Laminator (optional)
- Scissors
- Awl/Punch
- Yarn or String

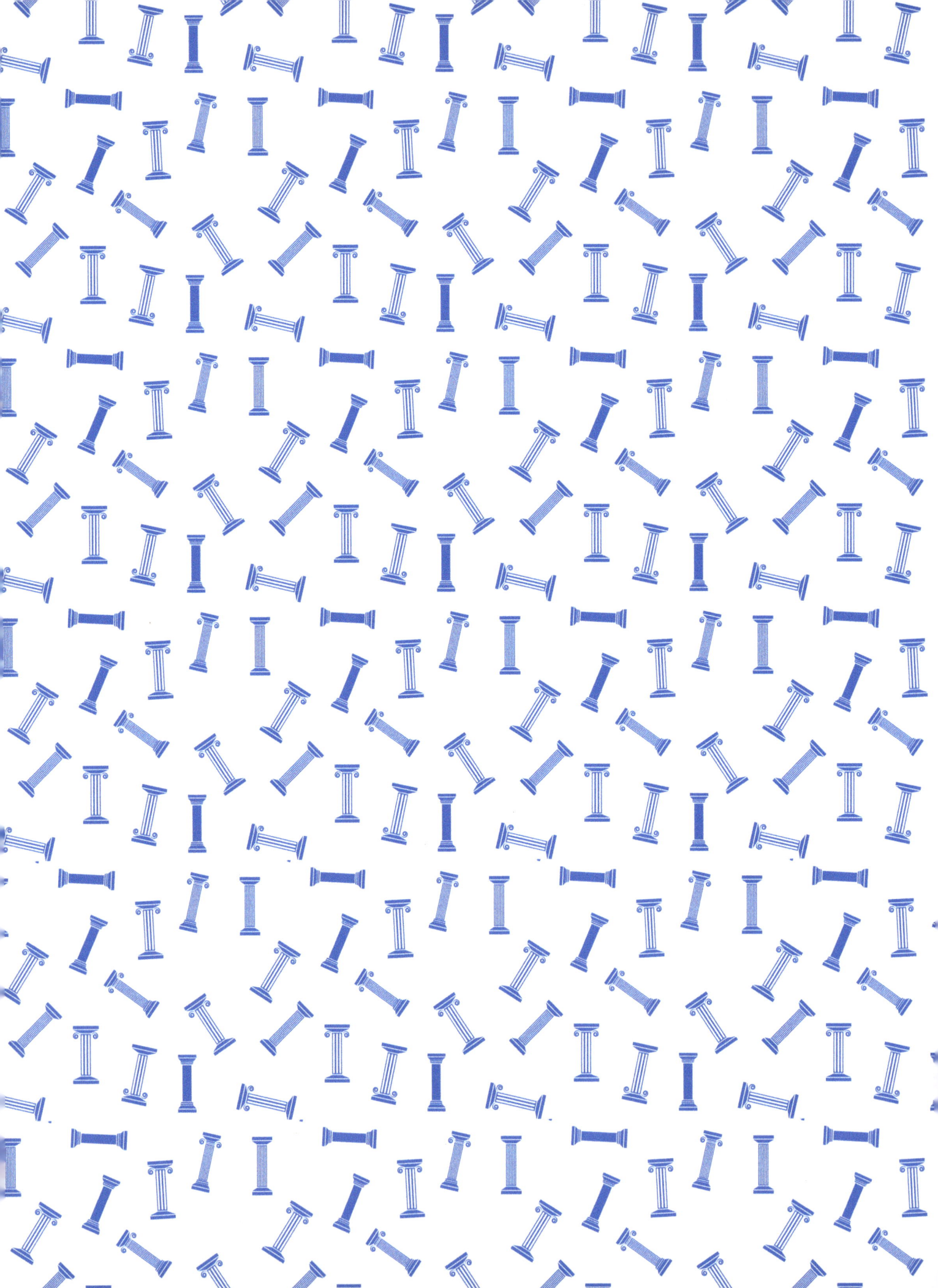

# Iynx Wheel

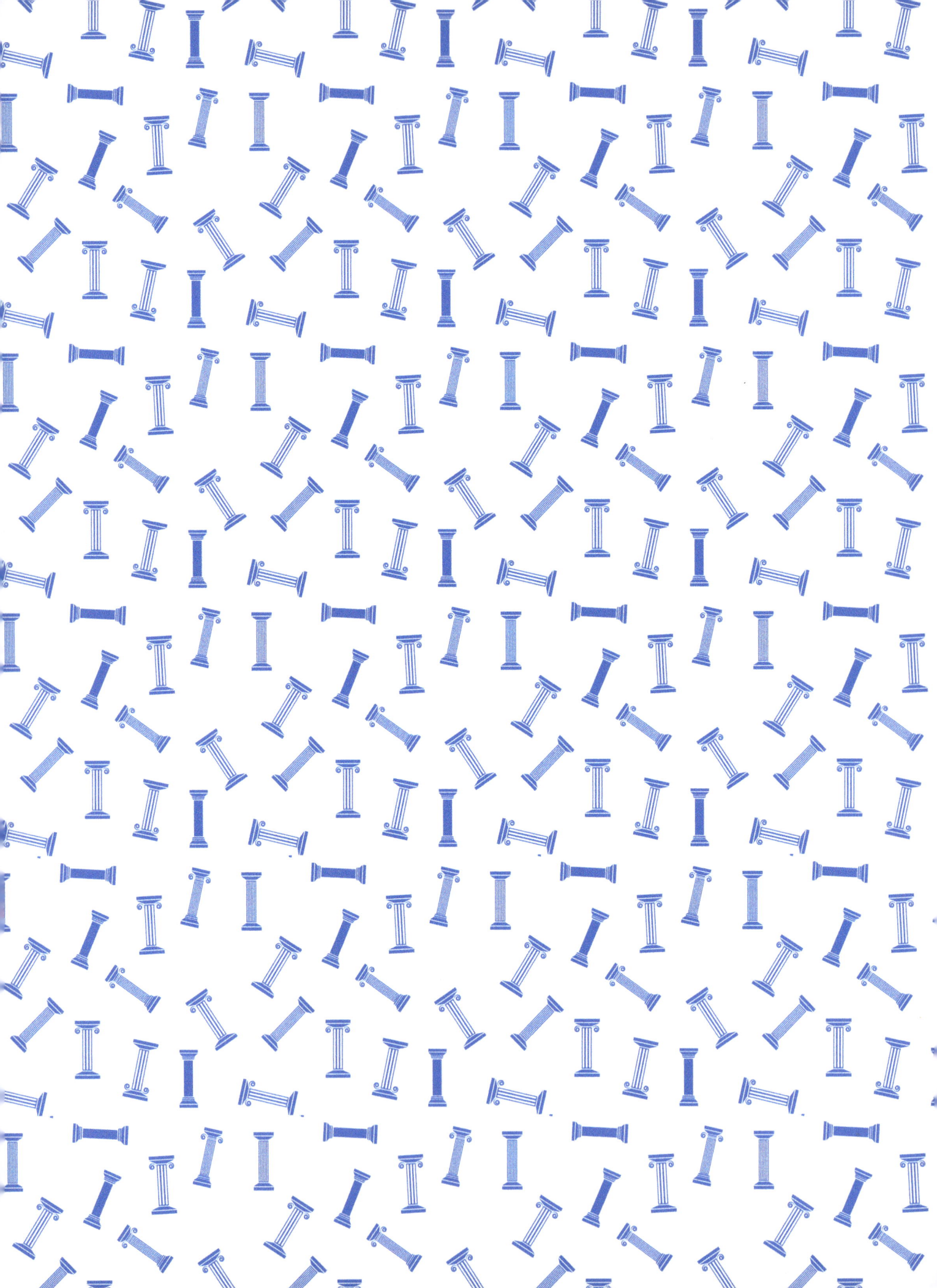

# CLEPSYDRA (WATER) CLOCK

## Instructions

**Materials**
- Plastic Bottle
- Knife/Scissors
- Drill or Awl
- Large Craft Sticks
- Marker
- Water

The water clock was developed to solve the problem of the first timekeeping device known as the sundial, which only worked when the sun was out. Around 325 BC work began on Clepsydra, the Ancient Greek water clock. The water clock was a bowl-like canister and made of stone. The device had a hole in the bottom to control the flow of pressurized water non-stop. These holes pointed to other similar canisters that the water overflow ran into. The Clepsydra was also able to keep up with the hour of day via markings on its side.

Cut the top of a plastic bottle off. Drill a tiny hole in cap. Glue two large craft sticks on and glue inverted bottle top so that cap falls just below the top of the bottom half. Allow to dry thoroughly. Pour water into top half and allow it to drip into lower half. Indicate on bottle every measure of time (minute, hour, etc) by using a stopwatch.

# PLATO (PLAYDOUGH) MATS

## Materials
- Philosopher Templates
- Laminator
- Scissors
- Playdough/Clay

### Instructions

Ancient Greece was inarguably affected by the teachings of many renowned philosophers, whose works continue to shape physics, logic, and ethics. Three of the most famous include Socrates, Plato & Aristotle. Hippocrates is known for his incredible early work paving the way for modern medicine. Statues of these people are all that is accurately left of their features. Laminate included templates. Cut each out and provide the child with playdough or clay in a variety of colors. Using the bust outline as designs, have the child form facial features, eyes, hair, etc. to create an illustration of the philosopher's face.

**Discuss:** What do you think these people really looked like? Consider skin, hair, eye color, etc... What examples in history point to what these men looked like?

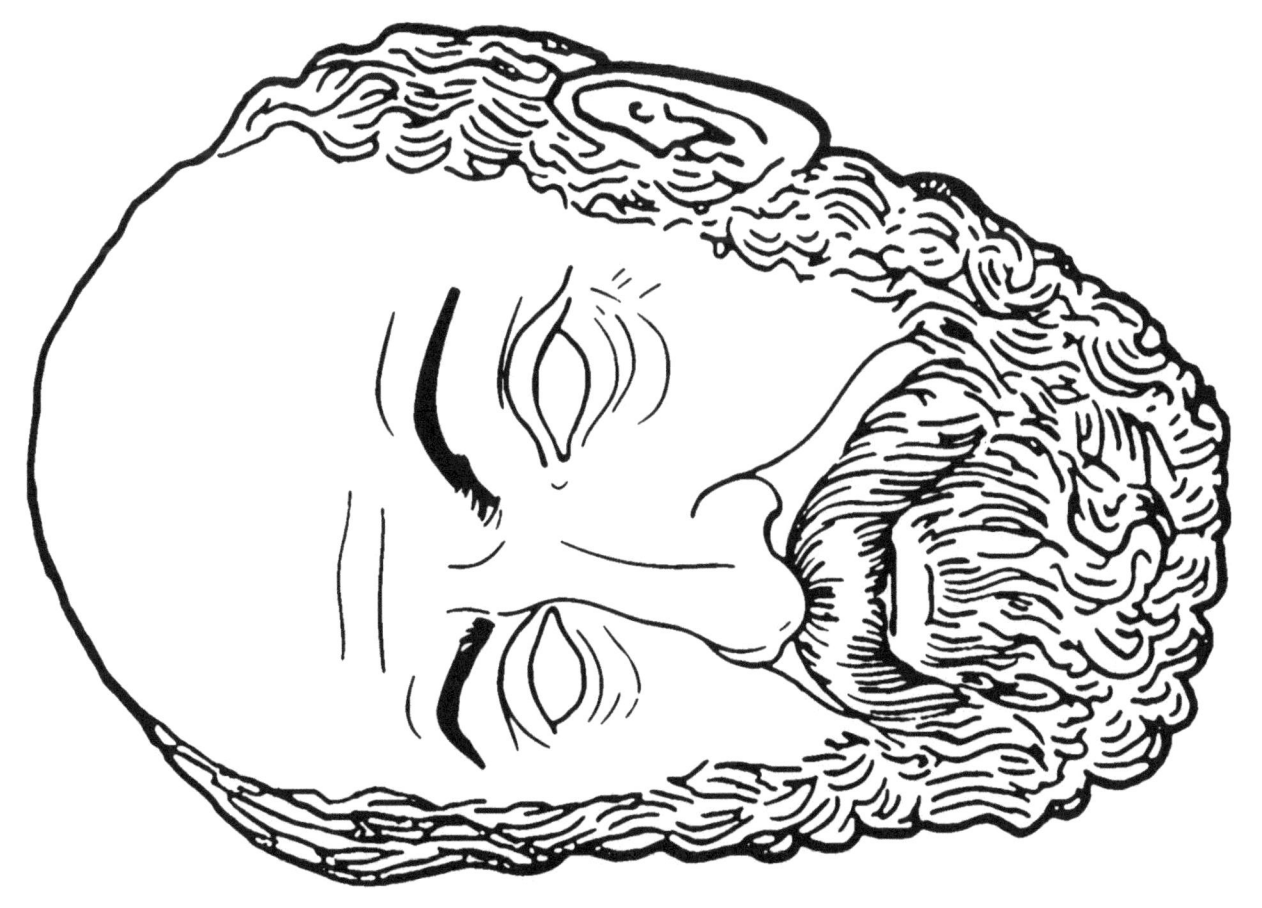

Socrates

Hippocrates

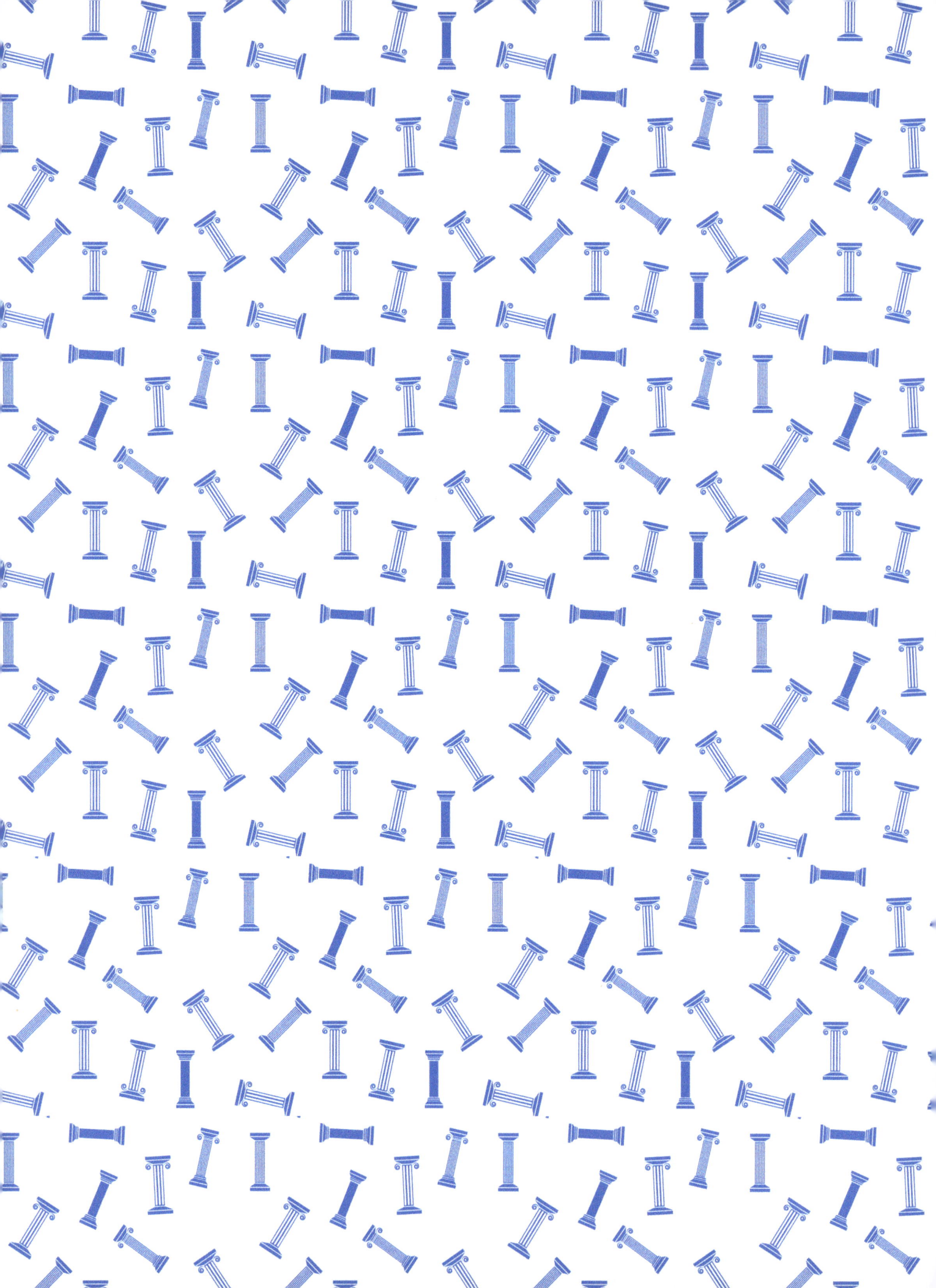

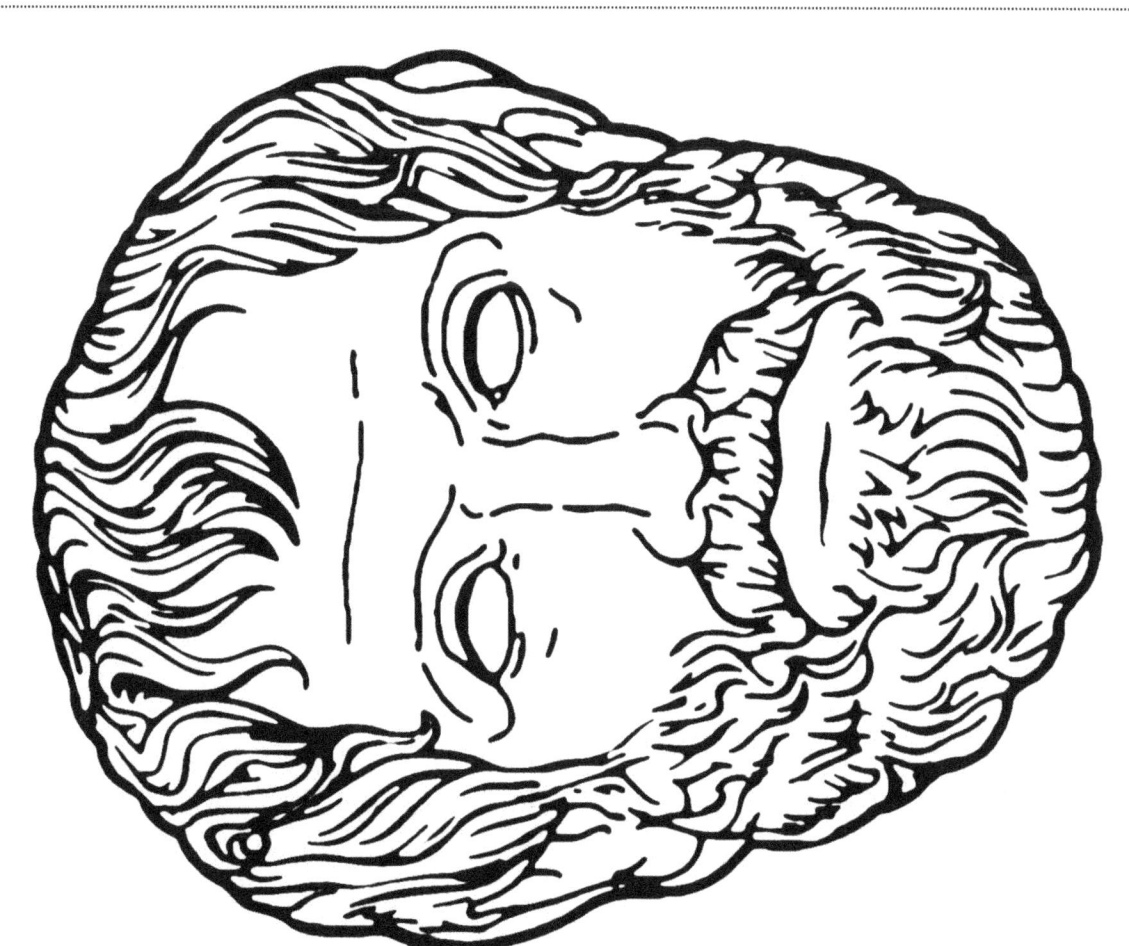

Plato

Aristotle

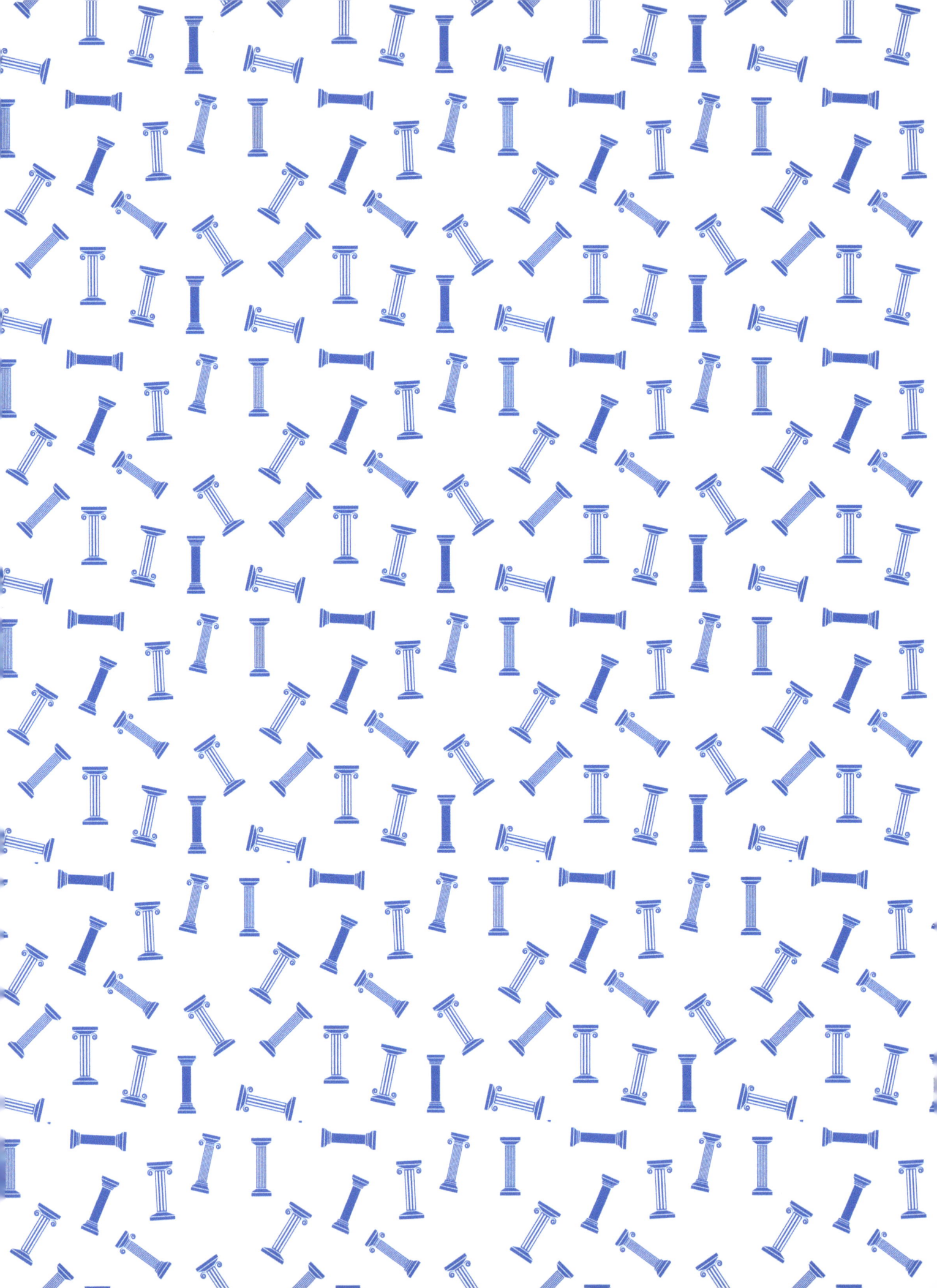

# Famous Greek Philosophers

**Socrates**
*469 BC–399 BC*

**Hippocrates**
*460 BC–370 BC*

**Plato**
*427 BC–347 BC*

**Aristotle**
*384 BC–322 BC*

# Famous Greek Philosophers

## Hippocrates

Hippocrates of Kos was a Greek physician of the classical period who is considered one of the most outstanding figures in the history of medicine. He is traditionally referred to as the "*Father of Medicine*" in recognition of his lasting contributions to the field, such as the use of prognosis and clinical observation, the systematic categorization of diseases, or the formulation of humoural theory.

```
"Walking is man's best
         medicine."
       — Hippocrates
```

## Socrates

Socrates was a Greek philosopher from Athens who is credited as the founder of Western philosophy and among the first moral philosophers of the ethical tradition of thought. Socrates exerted a strong influence on philosophers in later antiquity and has continued to do so in the modern era. Socrates played an important role in the thought of the Italian Renaissance, particularly within the humanist movement.

```
"The only true wisdom is in
 knowing you know nothing."
          — Socrates
```

## Aristotle

Aristotle was a Greek philosopher and polymath during the classical period. Taught by Plato, he was the founder of the Lyceum, the Peripatetic school of philosophy, and his views profoundly shaped medieval scholarship. The influence of physical science extended from Late Antiquity and the Early Middle Ages into the Renaissance. His works contain the earliest known formal study of logic and were studied by medieval scholars.

```
"Knowing yourself is the
beginning of all wisdom."
       — Aristotle
```

## Plato

Plato was a Greek philosopher born in Athens during the classical period. He founded the Platonist school of thought and the Academy, the first institution of higher learning in the Western world. Plato was an innovator of the written dialogue and dialectic forms in philosophy. Plato is also considered the founder of Western political philosophy. Plato's entire body of work is believed to have survived intact for over 2,400 years.

```
"Opinion is the medium between
    knowledge and ignorance."
             — Plato
```

# ANCIENT GREEK CATAPULT

## Instructions

Catapults were invented by the ancient Greeks around 500 BC. A catapult is a mechanism for forcefully propelling stones, spears, or other projectiles, and was used mainly as a military weapon since ancient times. Early versions were quickly used and improved upon by other civilizations, most notably the Romans. Glue five small craft sticks together by stacking them upon one another. Secure the ends with rubber bands for additional stability. Take two large craft sticks and glue/band together. Place large sticks as a base and the smaller sticks perpendicular with the spoon on top. Use a rubber band wrapped in an X-shape to hold the spoon in place. Glue the handle of the spoon to the base and secure with rubber bands. Allow to dry thoroughly. Place small soft object into spoon and pull towards base. Release and let object be propelled into the air. Try different items - what items fly the best?

### Materials
- Large/Small Craft Sticks
- Rubber Bands
- Plastic Spoon
- Craft Glue

# TOILET ROLL TROJAN HORSE

**Materials**
- Trojan Horse Templates
- Toilet Roll
- Craft Sticks
- Craft Glue (or Hot Glue)
- Scissors

## Instructions

The Trojan Horse refers to a wooden horse said to have been used by the Greeks, during the Trojan War, to enter the city of Troy and win the war. First mentioned in the Odyssey, it describes how Greek soldiers were able to take the city of Troy after a fruitless ten-year siege by hiding in a giant horse supposedly left as an offering to the goddess Athena.

Cover a toilet roll with craft sticks. Allow glue to dry thoroughly between stages or use hot glue. Glue four half-sticks on sides for legs and one full-size on each side to stabilize horse base. Cut out included templates. Glue head and tail to body using included tabs. Add additional sticks to hide tabs if desired. Cut out soldiers. Place inside hollow horse body and allow child to count the soldiers. Change the number of soldiers to continue counting work.

# Trojan Horse

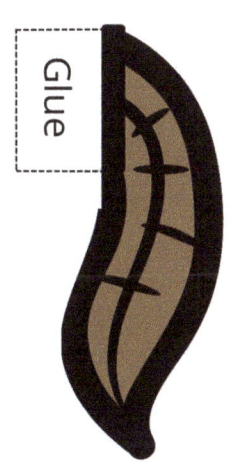

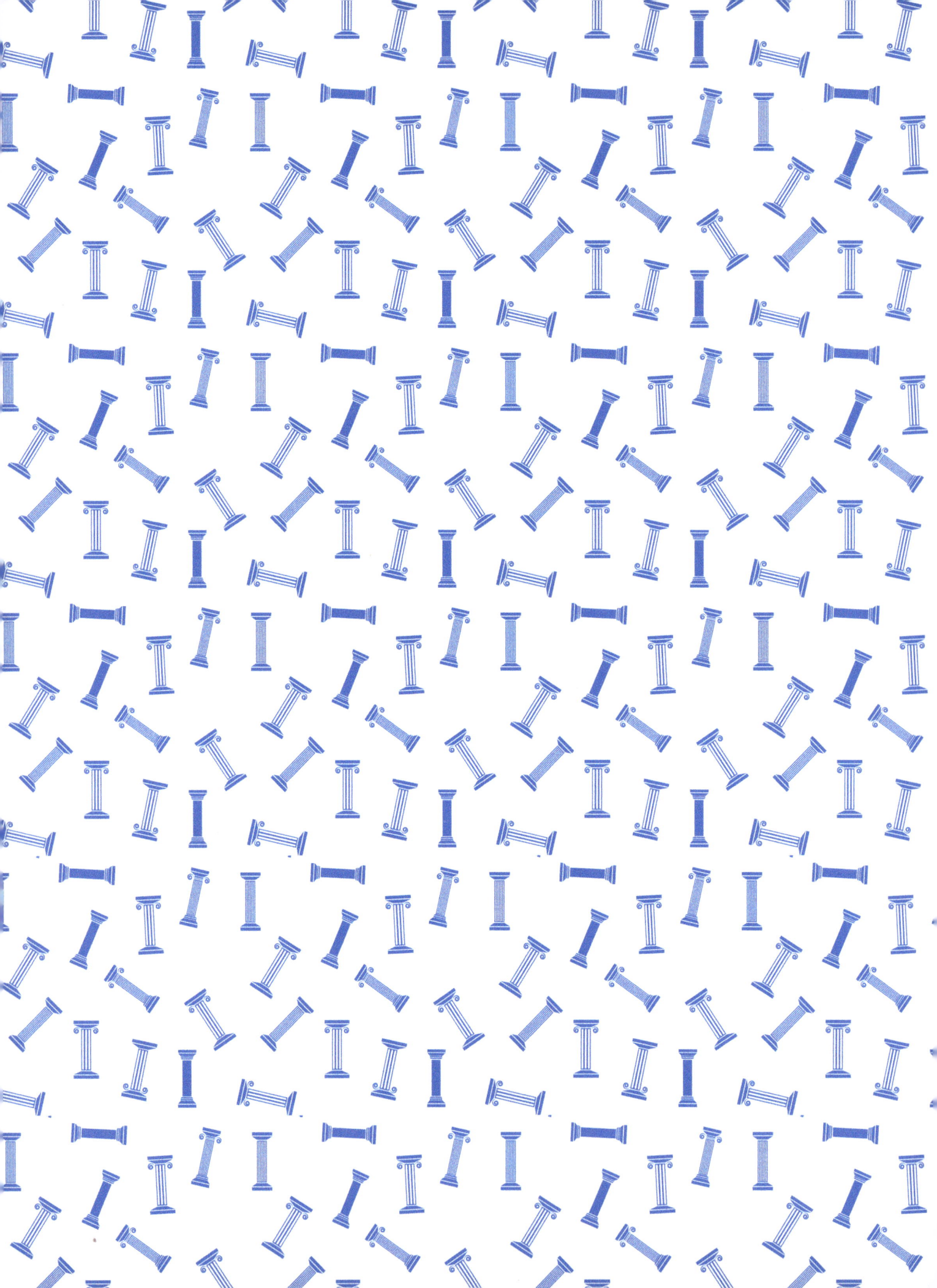

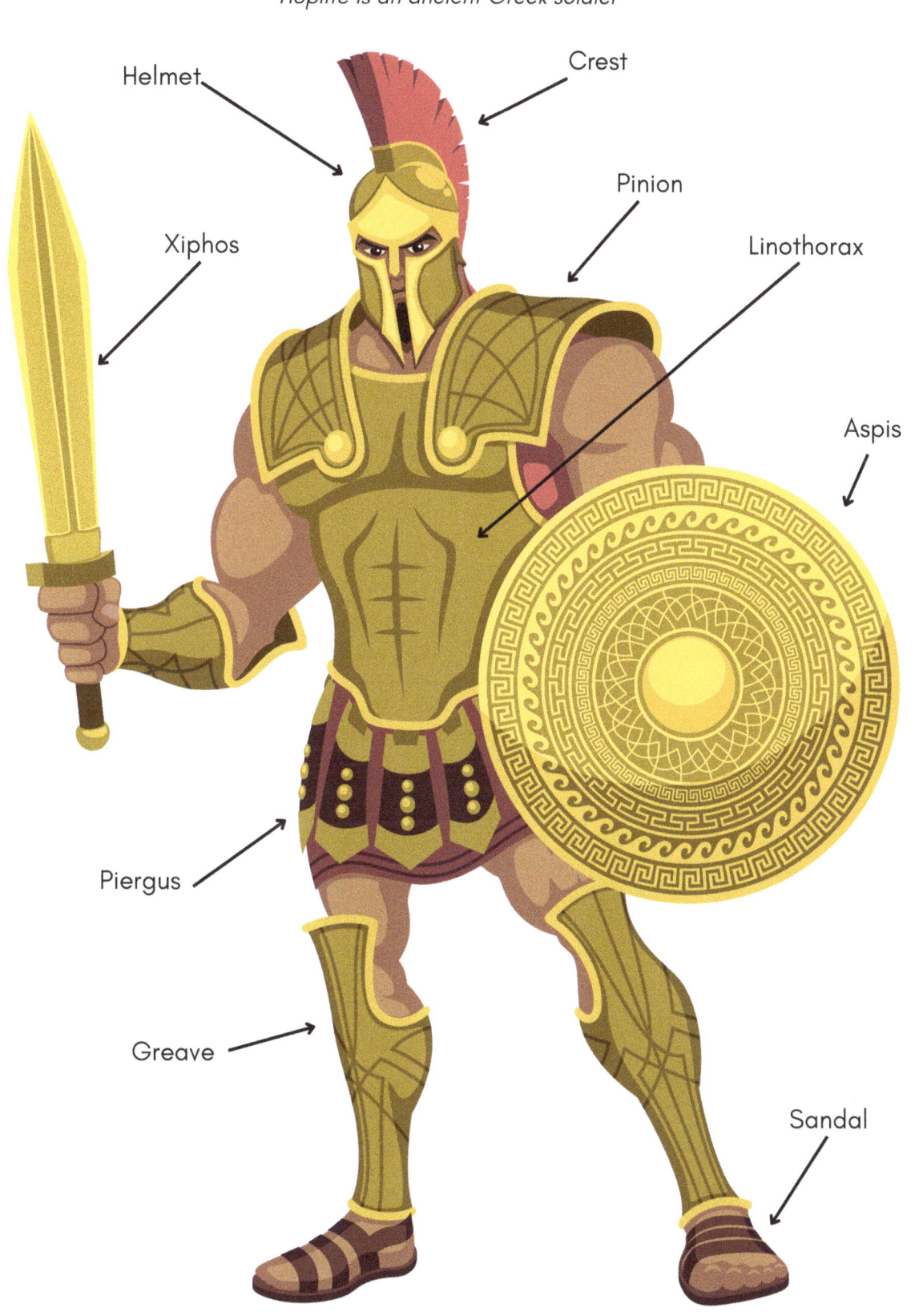

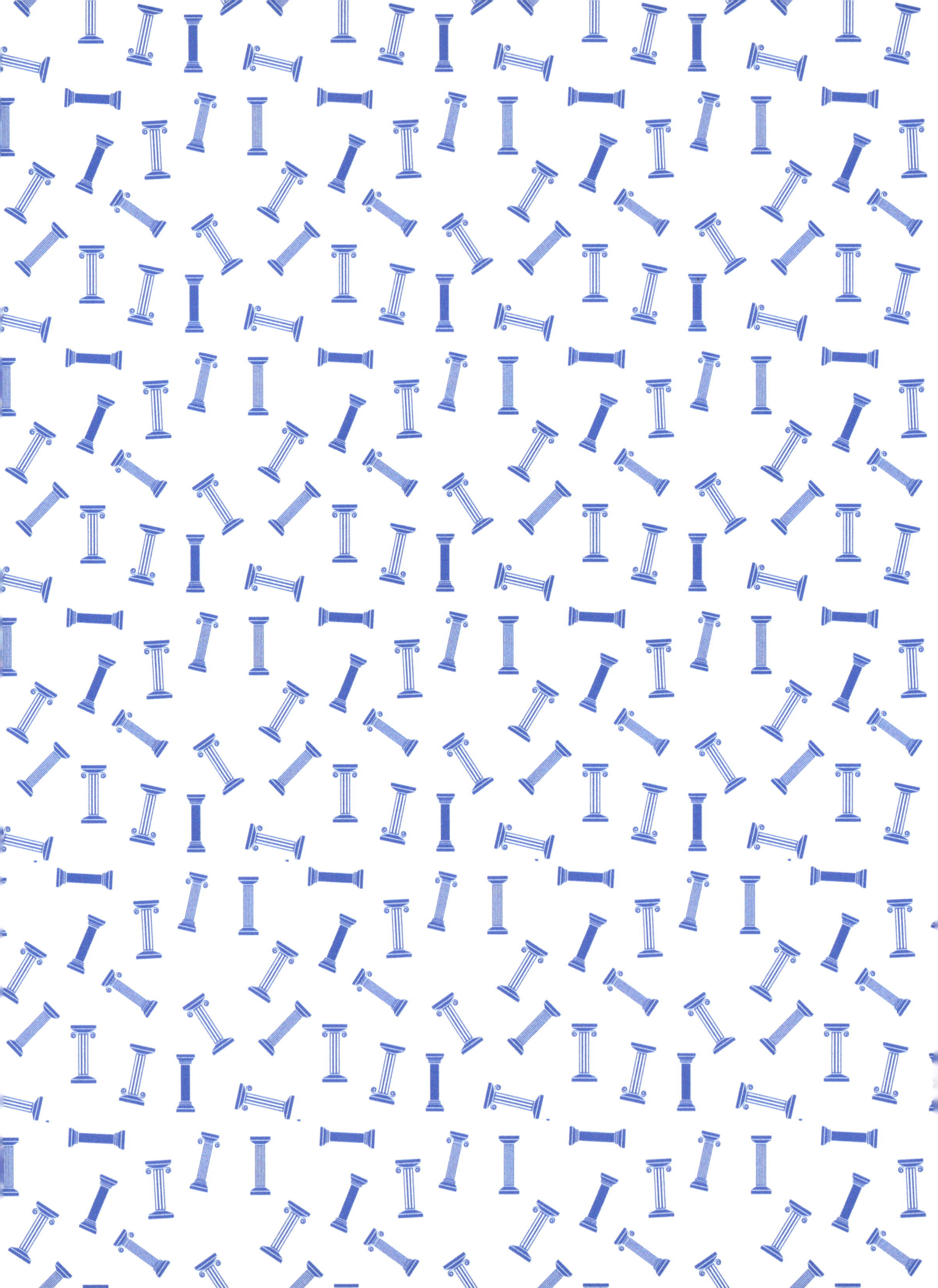

# DAEDALUS & ICARUS

As Icarus came closer to the sun, the wax holding the wings together began to melt and he started falling. Daedalus tried to catch his son, but he was too late, and Icarus was lost forever in the sea.

Daedalus had a son named Icarus, who was his pride and joy. Daedalus loved his son very much and Icarus wanted to be a great inventor like his father.

Once upon a time there was an incredible inventor, Daedalus. He lived on the island of Crete, Greece, where he worked for King Minos. Over the years, Daedalus invented many amazing inventions for King Minos.

**1**

And that is why it's important to follow good advice and not make bad choices in the heat of the moment.

THE END.

**10**

Daedalus had been born in Athens and wanted to return home. But King Minos wouldn't allow it, because he wanted Daedalus to keep working for him. Daedalus tried to leave, and King Minos put him in prison.

**3**

Farther and farther Daedalus and Icarus flew away from Crete, leaving their prison behind. As they approached Athens, Icarus had an incredible urge to fly higher and higher. Daedalus pleaded for him to stop, but Icarus ignored his father.

**8**

Before the guards could catch on to his new invention, Daedalus and Icarus took to the skies. Daedalus led the way, showing Icarus how to use his wings properly.

7

Life in prison was hard on Daedalus, and every day he plotted how to escape. His son Icarus visited him often, but Daedalus spent a lot of time watching the birds from his prison window. He studied the movements of birds and decided to make a device to allow him and his son to fly far away from Crete.

4

## Assembly Instructions

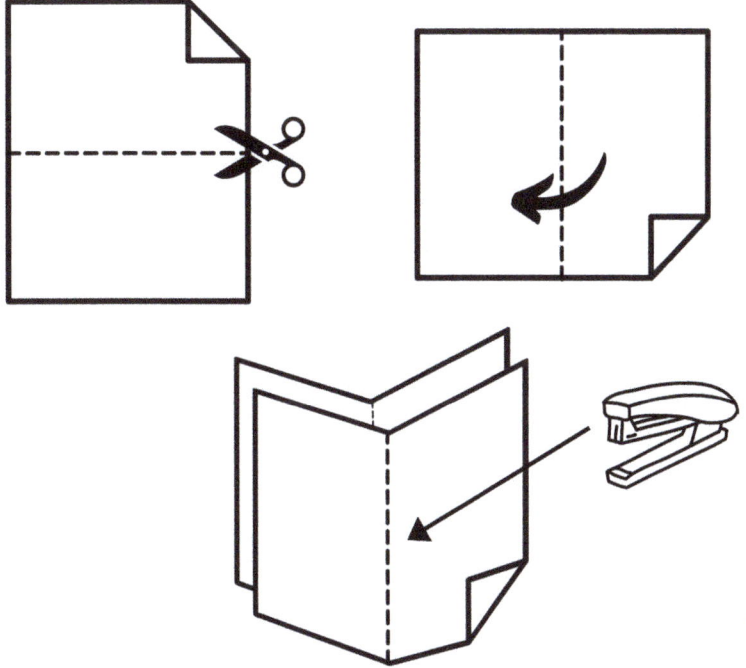

Cut paper in half on lines. Fold each page of book as indicated. Collate together so pages match up appropriately. Staple spine to hold together.

Daedalus started collecting feathers and attached them together using beeswax and thread. When he finished, he put on the wings and showed them to Icarus. Incredibly, the wings worked very well, and Daedalus went to work making a second set for his son, Icarus.

Daedalus knew that flying could be dangerous, so he warned his son to fly in the middle – not too low where the rain could weigh him down or too high where the sun could melt his wings.

## Olive Leaf Outline

# KOTINOS OLYMPIC WREATH

## Instructions

The olive wreath, also known as "kotinos" was the winner's prize at the ancient Olympic Games. Made from the sacred wild-olive tree near the temple of Zeus, these branches were cut with a pair of golden scissors, and then taken to the temple of Hera and placed them on a gold-ivory table. From there, the "Hellanodikai" (the judges of the Olympic Games) would take them, make the wreaths and crown the winners of the Games.

### Materials
- Olive Leaf Outline
- Green Foam or Felt
- Marker
- Scissors
- Green Pipe Cleaner

Cut out included olive leaf template. Trace leaf shapes onto felt (or foam) and cut out. Cut out a couple dozen in a variety of shapes using the different templates. Punch holes in each leaf. Using a pipe cleaner, have child "thread" the leaves onto the "stem" to form branches. Crimp the pipe cleaner to hold leaves in place. After making at least two branches, form into wreath, and place on child's head. With several children, create a small contest and provide the wreath as a prize.

# ABACUS CRAFT

## Instructions

The abacus is a calculating tool which has been used since ancient times. The exact origin of the abacus is unknown, but the Greek abacus was a table of wood or marble, pre-set with small counters in wood or metal for mathematical calculations starting as early as 300 BC. Traditionally, abacuses consist of rows of movable beads strung on a wire, which represent digits. In their earliest designs, the rows of beads could be loose on a flat surface or sliding in grooves. Later the beads were made to slide on rods and built into a frame, allowing faster manipulation. Cut four groves into craft stick sides with scissors or small knife. Glue craft sticks into frame with groves on outside of frame. Thread ten (10) beads for each line using different colors. Continue until four lines of 10 beads are completed. Secure tightly. Add additional glue if necessary. For additional durability, add additional craft sticks to frame. Each row represents 1, 10, 100, 1000 place. Slide the beads from one side to the other to represent different numbers. Test the child's knowledge. Can they recognize numbers based on the position of the beads?

## Materials
- Large & Small Craft Sticks
- Scissors
- Craft Glue
- Beads
- String

# Abacus Counting Clip Cards

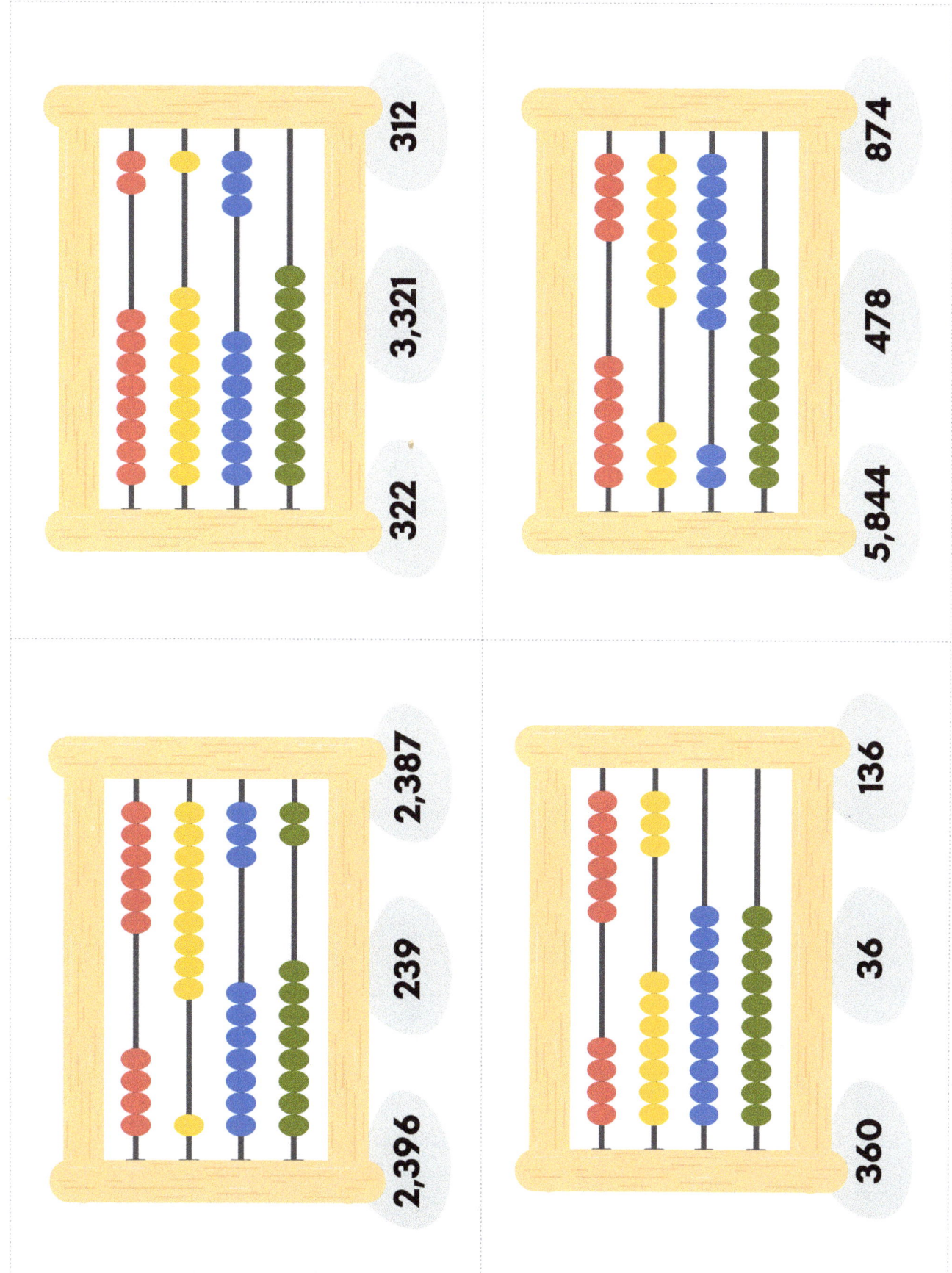

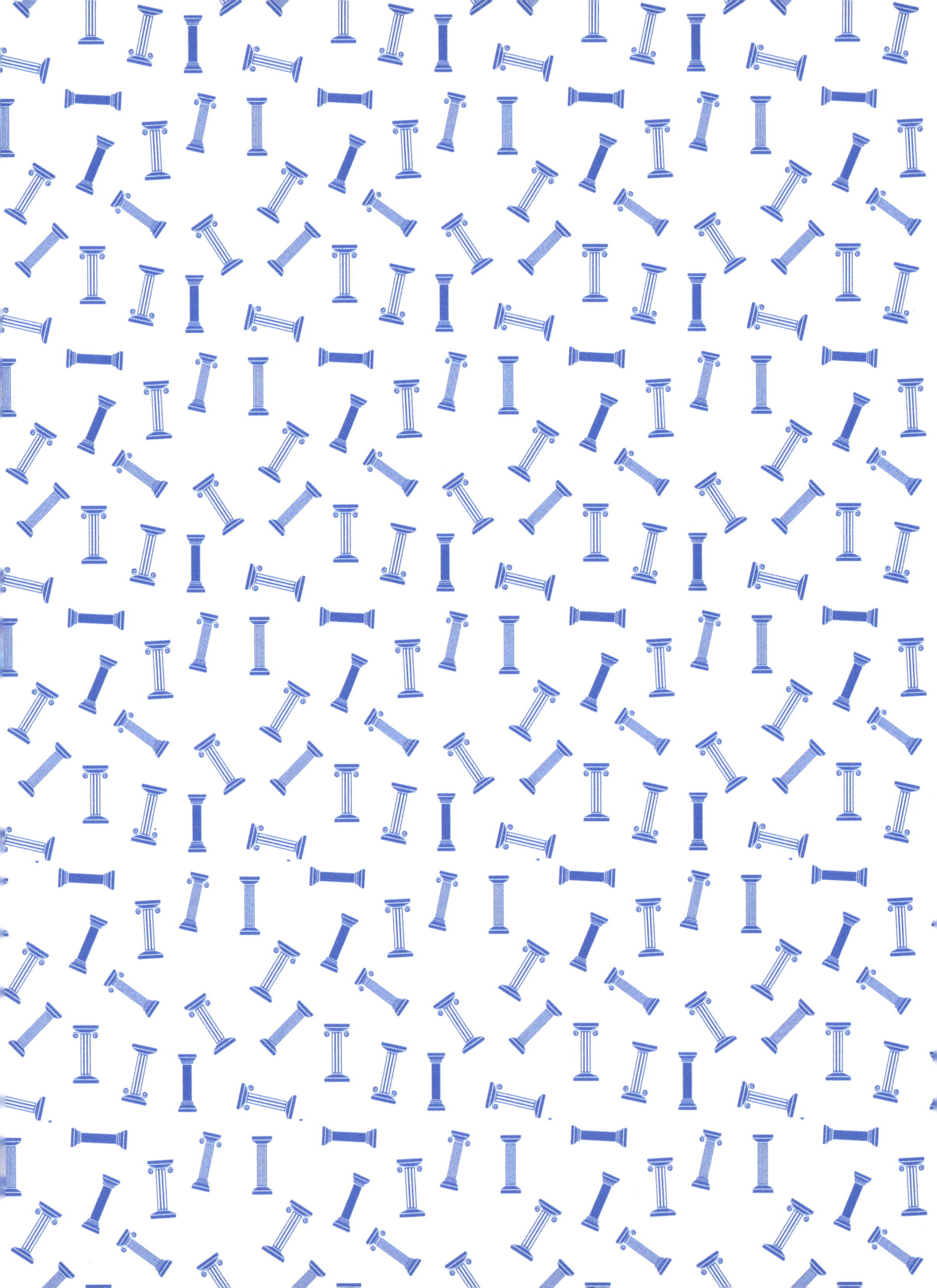

# Abacus Counting Clip Cards

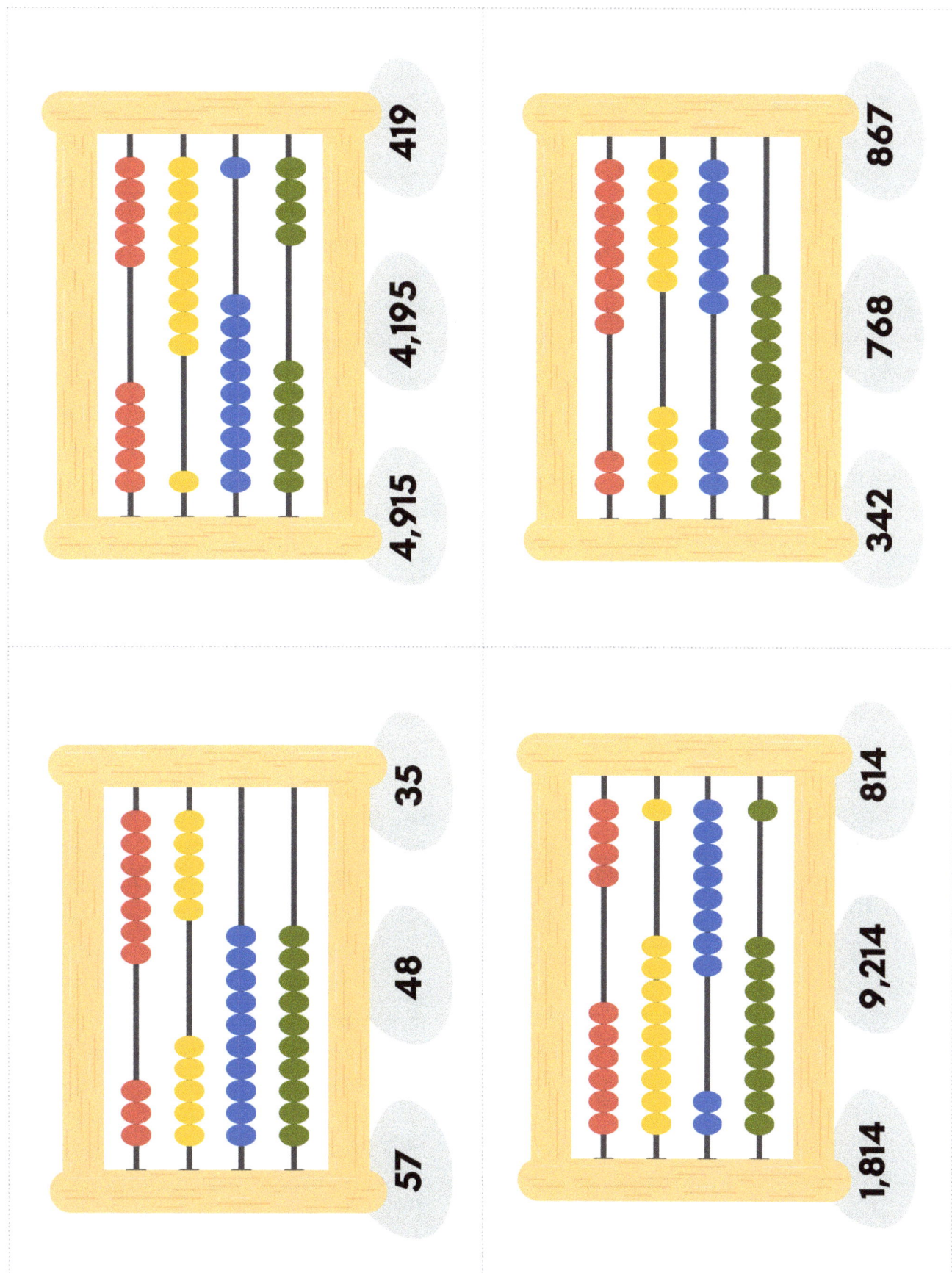

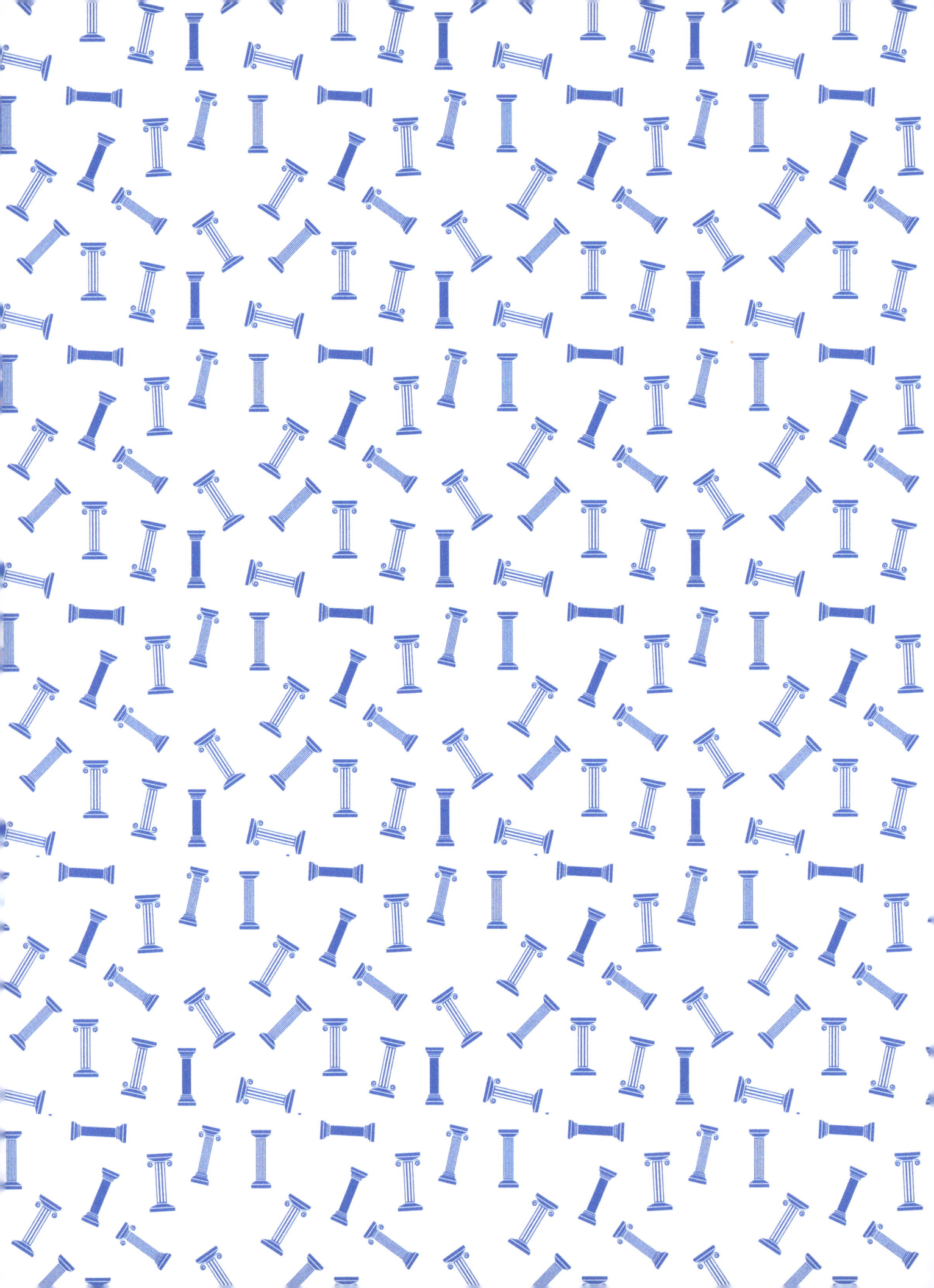

# Abacus Counting Clip Cards

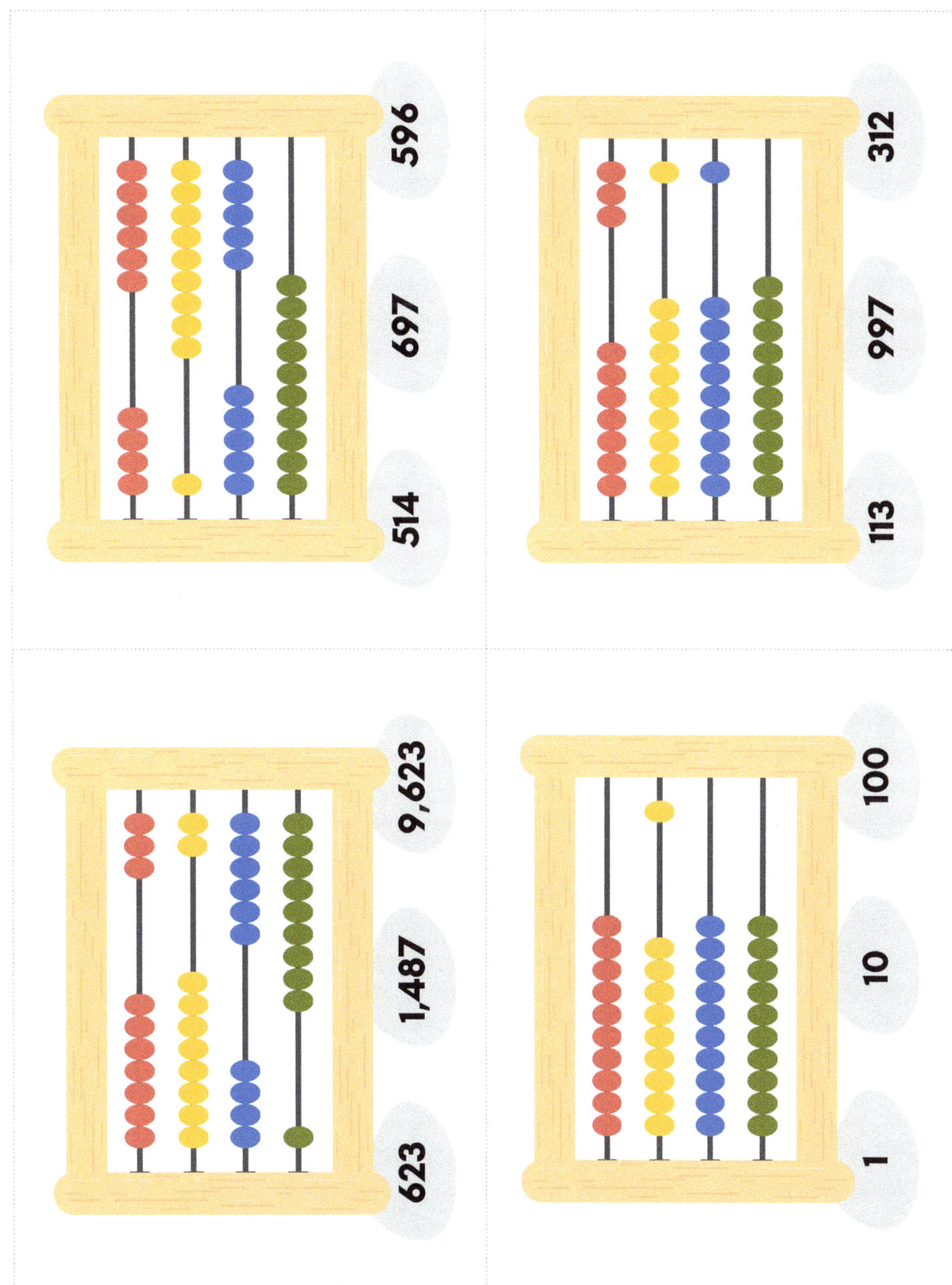

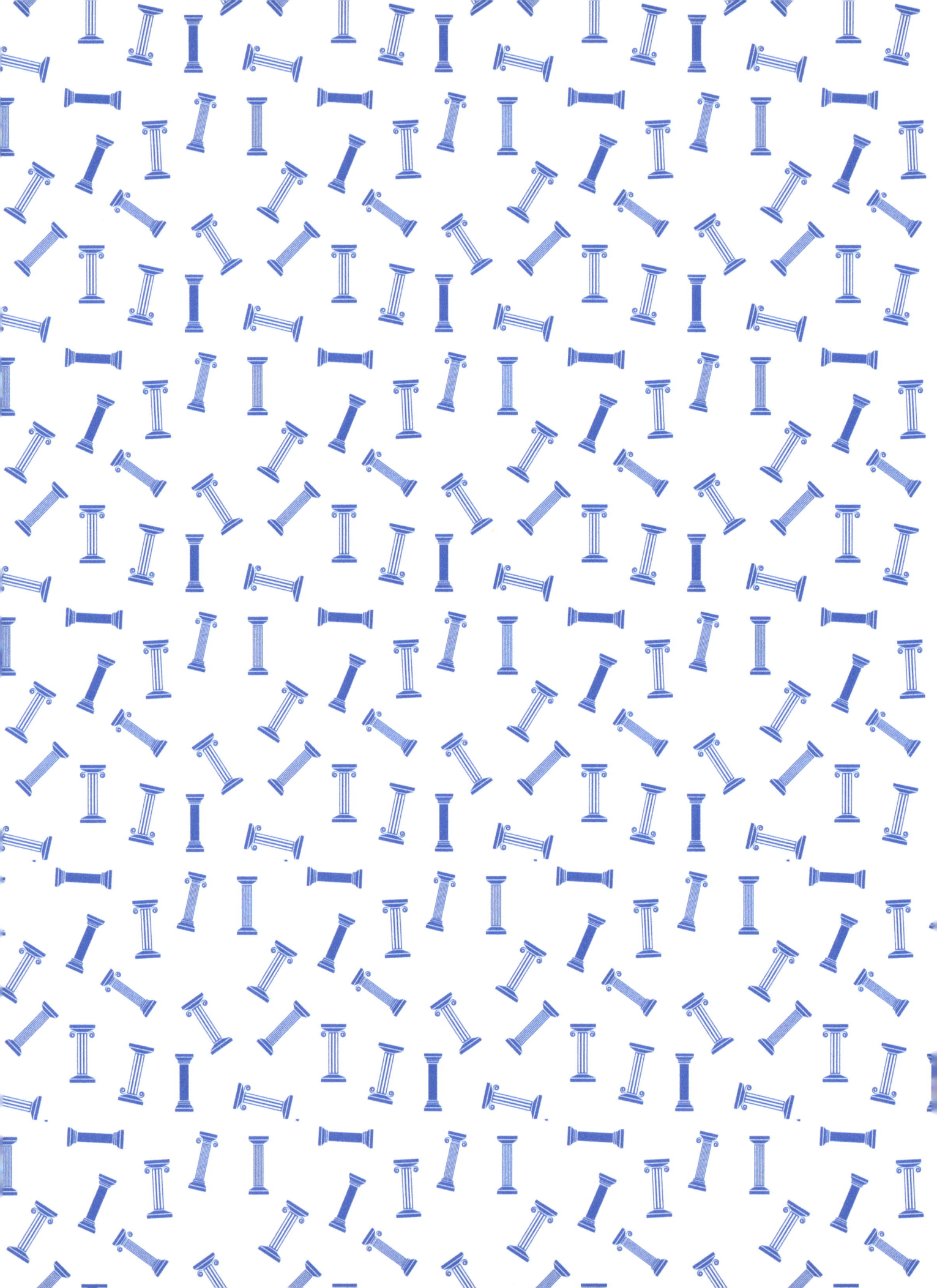

# EVIL EYE "MATI" PENDENT

## Instructions

The Greek evil eye, or mati, is a curse given by one person to another by way of a spiteful or bitter look. This usually happens when the person receiving it is unaware of what's happening. It is a negative energy, such as jealousy, anger, or hostility that creates the evil eye. To ward off the evil eye, a mati pendant is worn to protect the user from the negative energy. This practice actually dates back to the 6th century BC.

### Materials
- Blue Glass Charm
- Acrylic Paints
- Paintbrush
- E-6000 Glue
- Jewelry Wire/String
- String

Provide child with blue glass charm*. Have them paint the middle with white, then light blue and finally a black dot to create an eye-appearing design. Have each layer dry completely between. Glue a small piece circle of jewelry wire or string to the back of the glass charm with E-6000 glue. Allow to dry completely. String a piece of string through the pendant to create a necklace. Wear proudly.

*If unable to find a blue glass charm, use another color and/or clear and paint the charm dark blue.*

# MYKONOS WINDMILL

## Instructions

The Mykonos windmills are iconic features of this Greek island. Most of the windmills face towards the North where the island's climate sources its strongest winds over the largest part of the year. Most of them were built by the Venetians in the 16th century, and were primarily used to mill wheat, and an important source of income for the inhabitants.

Cut out included windmill template. Glue the base together in a tube and the roof into a beveled shape. Use clothespins to hold in place while drying. Punch a hole as indicated for windmill blades. Use measuring line to cut four skewer sticks into appropriate length. Measure an additional stick by placing into center through hole on side and gluing into place. Trim so it extends just beyond roof edge. Glue four sticks into cross shape to form windmill. Use hot glue for quicker/easier construction. Glue onto wood extension. Glue jute string around edge. Display.

## Materials
- Windmill Template
- Craft Glue (or Hot)
- Hole Punch
- Clothespins (optional)
- Skewer Sticks
- Jute String

Mykonos Windmill

Glue Here

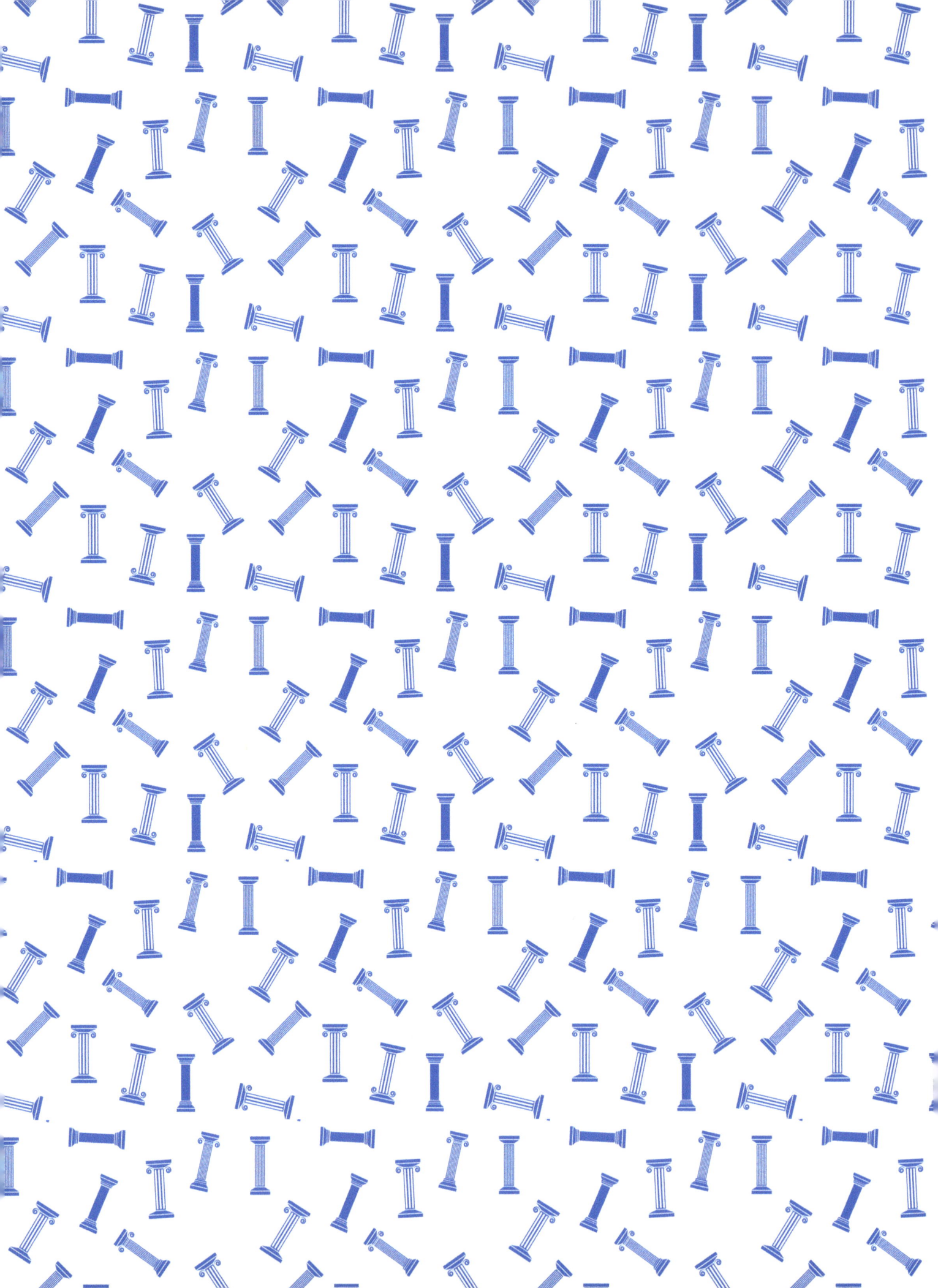

# Mykonos Windmill

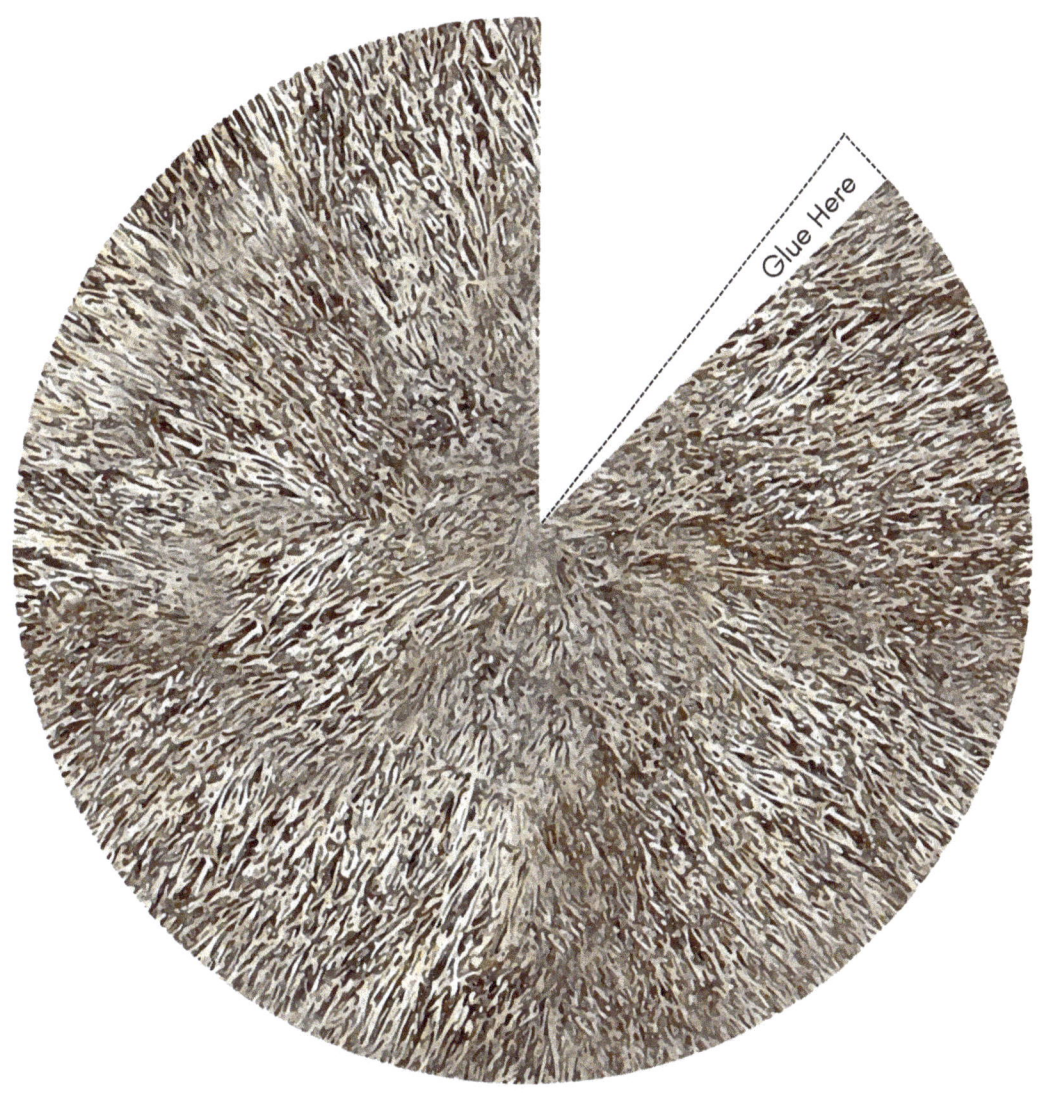

Cut Skewers This Long

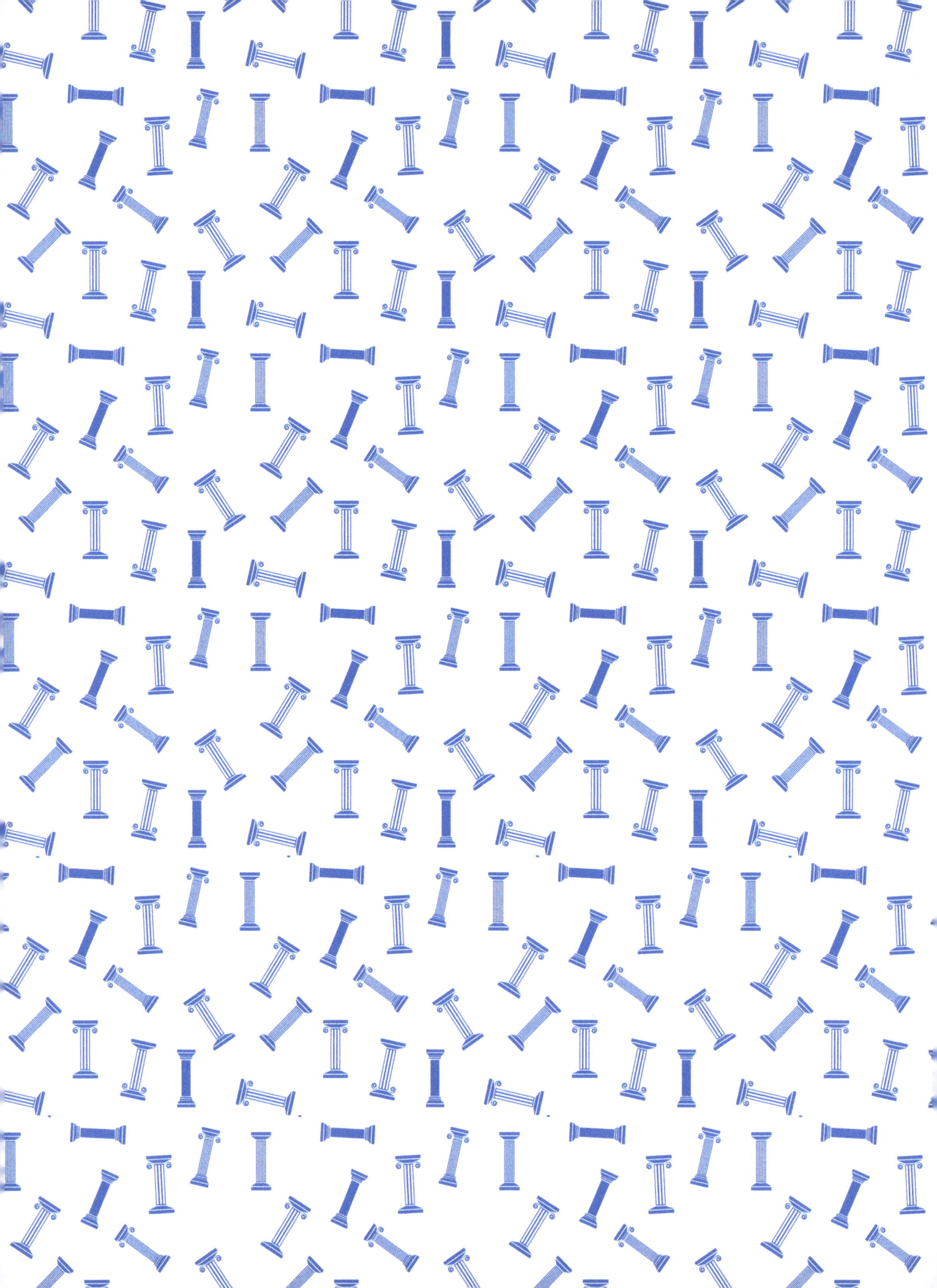

# Greek Alphabet

| | |
|---|---|
| **Α α**  Alpha | **Β β**  Beta |
| **Γ γ**  Gamma | **Δ δ**  Delta |
| **Ε ε**  Epsilon | **Ζ ζ**  Zeta |
| **Η η**  Eta | **Θ θ**  Theta |

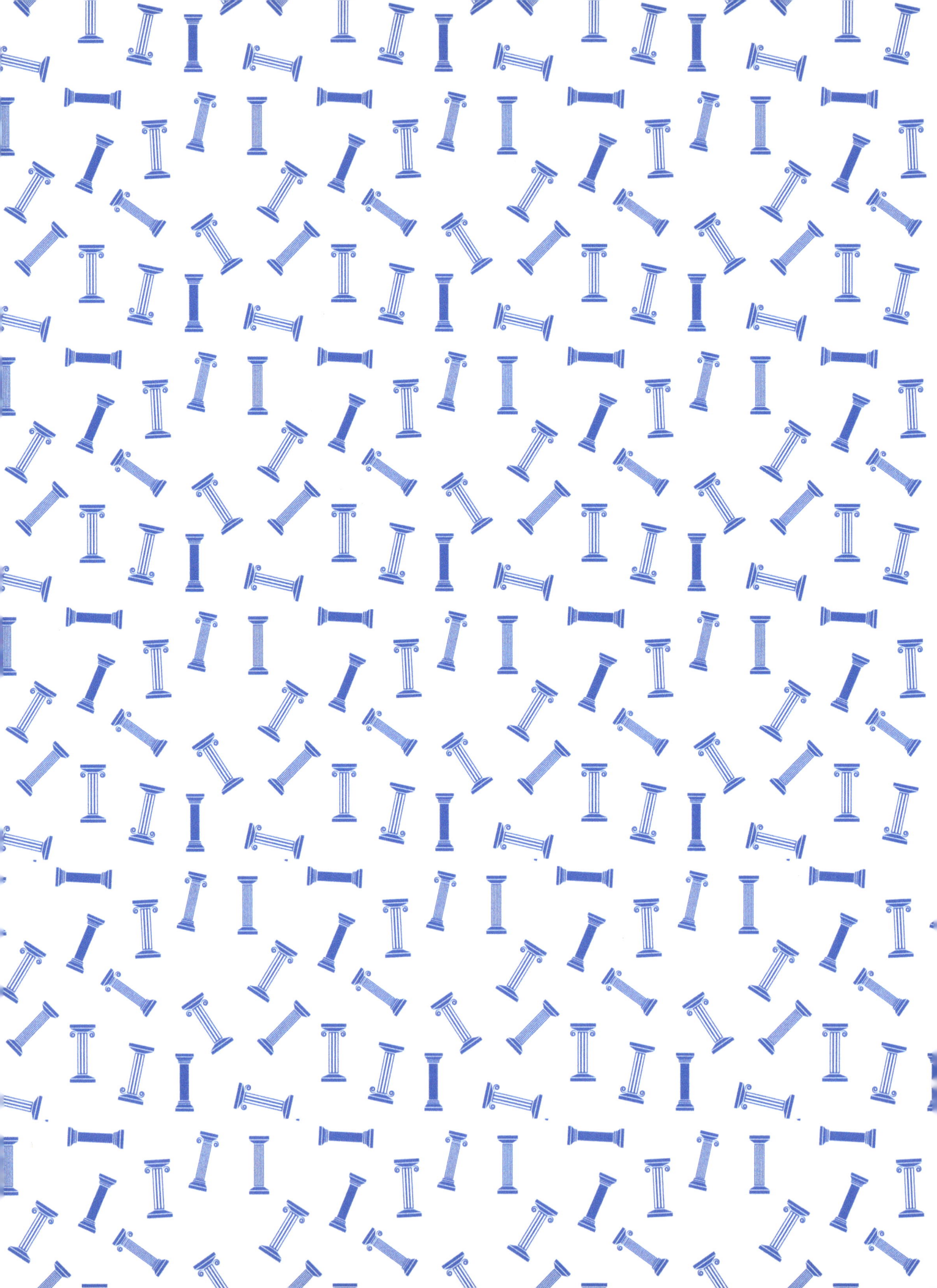

# Greek Alphabet

| | |
|---|---|
| **Ιι** *Iota* | **Κκ** *Kappa* |
| **Λλ** *Lambda* | **Μμ** *Mu* |
| **Νν** *Nu* | **Ξξ** *Xi* |
| **Οο** *Omicron* | **Ππ** *Pi* |

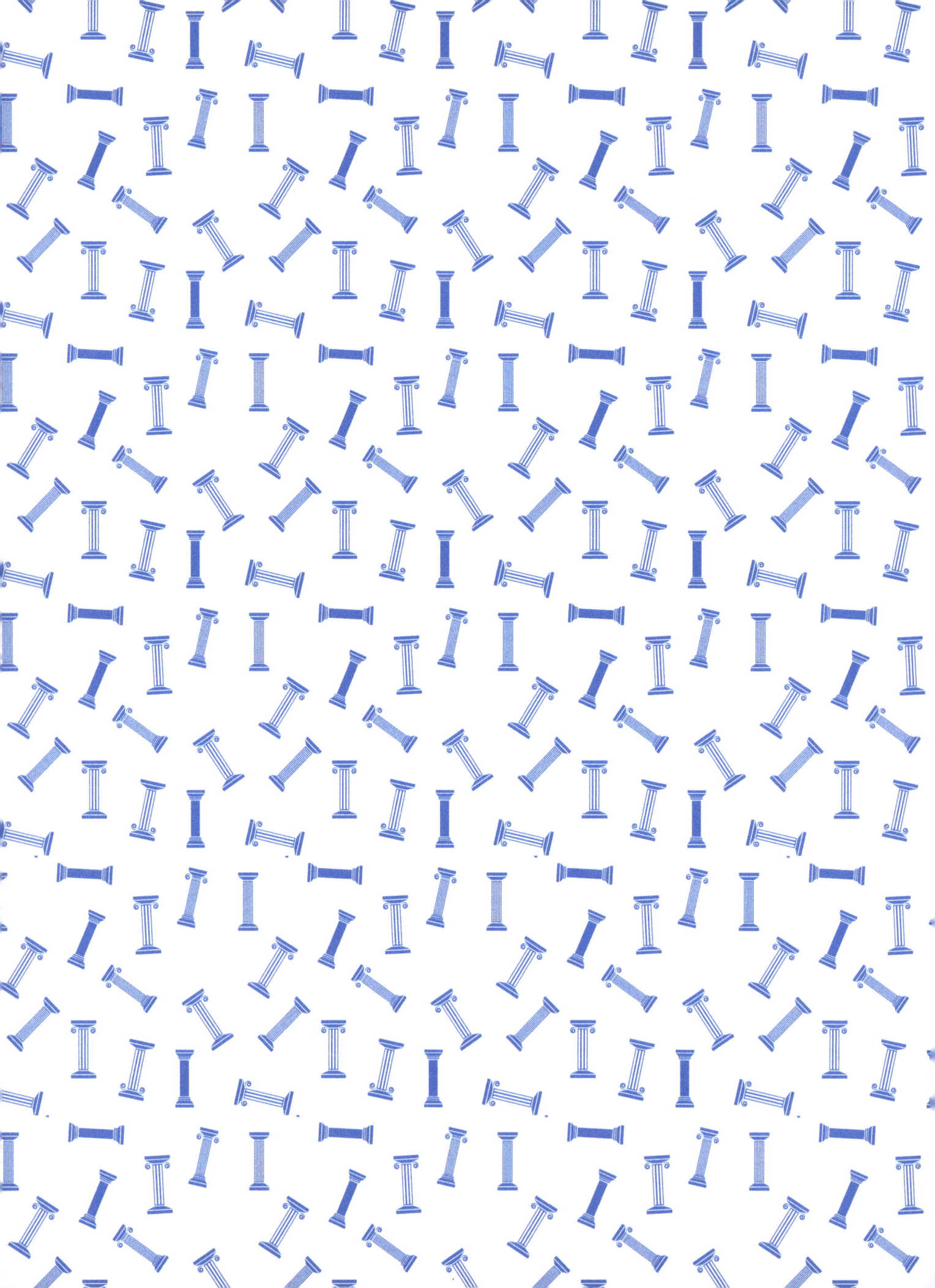

# Greek Alphabet

| Ρρ | Σσ |
|---|---|
| Rho | Sigma |

| Ττ | Υυ |
|---|---|
| Tau | Upsilon |

| Φφ | Χχ |
|---|---|
| Phi | Chi |

| Ψψ | Ωω |
|---|---|
| Psi | Omega |

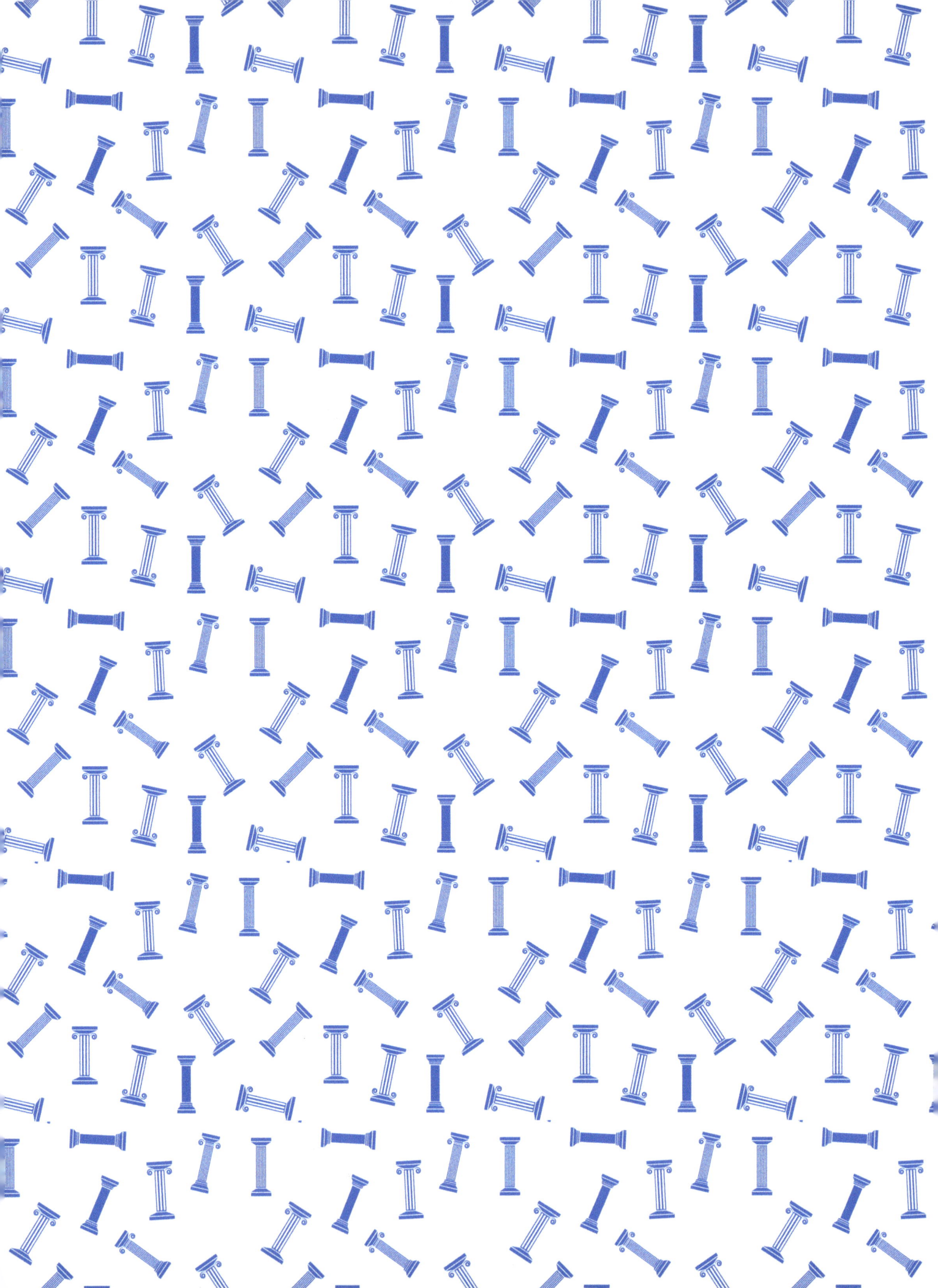

# MAGNETIC OR NOT? SENSORY BIN

### Materials
- Tray or Casserole Dish
- Large Magnet
- Assorted Items

### Instructions

According to Greek legend, magnetism was first discovered by a shepherd named Megnes, who lived in Megnesia, Greece. While tending to his sheep in the mountains, Megnes found that the nails in his sandals were attracted to a rock. The stone was named magnetite, after the name of the shepherd/country where it was found.

Three elemental metals are considered magnetic: iron, cobalt and nickel. Provide child with a tray or casserole dish filled with both magnetic and non-magnetic items. For metal trays, it may be helpful to line the bottom with a non-magnetic medium such as rice, legumes, cardboard or felt. Have the child guess if each item is magnetic or not. Have them test with the magnet to see if they are correct. For older children, make a list of items in the tray and have the child make a hypothesis if the item is magnet, then have them test their theories.

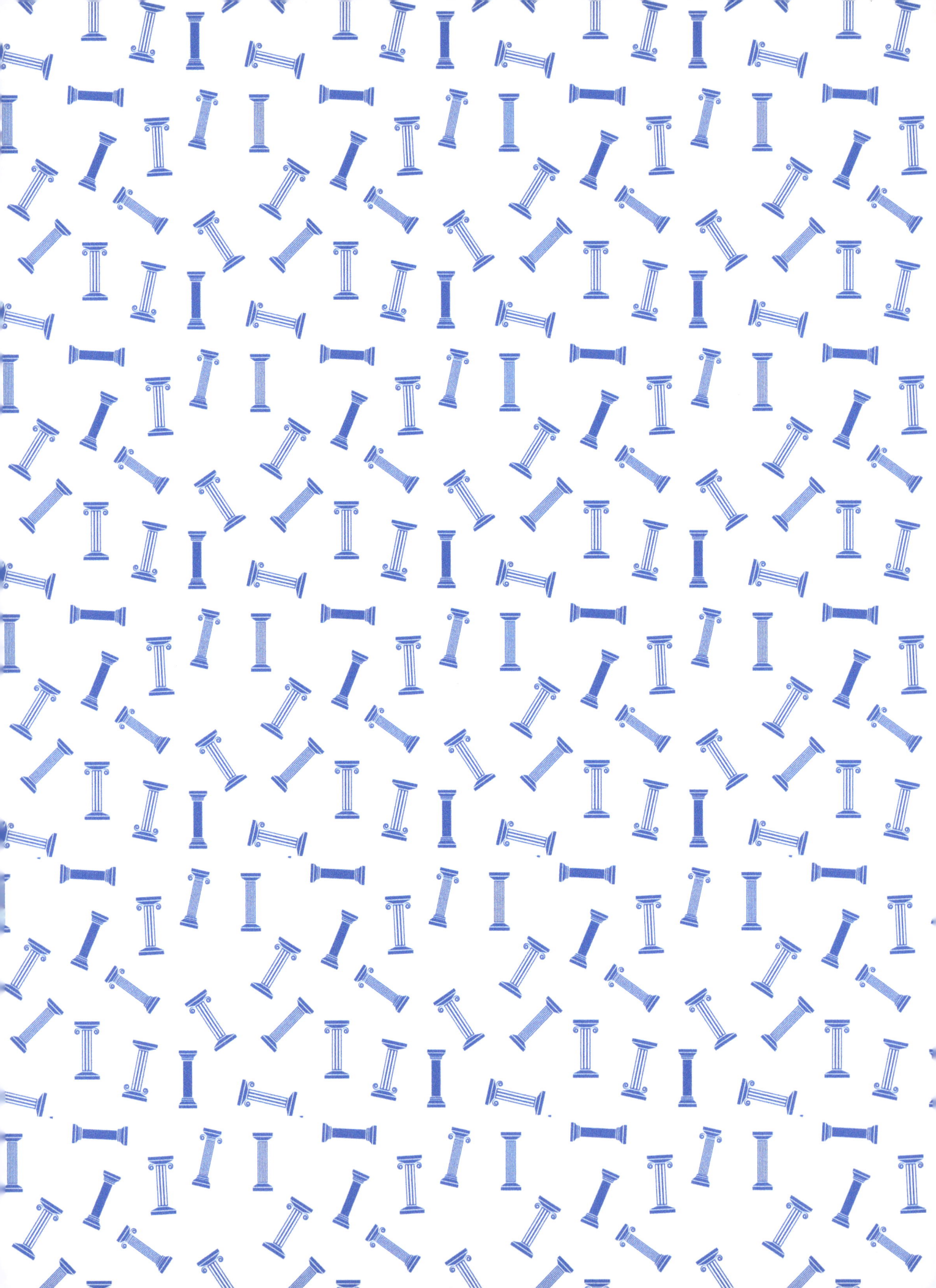

# ΓΎΡΟΣ (GYROS)

## ingredients

- sliced chicken nugget*
- tomatoes, sliced
- onions, sliced
- lettuce, shredded
- pita bread

**Tzatziki Sauce**
- ½ small cucumber, grated
- ½ cup plain Greek yogurt
- 1 tablespoon olive oil
- ½ tablespoon lemon juice
- 1 small garlic clove, minced
- ½ teaspoon sea salt

*Use a chicken substitute for vegetarian.

## directions

- Mix tzatziki sauce ingredients together and refrigerate overnight.
- Warm pita bread in microwave or oven.
- Layer chicken* and vegetables on pita bread and top with tzatziki sauce.
- Roll pita bread over ingredients to create a wrap. Serve with potato wedges or French fries.

# γύρος (Gyros)

## INGREDIENTS

CHICKEN NUGGETS · TOMATO · LETTUCE

ONION · PITA · PLAIN GREEK YOGURT

GRATED CUCUMBER · OLIVE OIL · LEMON JUICE

GARLIC · SEA SALT

# Greece Fauna (3-Part Cards)

**Dolphin**

**Mediterranean Monk Seal**

**Kri Kri**

**Balkan lynx**

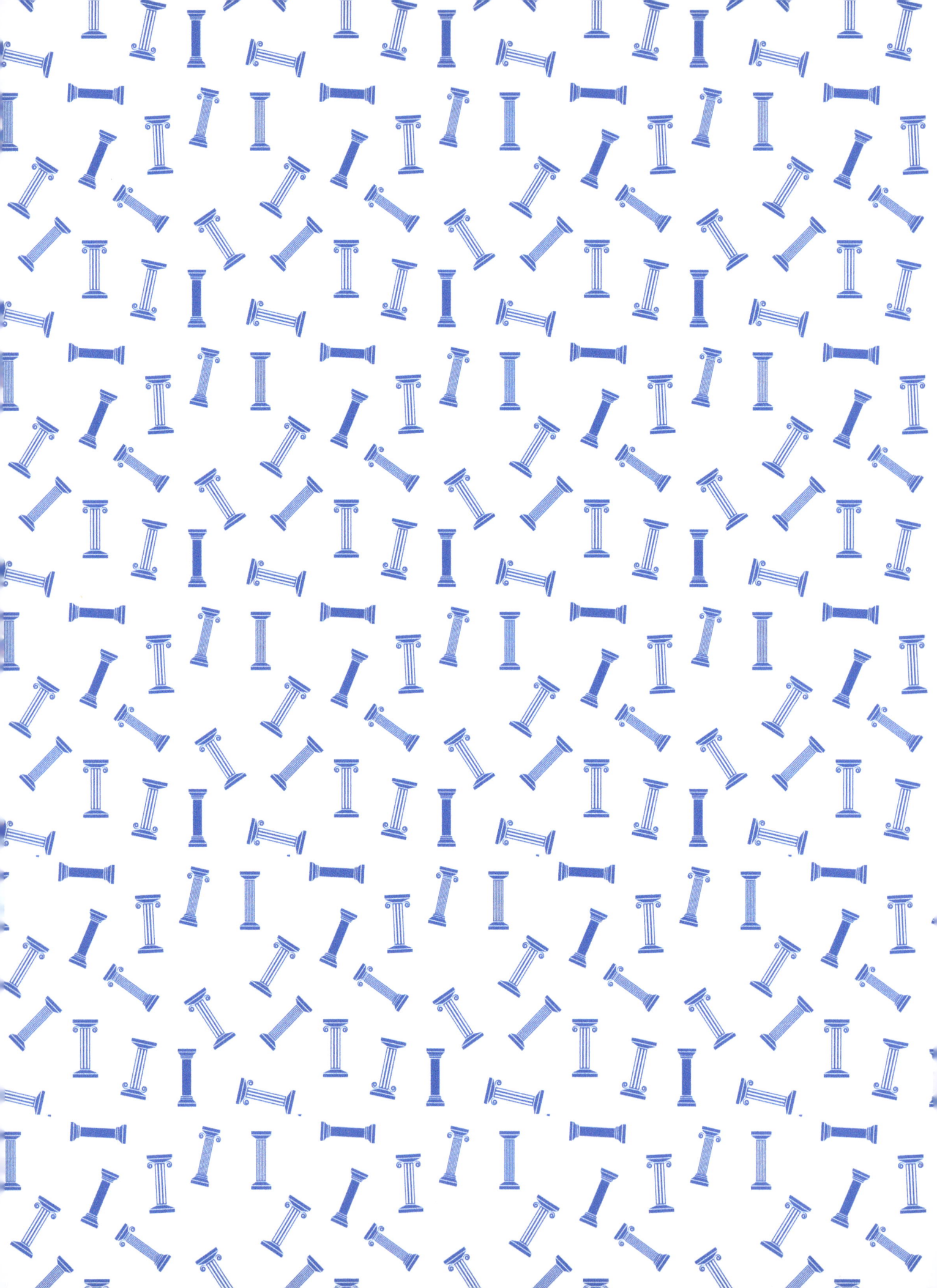

# Greece Fauna (3-Part Cards)

**Dolphin**

**Mediterranean Monk Seal**

**Kri Kri**

**Balkan lynx**

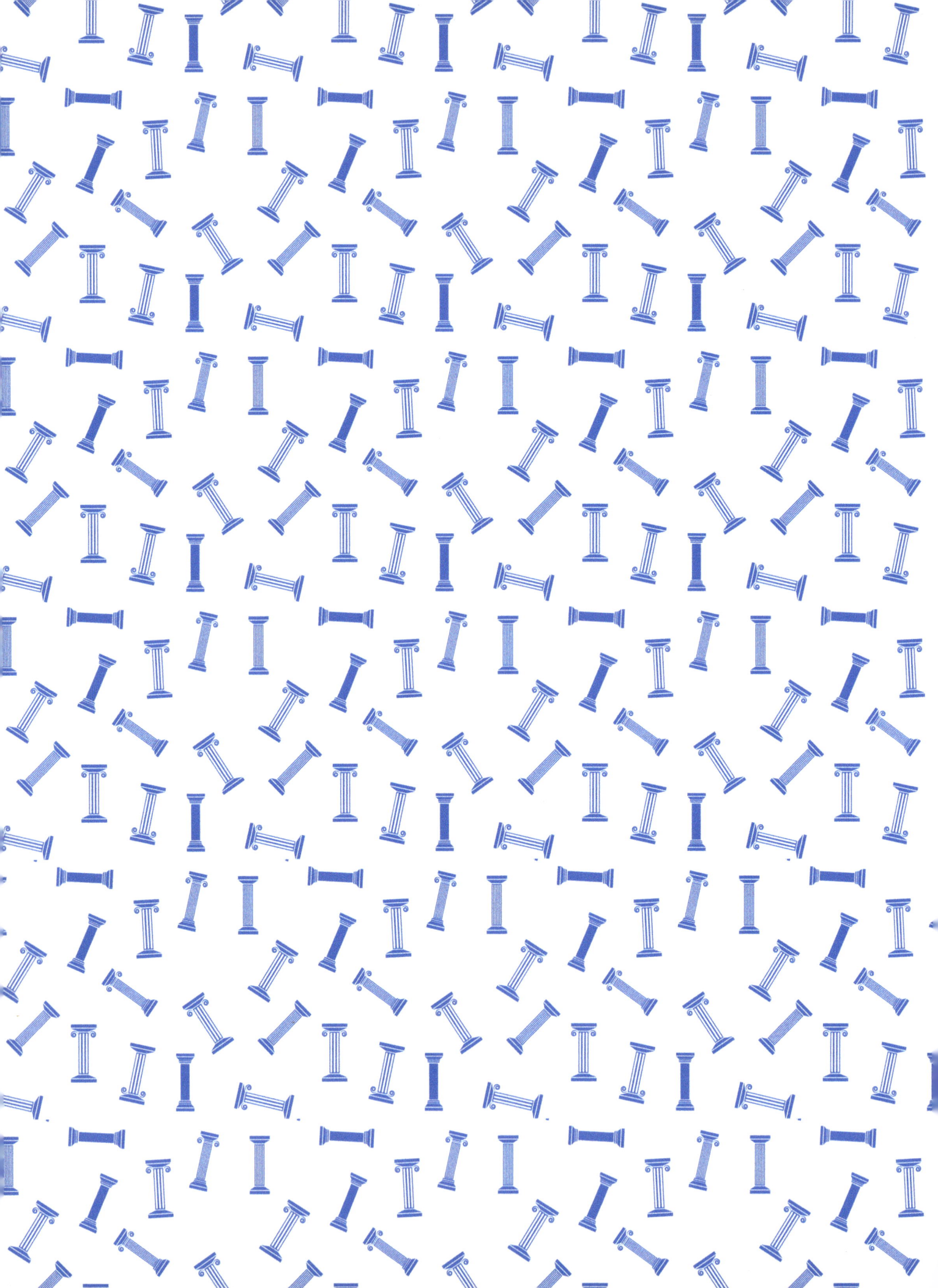

# Greece Fauna (3-Part Cards)

**Crete Pipistrelle**

**Beech Marten**

**Loggerhead Turtle**

**Kingfisher**

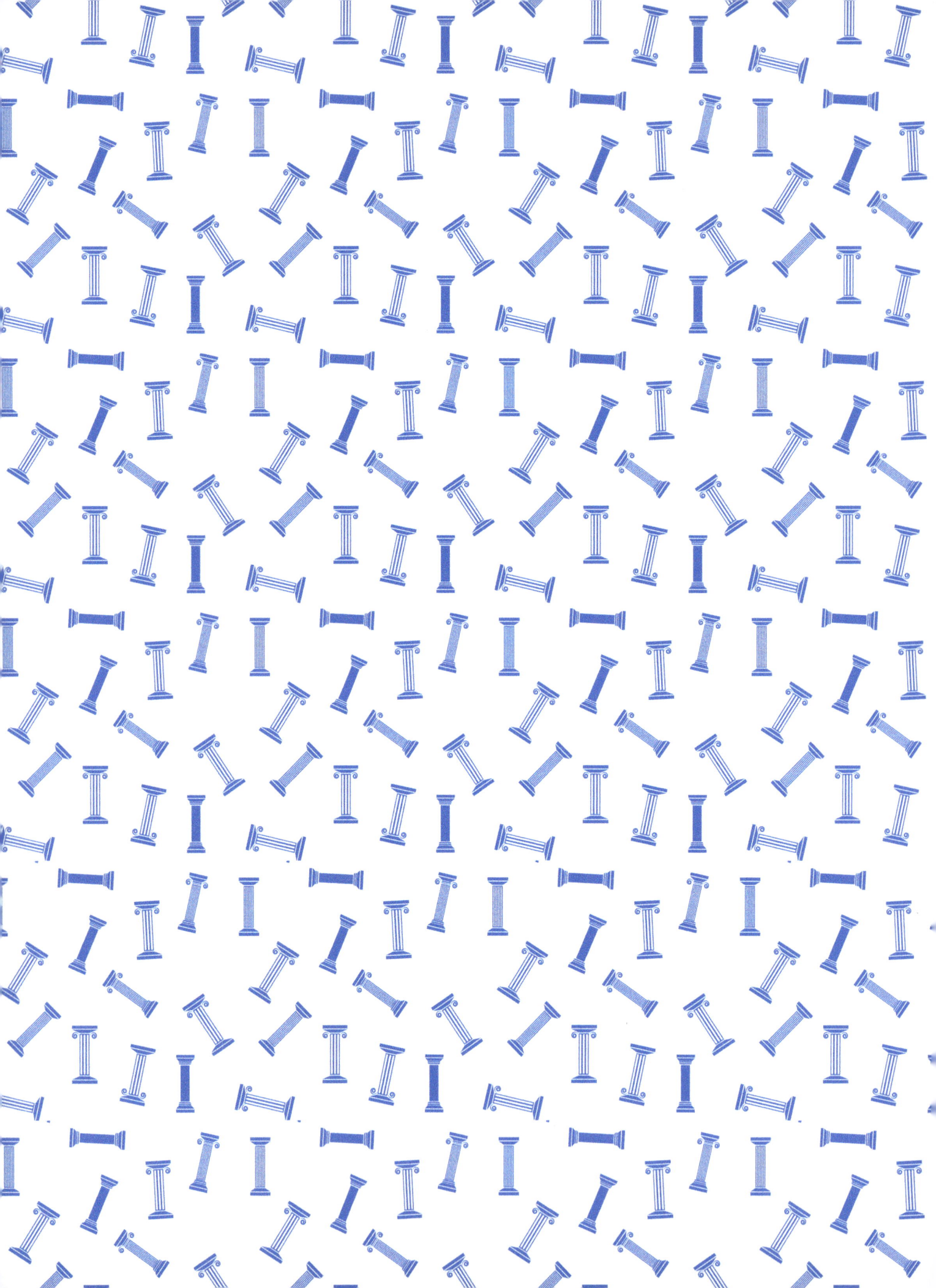

# Greece Fauna (3-Part Cards)

**Crete Pipistrelle**

**Beech Marten**

**Loggerhead Turtle**

**Kingfisher**

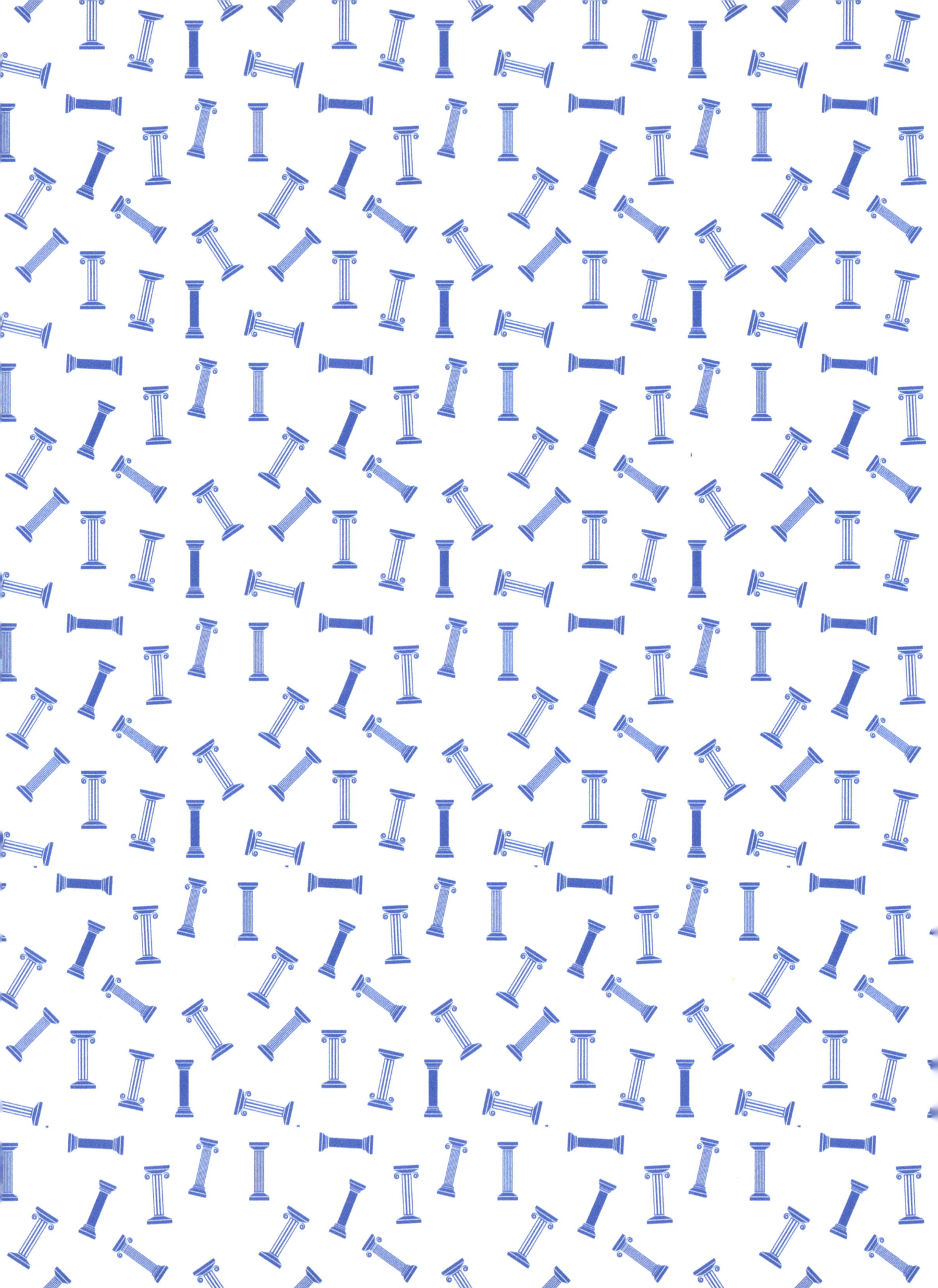

# Life Cycle Spinner

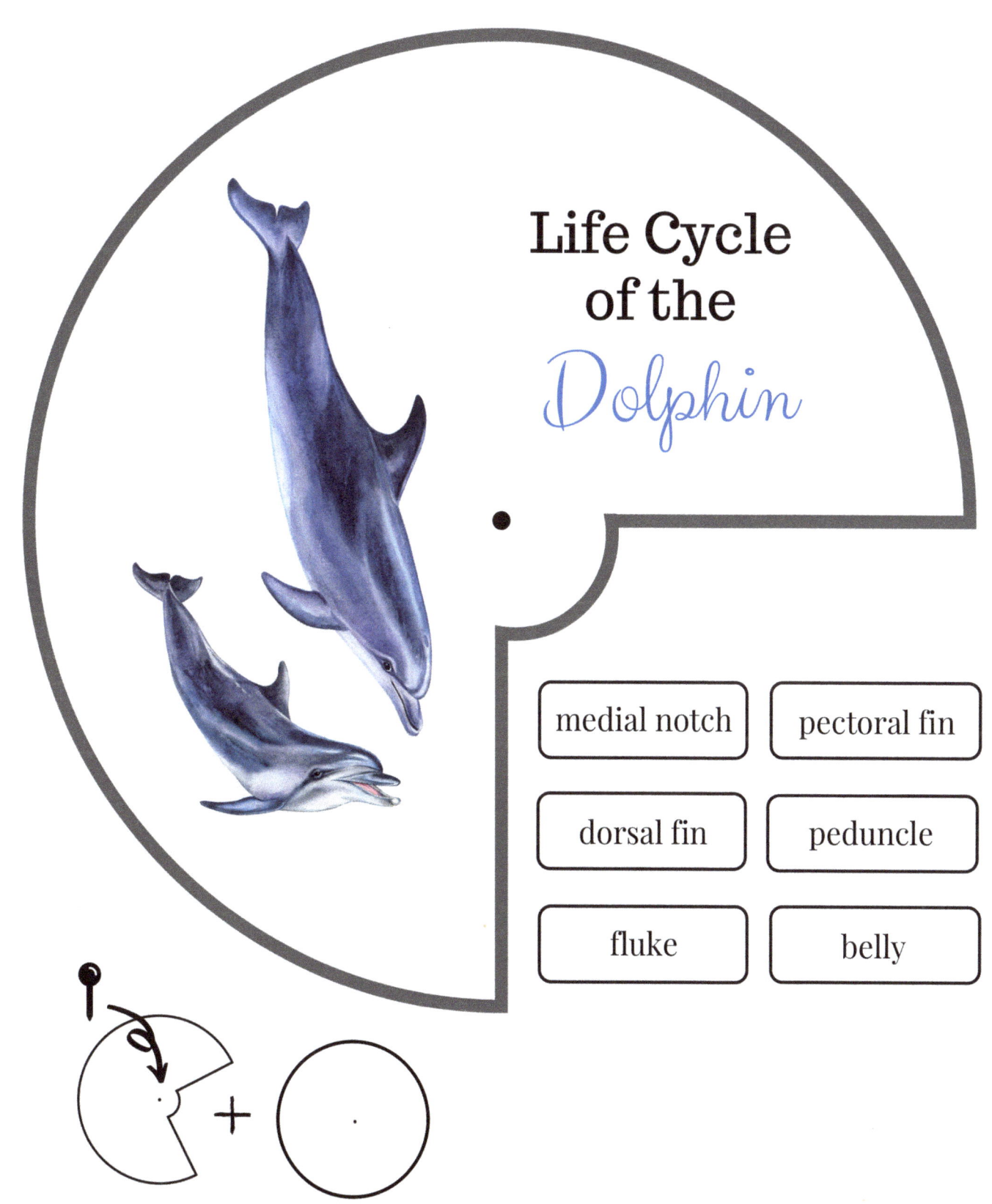

Life Cycle of the *Dolphin*

| medial notch | pectoral fin |
| dorsal fin | peduncle |
| fluke | belly |

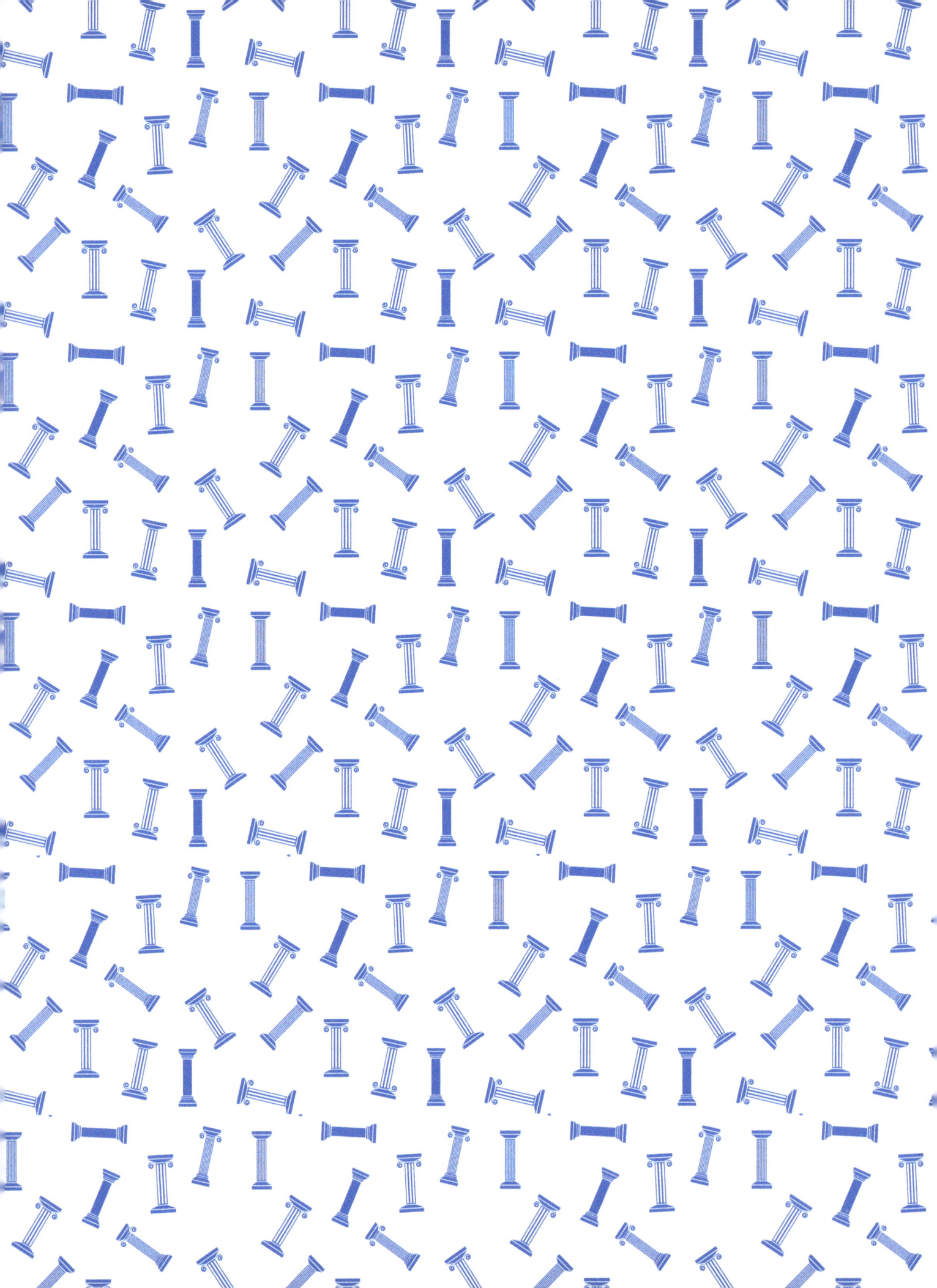

# Life Cycle Spinner

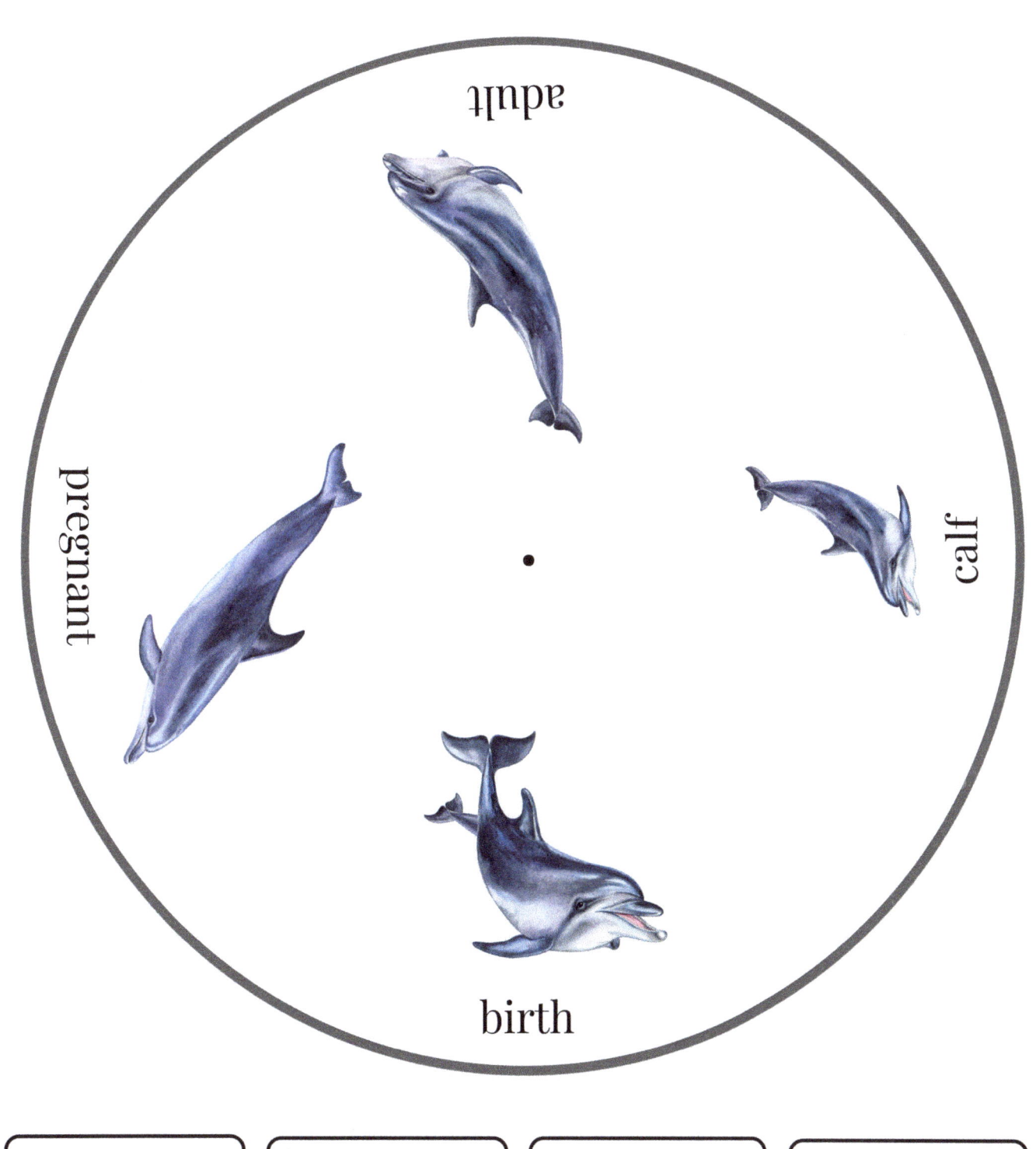

| blowhole | melon | rostrum | eye |

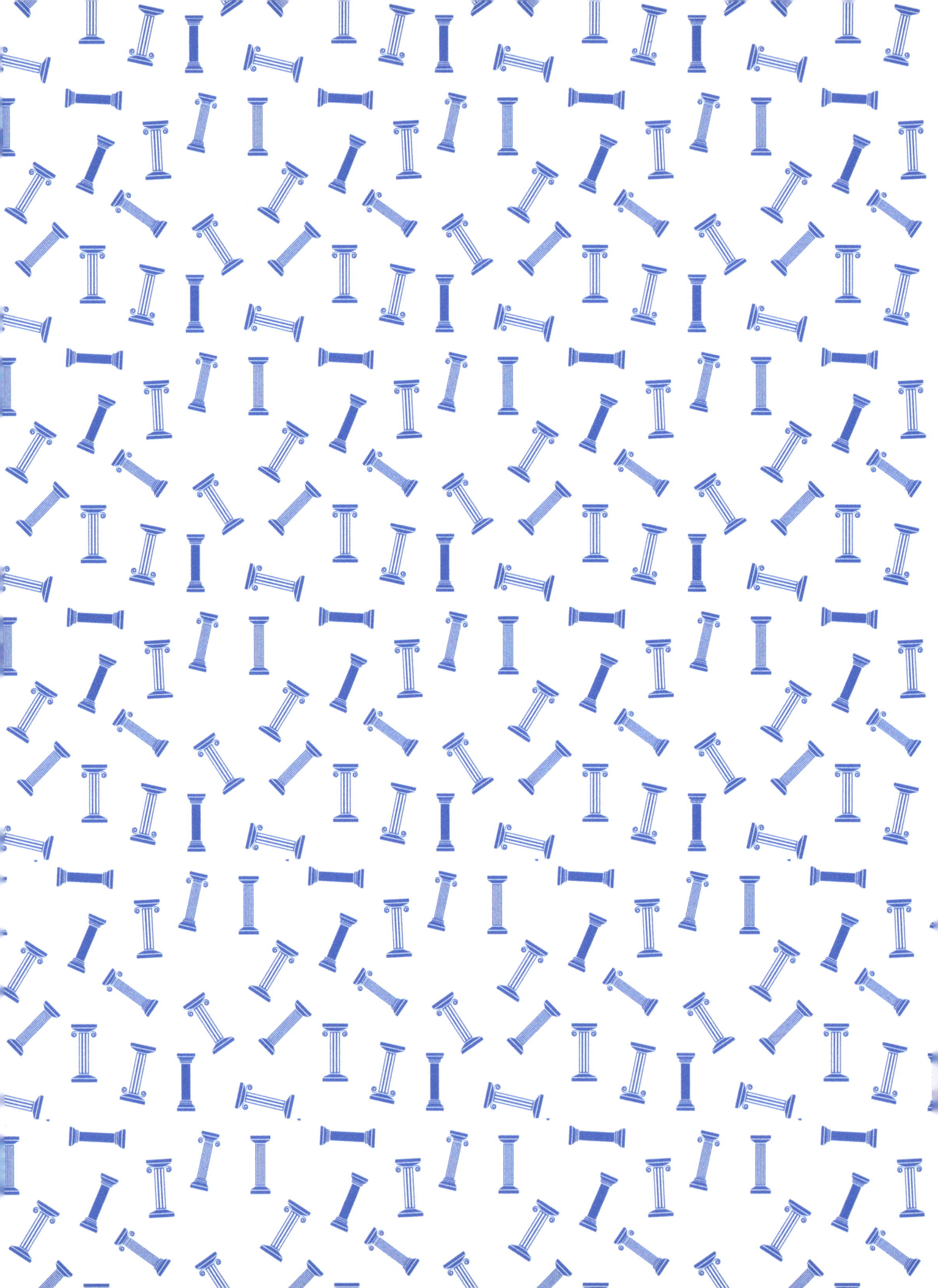

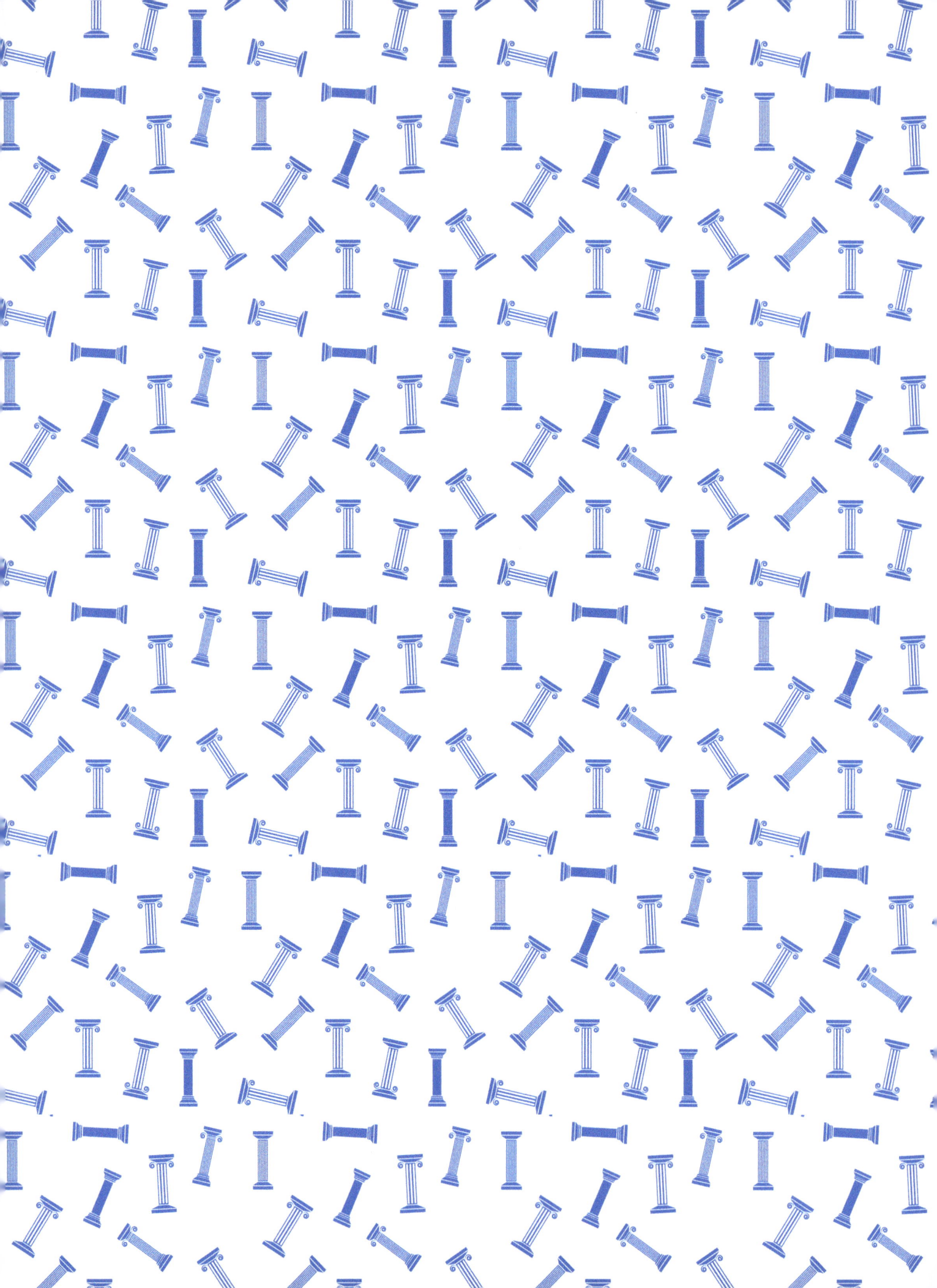

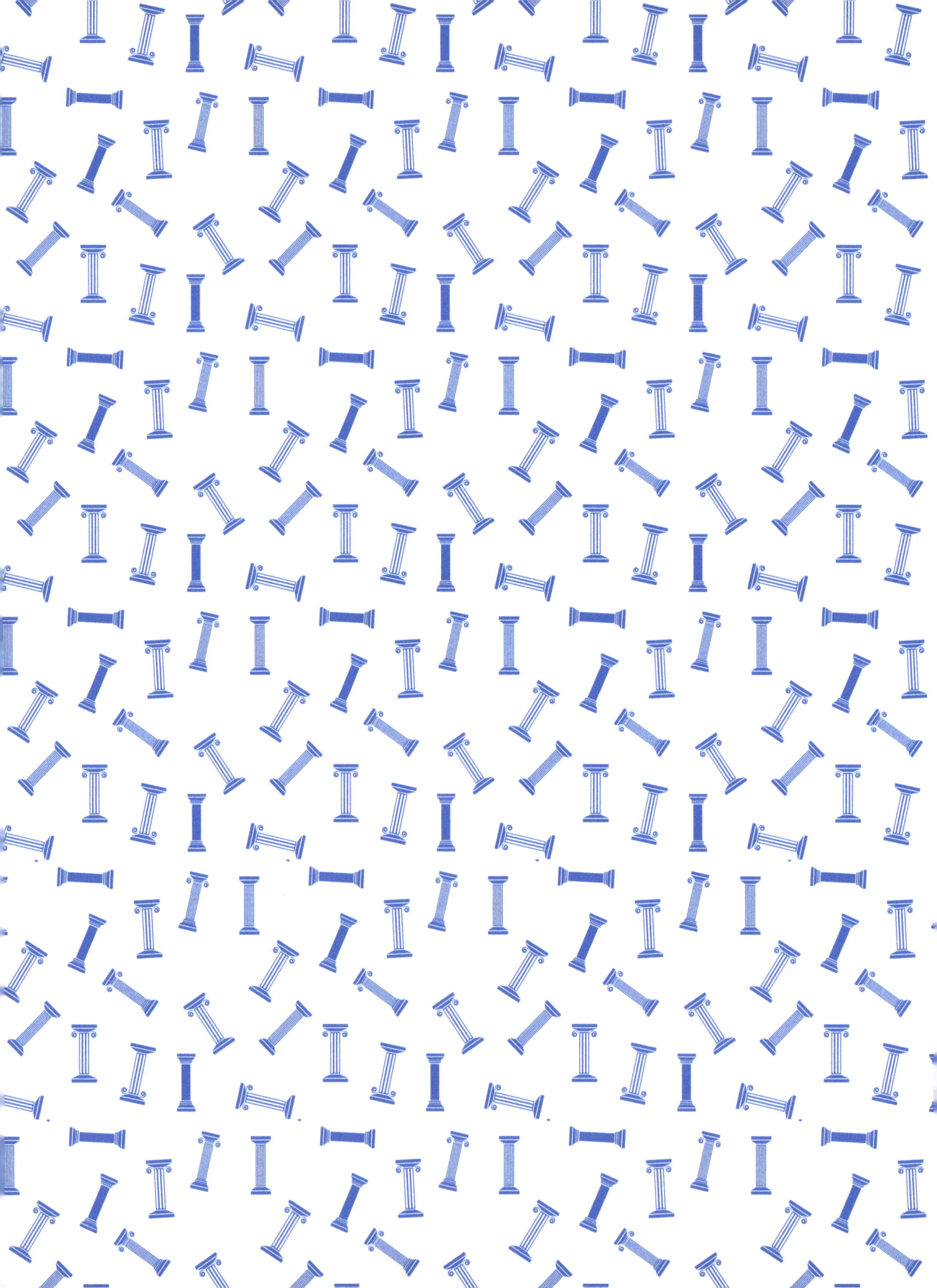

*Learning to Write*

Dolphin

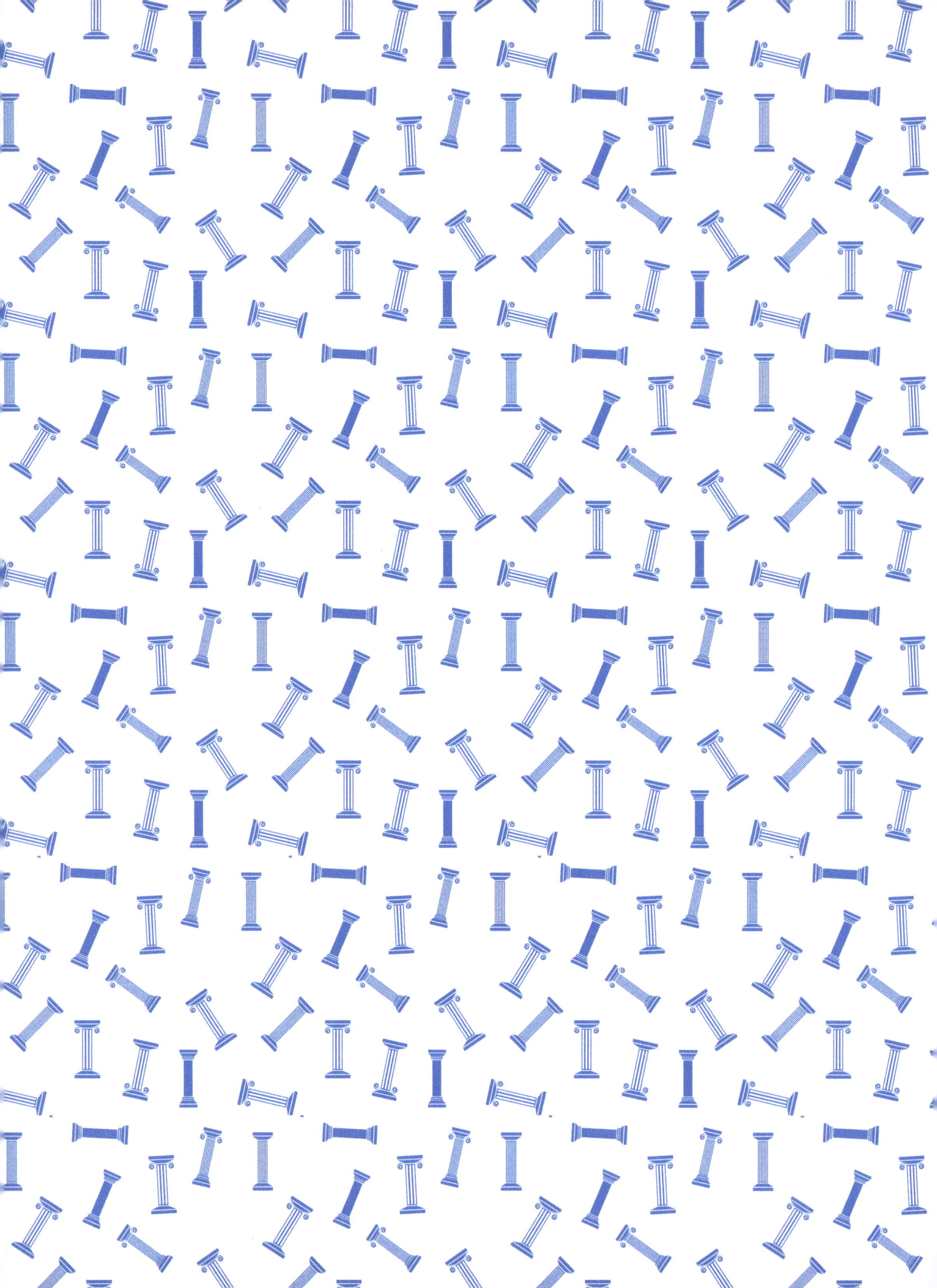

# DOLPHIN FELT PUZZLE

## Instructions

Greece's national animal is the dolphin, which has a long history in ancient Greek history in addition to being a popular sight around the Greek islands. The Greek seas enjoy the privilege of hosting four species of dolphins: the striped dolphin, the bottlenose dolphin, the Risso's dolphin and the short-beaked common dolphin.

Cut out included dolphin puzzle template. Trace onto appropriate colors and cut out with sharp scissors. Assemble puzzle. Use included anatomy tags to indicate the different parts of the dolphin. Use included color poster to assist if needed. For younger children, read the names of the tags and have the child appropriately tag the correct locations of each part.

### Materials
- Dolphin Puzzle Pattern
- Blue, Light Blue, Grey and Black Felt
- Marker
- Scissors

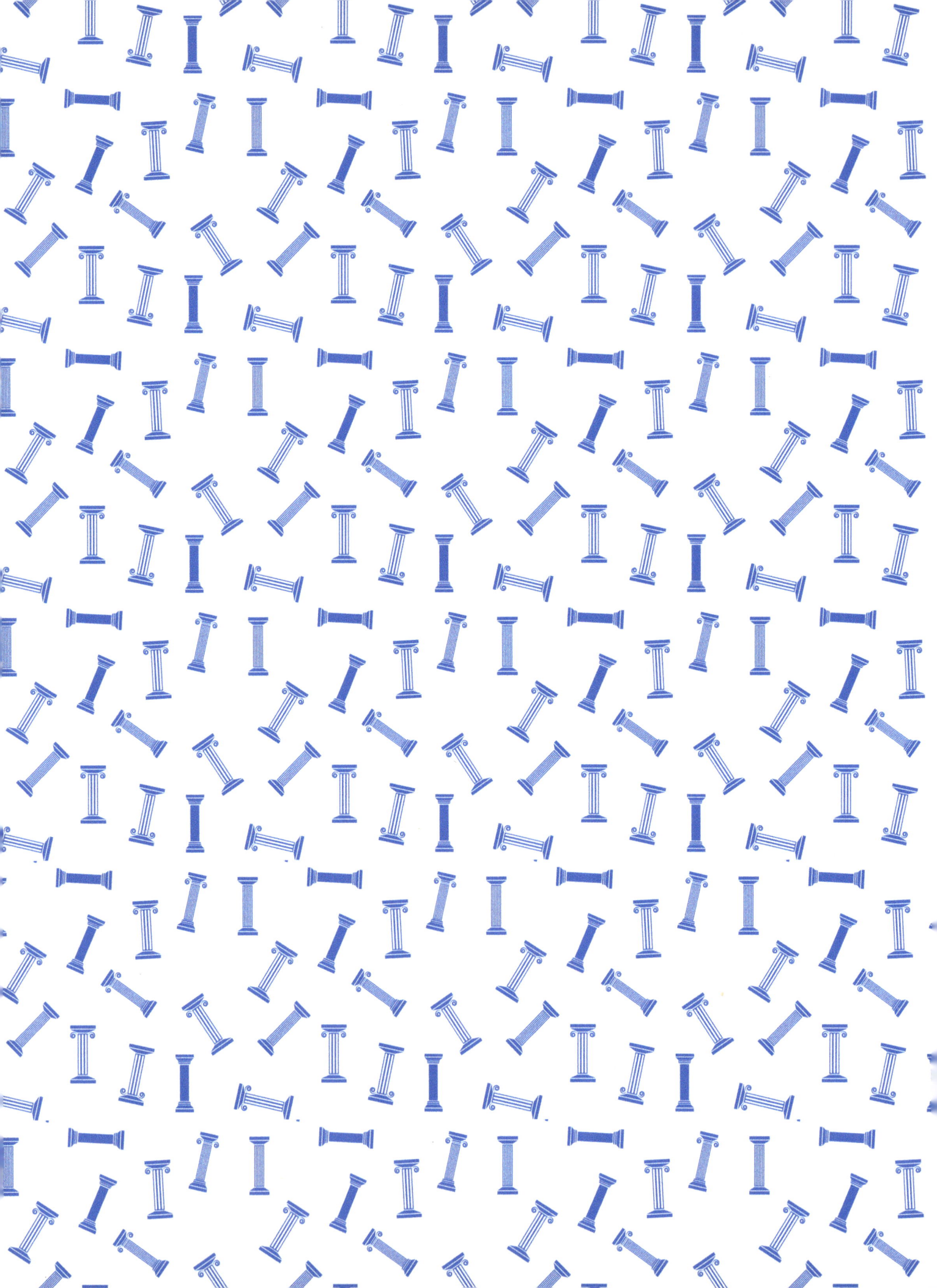

# Dolphin Puzzle Pattern

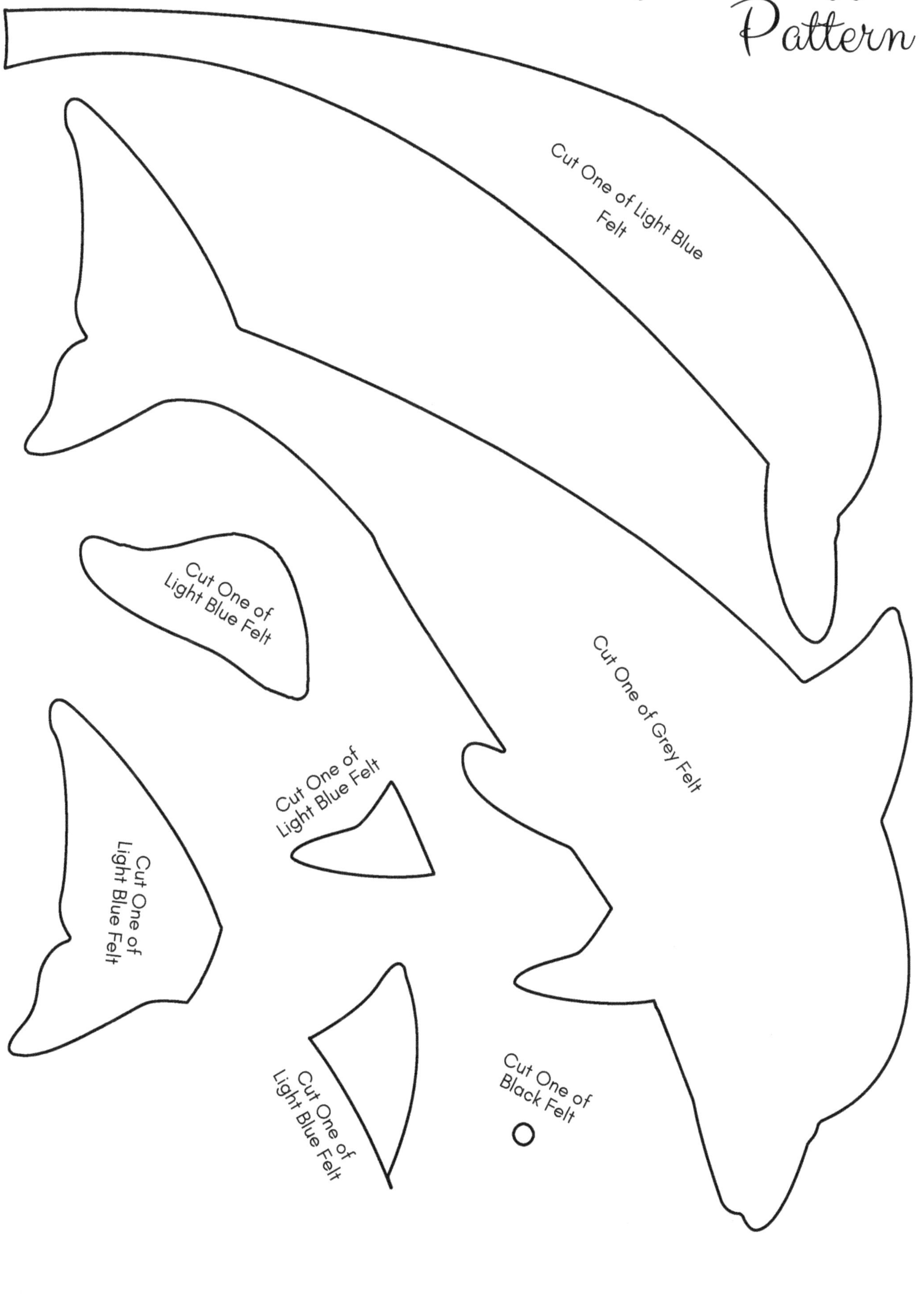

Cut One of Light Blue Felt

Cut One of Light Blue Felt

Cut One of Grey Felt

Cut One of Light Blue Felt

Cut One of Light Blue Felt

Cut One of Light Blue Felt

Cut One of Black Felt

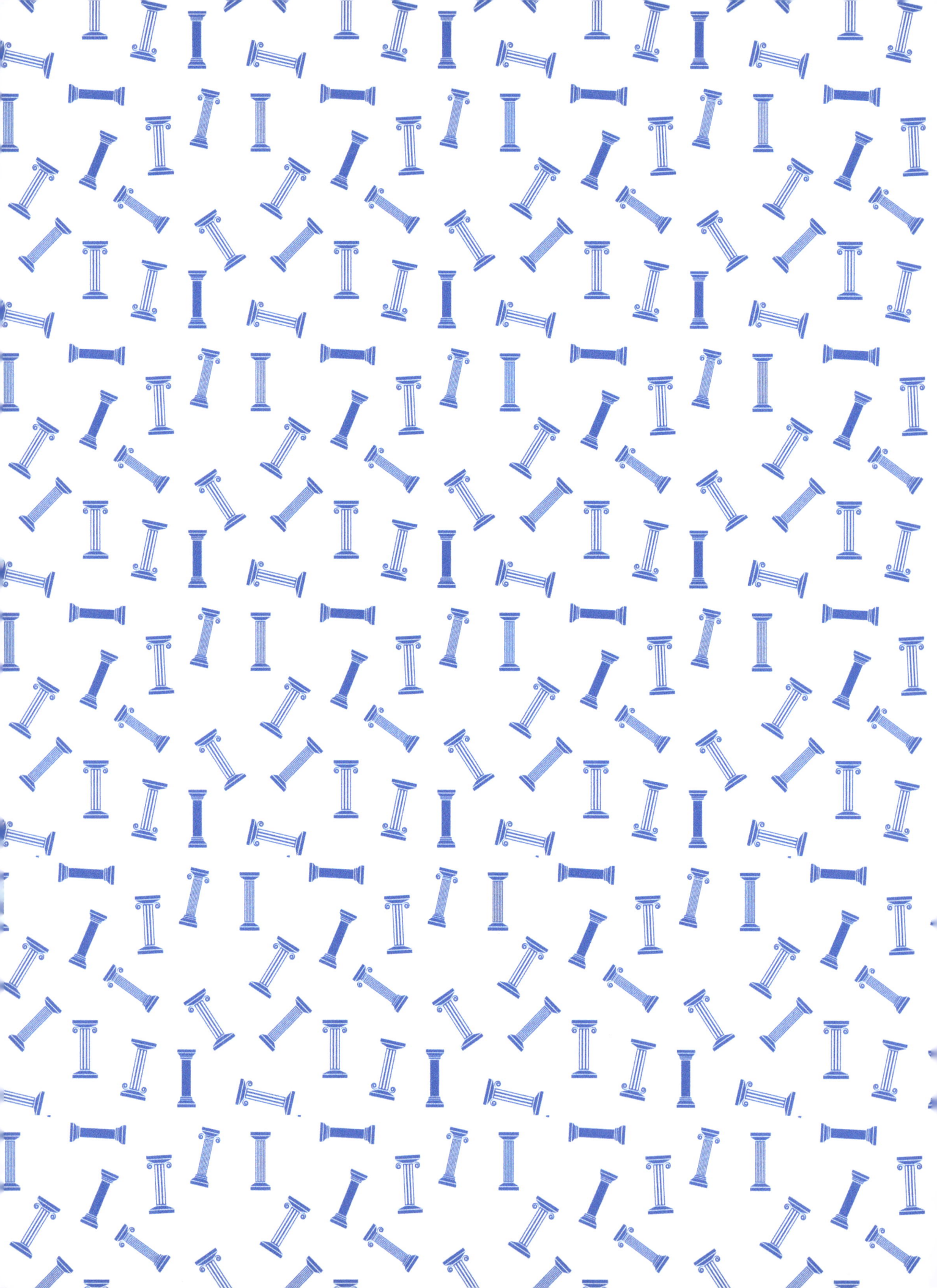

# Greece Currency
## European currency or Euro €

*The Euro € is the main unit of the European currency. The cent is a subdivision worth up to 1/100 of a Euro €.*

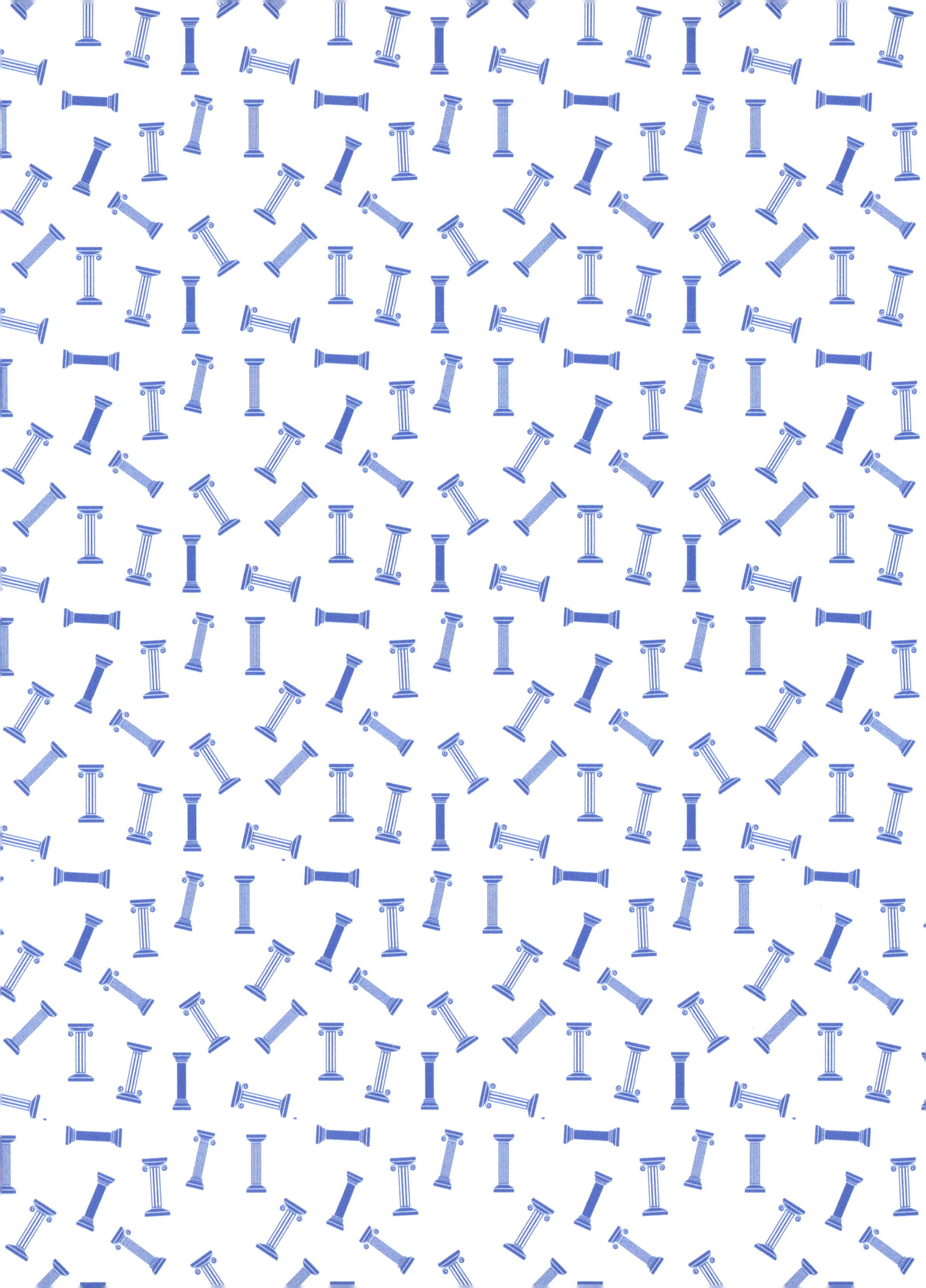

# Greece Currency
## European currency or Euro €

*The Euro € is the main unit of the European currency. The cent is a subdivision worth up to 1/100 of a Euro €.*

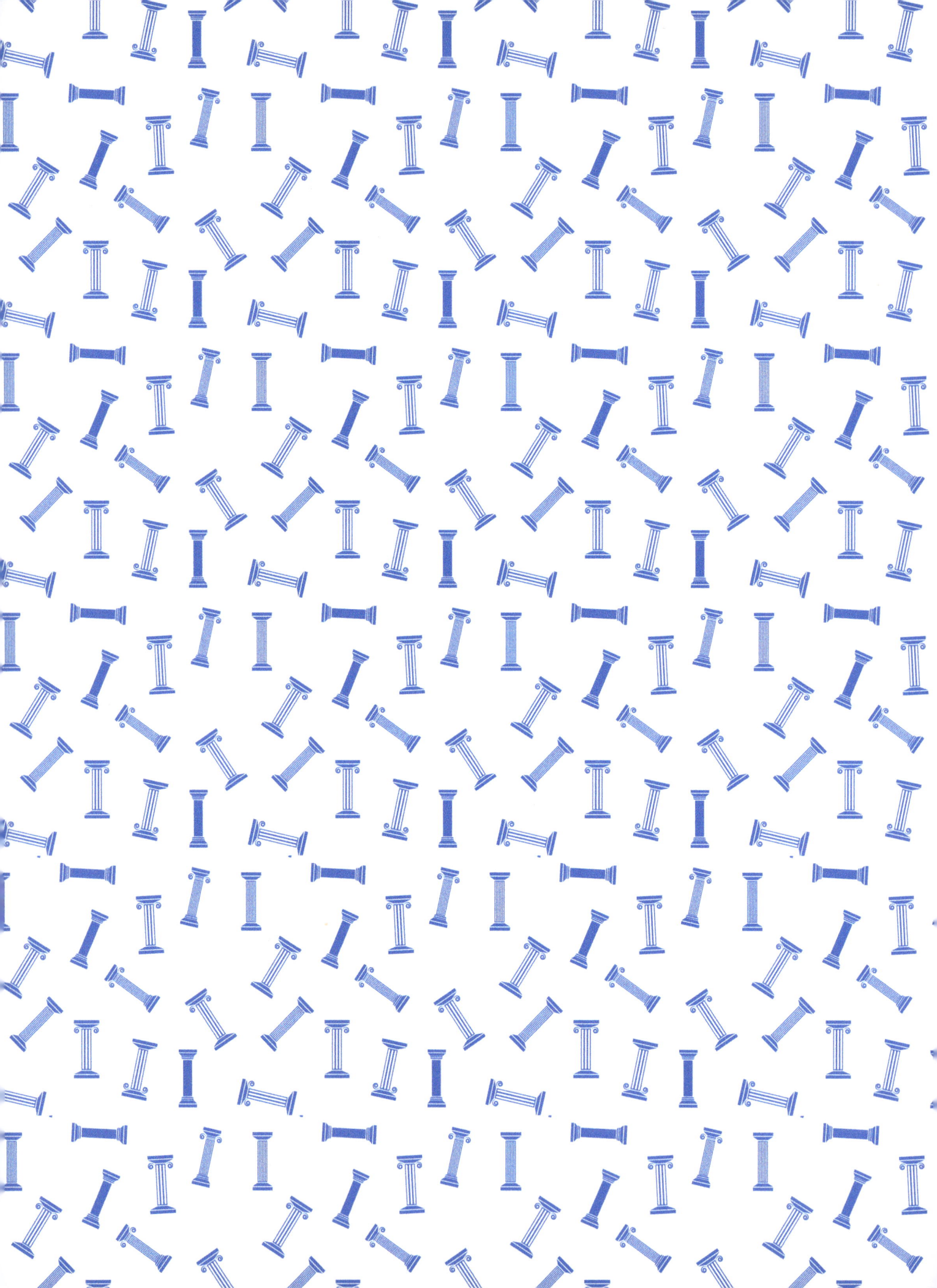

# Greece Currency
## European currency or Euro €

*The Euro € is the main unit of the European currency. The cent is a subdivision worth up to 1/100 of a Euro €.*

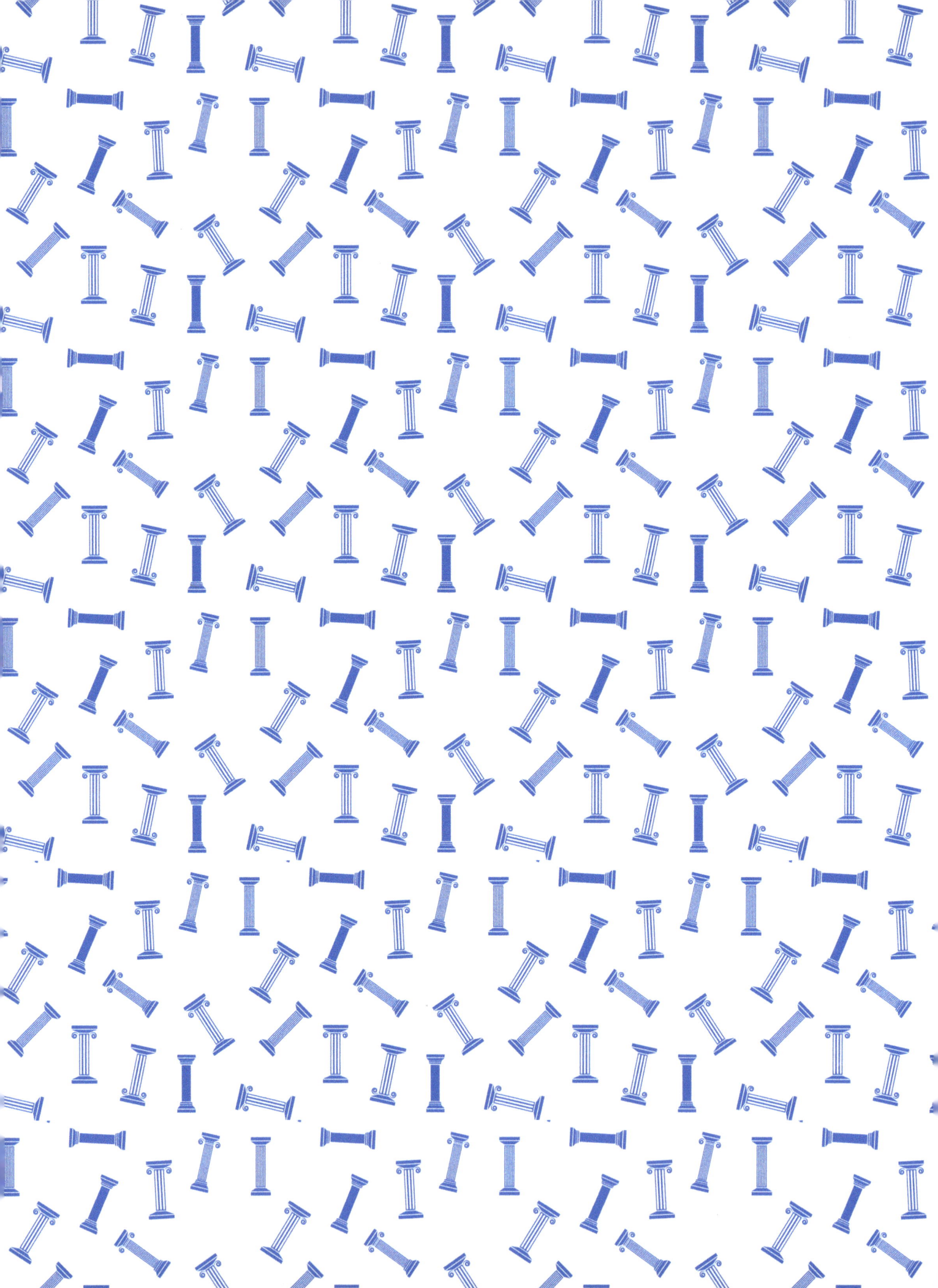

# Greece Currency
## European currency or Euro €

*The Euro € is the main unit of the European currency. The cent is a subdivision worth up to 1/100 of a Euro €.*

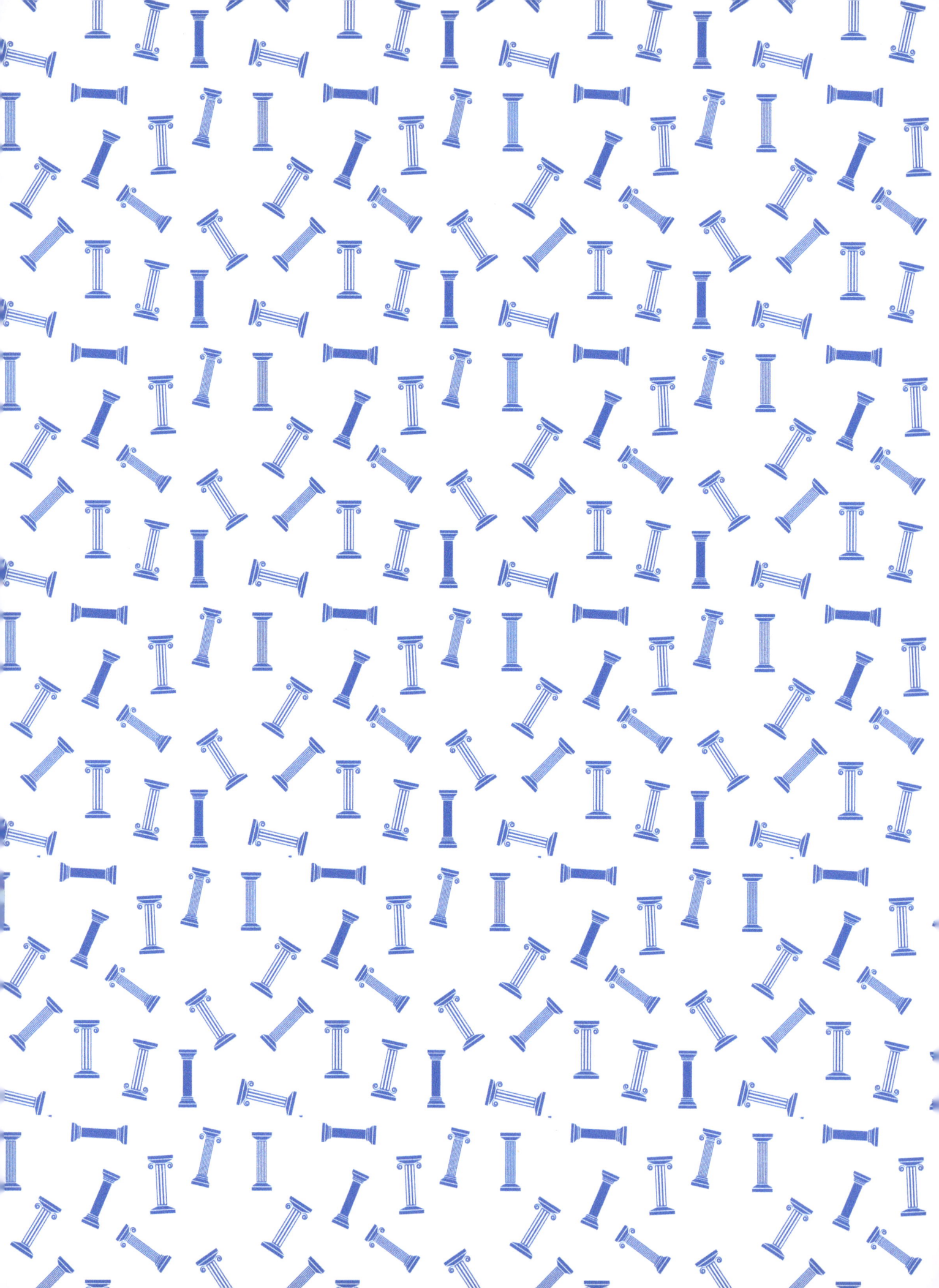

# Greek Language Cards

## Γεια σου
*YAH-soo*

Hello/Goodbye

## Τι κανείς
*tee-KAH-nis*

How are you?

## Χάρηκα
*HA-ree-ka po-LEE*

Nice to meet you

## Ευχαριστώ
*eff-kha-ri-STOE*

Thank you

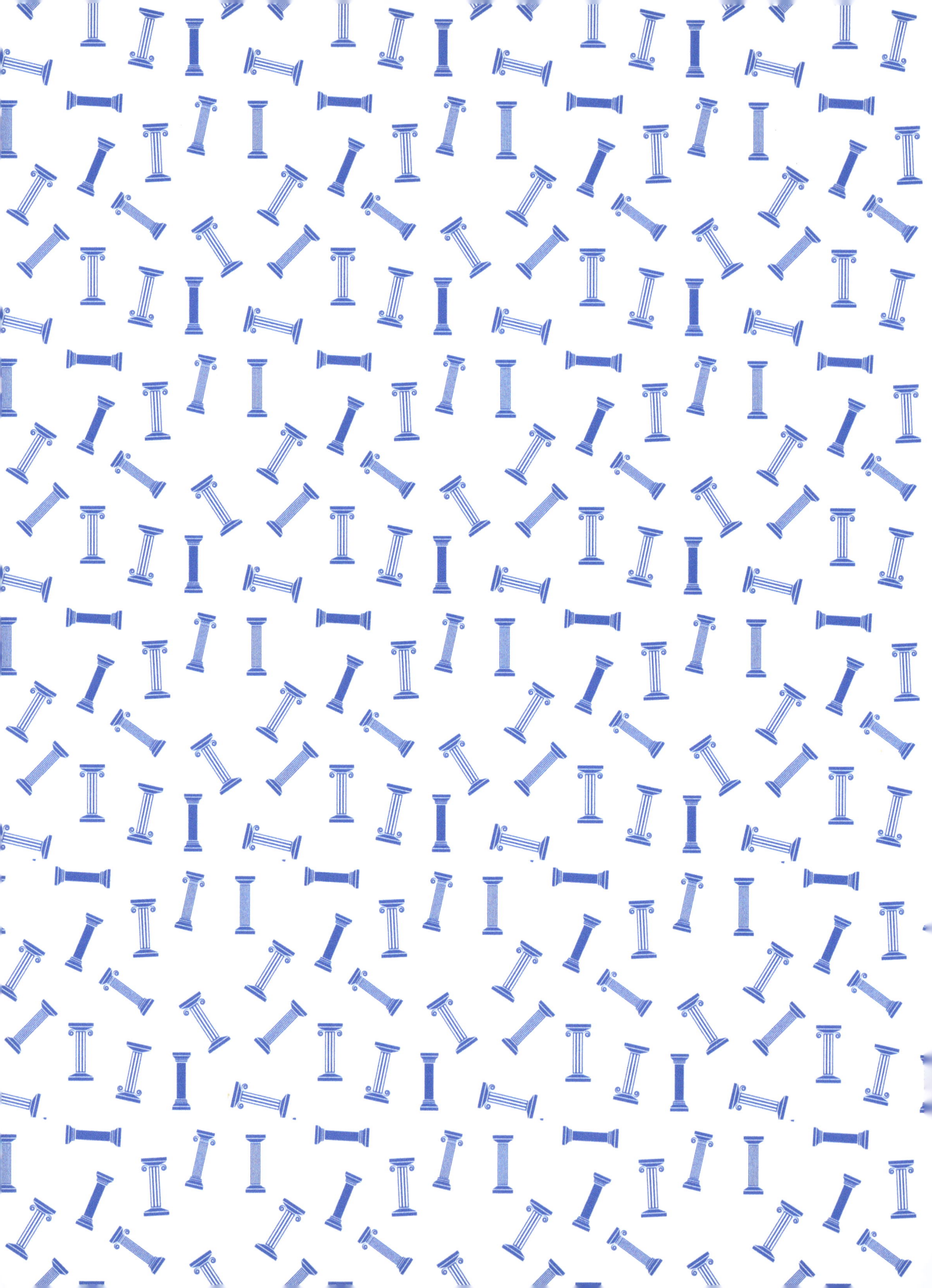

# Greek Language Cards

## Βοήθεια
*voh-EE-thee-yah*

Help

## Πόσο κάνει αυτό

*POH-soh KAH-nee af-TOH*

How much is it?

## Συγνώμη
*see-GHNO-mee*

Excuse me/Sorry

## Με λένε
*may LEH-neh*

My name is...

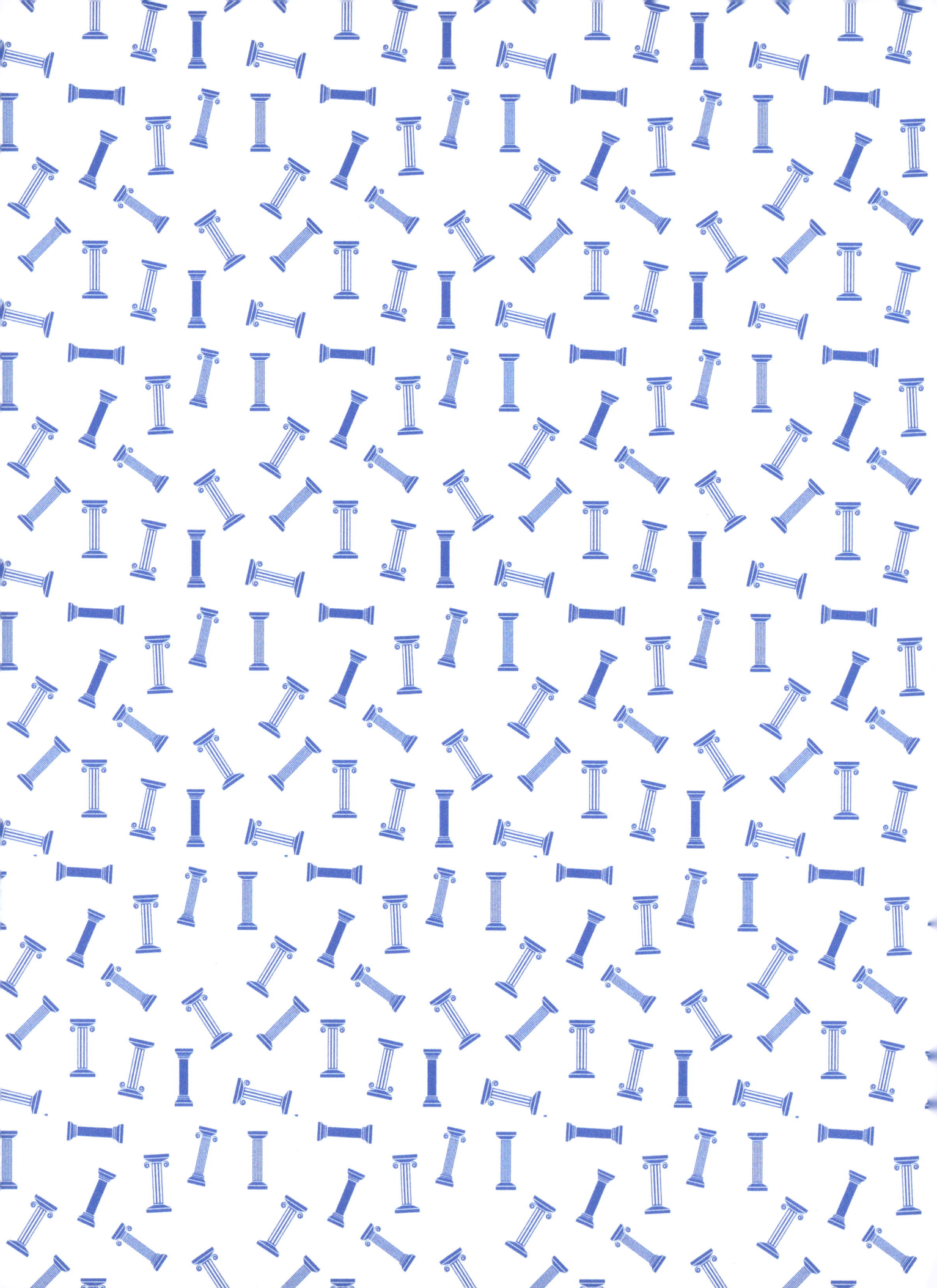

# Savy Activities

Travel the world through the interactive learning activities of **Savy Activities**; these hands-on resources provide parents, caregivers and educators practical ways to teach children about the world around them. Each book features a country, location or time period where subjects such as geography, history, vocabulary, reading, language, science, mathematics, music and art come alive by engaging auditory, visual and kinesthetic learning styles.

All activity books include geography with applicable maps, landmarks and locations. Historical events and time periods are visually represented with full color posters and flashcards, if applicable. Each book includes a set of fun-fact cards, poster and flag, if applicable. Paper models allow children to create 3D creations of major landmarks and structures. All books include a life cycle and anatomy of a plant, animal or organic compound, with flashcards and 3-part cards featuring important structures applicable to the theme.

Children learn scientific principles through active experiments and activities. Traditional customs, festivals, toys, clothing and art are also explored. Each book includes an exclusive themed mini-story featuring historical events or traditional mythology and folklore to promote vocabulary and reading. Where applicable, world languages are introduced through engaging flashcards, posters and tracing work. Each country has been meticulously researched by interviewing native persons and/or personal travel experiences to ensure the authentic culture is fully explored.

**Savy Activities** utilizes concepts from multiple educational methods to create unique resources allowing children a tangible and enjoyable way to explore their world. The **Savy Activities** series should not be viewed as a curriculum, but rather complimentary thematic resources to enhance traditional education. Because the individual needs and knowledge of children varies within standardized grade levels, **Savy Activities** resources have the flexibility to be used with preschool learners through early to mid-elementary years. For younger learners, adult supervision and/or assistance may be needed and activities presented in a simplified version. For older learners, resources may be paired with additional content from other materials to meet learning outcomes.

Check out our other products and resources at **www.SavyActivities.com**

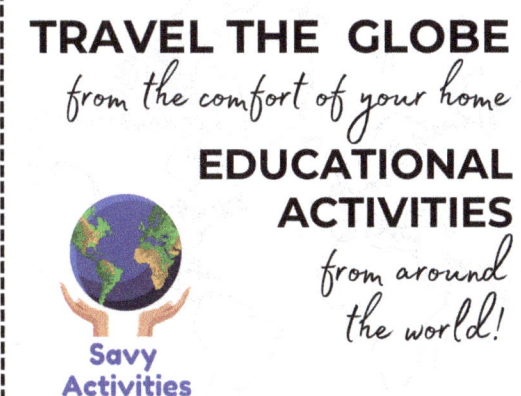

www.ingramcontent.com/pod-product-compliance
Lightning Source LLC
Chambersburg PA
CBHW061811230426
43665CB00033BA/2998